RICHARD HAMILTON

RICHARD HAMILTON

TATE GALLERY

Exhibition sponsored by SRU Ltd

SRU

The sponsorship of the *Richard Hamilton* exhibition by SRU Ltd
has been recognised by an award under the Government's
Business Sponsorship Incentive Scheme. The Scheme, administered
by the Association for Business Sponsorship of the Arts, is
designed to increase the level and effectiveness of business
sponsorship by augmenting sponsors' contributions.

Cover: detail from 'Soft blue landscape', modified on a
QUANTEL GRAPHIC PAINTBOX

Frontispiece: Richard Hamilton, self-portrait photograph, 1992

ISBN 1 85437 098 7 paper
ISBN 1 85437 099 5 cloth

Published by order of the Trustees 1992
for the exhibition at the Tate Gallery
17 June – 6 September 1992
and then touring to the
Irish Museum of Modern Art, Dublin:
28 October 1992 – January 1993
Published by Tate Gallery Publications, Millbank,
London SW1P 4RG
© Tate Gallery and contributors 1992 All rights reserved
Typeset in Photina by Servis Filmsetting Ltd, Manchester
Printed in Great Britain by Balding + Mansell plc,
Wisbech, Cambridgeshire

Illustrated works are copyright as follows:
Richard Hamilton © DACS 1992
Marcel Duchamp and Richard Hamilton © DACS 1992
Richard Hamilton and Dieter Roth © Richard Hamilton, DACS/Dieter Roth 1992
Rita Donagh © Rita Donagh 1992
Jean Dubuffet, Marcel Duchamp © ADAGP, Paris and DACS, London 1992
Jasper Johns © Jasper Johns/DACS, London/NAGA, New York 1992

CONTENTS

FOREWORD

Richard Hamilton has been a seminal figure in British art for more than forty years. His activity as painter, teacher, exhibition organiser and spokesman for artists has both shaped the development of art in Britain and reflected changing social conditions and attitudes.

This is the first major exhibition of his principal themes to concentrate on final statements, starting with three early paintings of 1940 and culminating in a painting completed this year, 1992. We decided to omit prints and preparatory works in order to concentrate on presenting the sequence of his final statements with the dignity and clarity they deserve. This we believe is the best means of disclosing the richness of thought, process and feeling that they comprehend. These paintings, objects and related environments work together to form one of the most important bodies of work in post-war European and American art.

It is the third retrospective exhibition of Richard Hamilton's work at the Tate Gallery. In 1970 the Gallery organised his first museum retrospective, showing 170 works in almost all the media he had till then employed, then in 1983 we showed a survey, titled *Image and Process*, of studies, stage and final proofs for Hamilton's graphic works.

Twenty-two years on from the first show when the emphasis was on Pop it is now possible to see that Pop is simply one aspect, however important, of Hamilton's work, but that his Pop works embody continuous preoccupations of his art which go far beyond the question of a work's specific sources.

The present exhibition will demonstrate the degree to which Hamilton has engaged with crucial themes underlying the public and community life of the periods in which he has worked. His art tellingly reflects changes in the atmosphere of the times and it does so with a sensitivity and insight which, for all the superficial detachment of his manner, are increasingly evident as time passes.

In his concern at all periods with the idea of myth and of archetype, Hamilton addresses many of the principal themes of ambitious painting across the centuries. His work is a dialogue at once with the transmission of imagery in our own culture, with all that its many inflections imply, and with great art of the past.

As the national collection both of British and of modern foreign art, the Tate is a particularly appropriate venue for this survey of the achievement of an artist who, while contributing significantly to the opening of British art to international currents in the post-war era, has also notably extended peculiarly British traditions of thematic complexity. In addition to holding memorable exhibitions here, and to being represented in the collection by outstanding works, it was Hamilton who curated the remarkable Duchamp retrospective at the Tate in 1966 and who made for that occasion the reconstruction of Marcel Duchamp's 'Large Glass' which has been an important part of the Tate Gallery's collection since 1975.

I should like to thank here the contributors to the catalogue, Sarat Maharaj, David Mellor and Stephen Snoddy, whose essays covering both the artistic and political background, will greatly broaden readers' understanding and appreciation of the artist's achievements. We are grateful too to Jackie Darby for her preparatory work on the catalogue entries. I am particularly grateful to Richard Morphet, Keeper of the Modern Collection, who is the curator of the exhibition in collaboration with the artist, and is also the editor of the catalogue and has written a general introduction.

As always we rely heavily on all our lenders, without whose generous support such an exhibition could not have been mounted. We are deeply indebted to them all. I should also like to thank Anthony d'Offay Gallery both for their loans and for their advice and assistance. We are grateful too to Nigel McKernaghan who has unobtrusively but with unfailing commitment helped both the artist and ourselves on many aspects of the exhibition over many months. But it is to Rita Donagh that we owe particular thanks for being so quietly and patiently supportive during the whole period leading up to the opening of the exhibition.

I am delighted that this exhibition will travel to Dublin, native city of James Joyce, whose work greatly influenced Hamilton's, and that this showing should be at the impressive new Irish Museum of Modern Art at Kilmainham, whose Director, Declan McGonagle, earlier so memorably presented Hamilton's and Rita Donagh's work on Irish themes to an Irish public.

It has been a great pleasure to work with Richard Hamilton. He has been unstinting in his help at every stage and has dedicated an enormous amount of time to the realisation of the project in addition to designing the cover for the catalogue and doing a new work for the show. We offer him our most sincere gratitude.

Nicholas Serota
Director

SPONSOR'S FOREWORD

We are delighted to celebrate SRU's twentieth birthday by sponsoring the *Richard Hamilton* exhibition.

SRU provides strategic advice about markets and things material. We feel a natural affinity with the vigorous, and sometimes astringent, commentary Hamilton has made on contemporary consumerism.

We are also pleased to support the Tate Gallery in its role as Britain's leading gallery of British and Modern Art – both of which are exemplified in this major retrospective of Hamilton's work.

Colin Fisher, Managing Director
SRU Ltd

RICHARD HAMILTON: THE LONGER VIEW

Richard Morphet

Richard Hamilton's first Tate Gallery retrospective, in 1970, was held in the year following a major international survey in London of Pop art. The present retrospective repeats this sequence of events. However, a further two decades of Hamilton's work and the perspective of time combine to make it irrational now – as it was always undesirable – for Hamilton's vision to be interpreted primarily in terms of Pop. While both Pop exhibitions rightly stressed the fundamental role of Hamilton's work in Pop art's achievement, his work both then and since exhibits preoccupations far wider and deeper than the notion 'Pop' can begin to suggest. This exhibition presents Hamilton as a painter engaged above all with many of the longstanding central concerns of art.

Since the mid-1950s the majority of Hamilton's motifs have been assertively contemporary. At the same time, his innovative assimilation to fine art of mass media imagery and of technological processes for the transmission of what we see have been strongly evident. Yet the content of any of Hamilton's works cannot be defined in terms of novelty, either of subject or of effect. The very appearance of a work belies the notion of the fleeting, and a close look discloses the extent to which Hamilton has given pre-existing images fresh form and, in that guise, a long-lasting potency that is one of the hallmarks of important art.

A RICHER CONTENT

Hamilton's mature painting career began with abstract works, and at all subsequent periods the abstract element has been significant in his paintings. At the centre of his concerns, however, has always been richness of content and for this, in his view, abstraction, on its own, cannot be a fully effective vehicle. Hamilton's own abstract paintings of 1950 were in fact the beginning of a systematic progress towards the act of representation. At that time, abstract painting was experiencing a major revival. But to Hamilton the forms it offered seemed incapable of embodying the sense of necessity, in terms of experience of life, which he felt all art should have. Thus his personal development of Pop art was in part a search for the fullness which he felt to be lacking in the dominant art forms of the day. In place, as he saw it, of formal exercises or decorative hedonism he sought to make paintings that would convey a stronger sense of contemporary reality. But in these works he wished also to rediscover, in the present, the element of myth which for so many centuries had been central in art.

Paradoxically, a concern with myth and with the search for authentic subject was at the heart of the very tendency – Abstract Expressionism – which at the period of the genesis of Pop art constituted the received idea of modern art. For Hamilton, however, this form of abstraction, so greatly concerned with feeling and, as he saw it, with style, gave insufficient weight to another of art's key components, thought. Moreover, he was disturbed that as the influence of Abstract Expressionism grew, recognition of the insights of Marcel Duchamp declined proportionately. An important element in the emergence of this new American art had been the influence of Surrealism. This was a factor which sustained the esteem in which Duchamp had long been held. Though not a Surrealist proper, Duchamp was the creator of a richly mysterious and allusive art. As Abstract Expressionism developed, however, its climate changed, moving away from preoccupations shared with Duchamp. It was at this time that Hamilton discovered Duchamp. By lecturing, by creating a typographical rendering of the *Green Box*, by reconstructing the 'Large Glass' (fig. 1) and by curating the largest retrospective exhibition held in Duchamp's lifetime, he would go on to play a major role in Duchamp's rehabilitation. Hamilton conducted this enterprise in tandem with the development of his own work as an artist. It is not surprising, therefore, that Duchamp's art, with its layers of meaning, was a fundamental example underlying the formulation of Hamilton's own images as a Pop painter. Hamilton's undertaking, as a Pop artist and after, should in fact be seen in terms of a quest for fullness and complexity and as a declaration against shallowness and superficiality. Something of his underlying inspiration can be sensed in Hamilton's recollection, years later, of concurrent exhibitions of Robert Morris and Joseph Beuys, held in 1968, in which ostensibly the two artists could be seen as sharing similar concerns (for example, both showed works of similar scale using an identical grey felt). To Hamilton, however, 'the twinned personalities were bared. The American cool, thoughtful, abstract, minimal. The German white hot, visionary, arcane, multi-referential'.[1] Thoughtful though his own work is, and often cool in manner, Hamilton's heart lies with the latter alternative, as examination of his paintings will reveal.

fig. 1 Richard Hamilton reconstructing Duchamp's 'Large Glass' 1965 (photograph by Mark Lancaster)

One factor which made Pop art difficult for many people to accept was the shock of seeing, in works of fine art, imagery which hitherto they had encountered only in quite different contexts. They tended, as a result, to regard a Pop work in the same way as they did its sources. But Hamilton was, of course, using imagery originally created for one purpose for different and more complex purposes of his own. In the mid-1950s there were widespread fears of 'the dehumanising consequences of technical mass civilisation'.[2] Yet, in another paradox, the very thing that Hamilton was able to generate as a result of refusing to turn away from this mass culture and, indeed, of drawing on it extensively was a new approach to the creation of the thoughtful human image. As his post-Pop development shows even more clearly, this image went far beyond simply repeating the context of its sources. Instead, it encouraged the exercise by the viewer both of a critical intelligence and of the affective sensibilities.

BREAKING BARRIERS

Although Hamilton had more than five years' training as a fine artist, much of it very traditional in character, his principal time at the Royal Academy Schools was preceded by work in a design studio and followed by five years' work as a jig and tool draughtsman. During his subsequent years at the Slade School he was already working on the conception and organisation of exhibitions not of fine art. The fusion of these contrasting experiences of the visual resulted in a distinctive approach to the production of paintings. It meant that Hamilton's works had a 'look' which, when they were first shown, prevented people being able readily to place them in terms of art.

Early in their careers, the majority of artists of Hamilton's generation formulated a manner, which they then proceeded for decades recognisably to develop. But Hamilton's attitude did not have such a result. To him, manner was at once a subject – part of the landscape – and a raw material.[3] The result was a body of early work which, though it now looks all of a piece and also to have followed a logical course, appeared to many at the time as a sequence of disconnected experiments. It was also unclear in what discipline these operated. None of Hamilton's teaching appointments was in painting, and to some his Pop works looked like exercises, albeit of an unfamiliar kind, in the subjects he taught – design and interior design. Such a misconception is understandable if the works are viewed in the context simply of Tachisme, Kitchen Sink, St Ives and other contemporaneous art. But one of Hamilton's historic achievements was significantly to broaden the context of fine art.

Hamilton intended that the homage his work paid to outstanding precursors should be as clear in the field of design as in that of fine art. As he wrote in 1989, 'Domestic appliances, audio equipment, chairs, automobiles, planes, computers have been submitted to some of the best and most inventive minds of our time; for me to place the achievement of a few industrial designers above that of most practitioners in the fine arts implies a recognition of the fragile boundaries between specializations in the plastic arts today.'[4] In the 1950s and early 1960s, painting displayed in an art gallery was an unfamiliar vehicle for abundant homage to sophisticated applied art. Some early viewers could not see beyond such references to more complex aspects of the content of Hamilton's work. The problem calls to mind the uncertainties which, as Hamilton recalled in a lecture on Duchamp, viewers had originally had as to what kind of thing the 'Large Glass' could be, not appreciating that it was at once 'an epic poem, a technical treatise and a pictorial masterpiece'.[5]

In Hamilton's work the poetic idea, which is crucial, is transmitted both through the painterly act and through the filter of a meditation on codes of communication peculiarly of our own era. Physical refinement is a component of a successful painting no less vital to Hamilton than effectiveness of intellectual engagement. In Manet, for example, he admires always the sheer expressiveness of the mark and feels close to the painter of flowers as well as to the painter of 'Olympia' and 'A Bar at the Folies Bergère'. Clear though this engagement is with the act of painting, some have been blinded to its centrality by their resistance to the idea of easel painting openly addressing mass media themes. But Hamilton is transmitting a sense not of enslavement to modern media but of wonder, and of celebration of expanded possibilities. As he has written, 'We must all have found that contact with the fantasy world is made all the more memorable when the bridge is a newly-experienced technological marvel'.[6]

These three elements – reflection on modes of communication, engagement with the painting's physical means and imaginative content – are among the constants in Hamilton's work which it is helpful to keep in mind, in view of the fact that another constant is its idiomatic variety. From an early date he has been impelled by the urge, having done one thing, to move on to its opposite, or, correspondingly, to repeat a work, but in a contrasting medium. Harold Rosenberg remarked of him in 1973: 'He has divined that the only stability for "the painter of modern life, in the Baudelairean sense", as John Russell calls him, is to keep moving. For an artist so orientated, the fading of the vanguard art movements need not be a disaster'.[7]

This exceptionally active quality in Hamilton's output is one of many innovative features which he introduced into British art. A brief outline of others may be helpful, not least to show how remarkable is their range.

Hamilton was determined that art should openly embrace the reality of its own period. He saw no reason why it should fail to reflect – and where possible assimilate – either the striking mass imagery or the technological discoveries of the age. These he saw as reality in the sense not only that they existed but also that they formed part of that continuous evolution of which he traced stages in successive exhibitions – *Growth and Form* (1951), *Man, Machine & Motion* (1955) and *This is Tomorrow* (1956). In what sense this evolution, in its latest stage, constituted progress, however great the increase in sophistication, was one of the questions posed by his art. Hamilton's intention in using such material in his paintings was not to subvert the goals of high art as it had evolved hitherto, but rather to realise some of these anew, to rediscover them in terms of contemporary experience, as artists had done in every age.

At the same time, by the focus he enforced both on the picture surface and on the range of techniques necessarily undertaken to employ the sheer variety of modes of representation that he presented within a single painting, Hamilton drew enhanced attention to the processes by which each work had been made. The many precedents for this emphasis extend back into the nineteenth century and are central, ironically, to Abstract Expressionism, with which Hamilton's work contrasted so sharply. His originality was that the vehicles within which he insisted so greatly on this aspect of art should have been paintings of such careful finish and outward detachment. The work of Jasper Johns (of which Hamilton was unaware till well into his Pop period) provides an interesting American parallel in terms of this major shift in focus on the role of process in art (fig.2). Significantly, Johns, like Hamilton, was a younger friend and admirer of Duchamp.

fig.2 Jasper Johns with his **Target with Four Faces** 1955 (encaustic and collage on canvas with objects, *Museum of Modern Art, New York*)

The character of a work by Hamilton was often puzzling. It ranged from the unfamiliar form, for art, of the Pop paintings, through the enigmatic 'Epiphany', 1964 (no.27) to the hybrid 'The critic laughs', 1971–2 (no.69) and the mysterious sound-emitting painting, 'Lux 50', 1979 (no.80). It thus compelled the viewer to ask 'What exactly am I looking at?' Examination of the picture swiftly undermined any sense of the image having been 'conjured up', since the physical nature of its discrete component marks was so insistent, as was the fact of their being located on the surface. Alternatively, when the paint surface was so immaculate as at first glance to seem similar to a photograph, attention was directed to painting processes of a different kind; the work then provoked the viewer to question the 'truth' of the representation.

Each finished work made clear that Hamilton's images did not spring purely from his imagination, but had specific sources. The viewer had the sense not only that Hamilton had manipulated his sources but also that at an earlier stage in the history of the subject others had used these images, to other ends (and, in fact, had often used people, in various ways, to create these images). This in turn caused the viewer to consider his or her own opinion on these antecedent events. Thus any work by Hamilton brought into sharp focus both the sense of the completed work as a decipherable encapsulation of a long succession of actions and the question of how, on every level, it was that things came to be how they were. The ways in which Hamilton posed these issues through painting were an original contribution to the art of his time.

fig. 3 Jean Dubuffet **Dhotel with Yellow Teeth** 1947 Mixed media on canvas *Private Collection*

They were also in extreme contrast to those brought together in, for example, the widely noticed exhibition *New Images of Man*, held at the Museum of Modern Art, New York in 1959, and which brought together work by twenty-three artists including Bacon, Dubuffet (fig. 3), and Golub. There shown often as battered or fearful, man seemed to come from a different planet from the new image of [wo]man proposed by Hamilton. Whatever demeaning processes her image might earlier have undergone, Hamilton's woman, by contrast, gave every appearance (at least) of being cheerful and at ease in the world of the urban present. And however ambiguous her meaning, it was clear that on looking at the world of admass Hamilton registered not fear but curiosity, discovering in its 'mundane' milieu even a certain beauty and magic. As Hamilton observed in 1961, 'popular culture [has] abstracted from Fine Art its role of myth-maker', and is able 'to project . . . the classic themes of artistic vision and to express them in a poetic language which marks them with a precise cultural date-stamp . . . If the artist is not to lose much of his ancient purpose he may have to plunder the popular arts to recover the imagery which is his rightful inheritance'.[8] In drawing on these sources in his paintings Hamilton showed, influentially, that art could be fun and could also have a strange new kind of optimism.[9]

In a period when the act of painting was widely held to be one of psychological drama, he also showed that the artist need not struggle to form the image, and further that a degree of detachment could yield substantial and long-lasting results – detachment both in the nature of the artistic process and in the artist's attitude to his subject matter, with which, nevertheless, he remained keenly involved. In place of the exercise of pure feeling, Hamilton proposed problem-solving as the model for the making of art; in place of instinctive gestures he proposed intellectual acts. From this summary it should be clear that in addition to being one of the creators of Pop art, Hamilton strikingly foreshadowed Conceptual art, with its heightened awareness (indeed, explicit exposition) of all stages of the artistic process, and not least in its crucial (if insufficiently recognised) role as a vehicle for transmitting human experience and disclosing social relationships.[10]

Also innovative was the openness and zest of Hamilton's merging of the role of fine artist with that of consumer of the products projected by sophisticated advertising, as well as of popular culture. Both of these were American-dominated. He was openly unenthusiastic about the revival of interest in indigenous folk-culture shown in exhibitions such as *Black Eyes and Lemonade* held at the Whitechapel Gallery during the Festival of Britain.[11] His creative consumerism, by contrast, was evidence of his wish to look beyond the constrictions of a narrowly British culture in the period of Neo-Romanticism, Kitchen Sink and the landscape-based art of St Ives. As well as American-styled goods Hamilton was a consumer of high design products emanating from the Continent, particularly from the Hochschule für Gestaltung, in Ulm. These preferences were symptoms of an instinctive internationalism. His belief that ideas cannot be confined by national boundaries would lead to wide-ranging professional friendships, from Vostell to Warhol and Tinguely to Beuys. It identifies Hamilton as one of the significant architects of Britain's expanding cultural relationship with the wider world in the post-war era. The wish to break down restrictive barriers is a motive which links all aspects of his work.

Hamilton was a leader in the reaction against what he saw as the purist morality dominating British culture, for example in the viewpoint of Sir Herbert Read. Though many of his works show the strength of his views on moral issues, Hamilton was opposed to any restriction, according to criteria of aesthetic taste or moral tone, on the range of material an artist could validly employ.[12] This standpoint of 'no hierarchy of value' sanctioned a revision in the role of style. From being a criterion to which a work sought to conform, it became one material among many which was there simply to be used, as eclectically as desired, according to the needs of the particular purpose in hand. Moral neutrality, in this sense, suggests numerous links between Hamilton's work and that of artists in other disciplines, from Robbe-Grillet to Straub. It also leads to a willingness to mix categories previously considered distinct, and foreshadows developments in art more recent than Conceptual art. These include Appropriation and Simulation, which enigmatically transfer an object, intact in one sense yet also transformed, from one context to another, and, more broadly, Post-Modernism, in which a single work may contain images in mutually contradictory styles.[13]

Hamilton is therefore a pioneer of the propensity in an increasing amount of the art of recent decades for a given work to do a large number of different things simultaneously. This is a function both of the new relative detachment which Hamilton exemplified and of the more extensive engagement with subject for which he hungered. It also carried the implicit expectation that the viewer of a painting would engage with it on several levels and, indeed, be happy to work in order to experience it to the full.

AN OPEN QUESTION

In taking a decisive stand against the idea of limitation on the content of a work of art or on its mode Hamilton asserted, too, that art could often best reflect the complexity of human experience by avoiding a hard and fast statement. Using the work, instead, to pose questions was a further means of enabling the viewer to experience it more richly. Thus in every Hamilton, as in his output as a whole, quite opposite ideas co-exist, resulting in a creative balance which itself expresses his view of life.[14] It is therefore hardly surprising that, while undermining traditional concepts of the work of art, Hamilton simultaneously reiterates and reinforces them. In such a play with ideas his ultimate purpose is not the satisfaction of an intellectual process, significant though that is, but rather the fuller revelation of the content that his art exists to disclose.

Hamilton's paintings merge fine art with the techniques, and sometimes the forms, of many non fine art media. They incorporate both movement and sound. Those of his works that constitute environments further dissolve clearcut distinctions between art and other aspects of life. Hamilton's admiration for artists such as Beuys, Tinguely, Latham and Cage, who have created new art forms, and his enthusiasm for such manifestations as Fluxus and the Destruction in Art Symposium attest his conviction that anything can be art. Yet at the same time he deliberately reasserts in contemporary terms the traditional genres of art and, while stressing the need for art to engage with the actualities of the present, sees his work in relation as much to that of past centuries as to that of his contemporaries. He has always insisted that he is a traditional fine artist and his work has a cohesion consistent with that concept. Even as he instinctively assimilates new types of material to art, an equal instinct compels him to reexamine and redeploy his own art's earlier content. His oeuvre can thus be read as a continuous dialogue between change and stability.

Hamilton's paintings contain, sometimes in the same work, immaculately impersonal-seeming passages and assertively autographic facture. When a work is confined

fig.4 Richard Hamilton and Dieter Roth **D.R. with suitcase, R.H. supporting** 1976 Enamel, oil-pastel, synthetic oil primer, tape and pencil on silkscreened paper
Private Collection

to one of these modes it is often the case that at the same period Hamilton was making another in the most contrasting manner. The calm and subtlety of touch in 'Still-life', 1965 (no.32) (a painting of a machine) was concurrent with the anthology of paint marks in 'My Marilyn', 1965 (no.31), which variously recall Fragonard, de Kooning and Rainer and evoke grave disquiet and a sense of human frailty. The designer of the refined 'Lux 50', 1979 (no.80) is the co-creator of the anarchic and scatological collaborations with Dieter Roth. The self-assertion of 'Marilyn Monroe's' crosses, tick and arrow confirms life, yet in its implication of self-cancellation reads also as foreshadowing her death. The rumbustiousness of the Hamilton/Roth collaborations (fig.4) has the character of an all-encompassing embrace of life, yet its powerful emphasis on the material, on consumption and bodily process, conveys a strong sense of life's cycle and of the fact that human beings, like the materials here so extravagantly consumed and daubed, are themselves, on one level, mere matter. Hamilton's work as a whole often gives a feeling at once of the abundance of this cycle and of its inevitable completion. In images many of which do not at first suggest such a preoccupation, his work abounds in reminders of mortality.[15] Though the most deliberate of artists, Hamilton – as this theme of mortality recalls – can combine an awareness of the Dionysiac with a feeling for metaphor in ways which link his work with that of the Viennese artists Günter Brus and Hermann Nitsch and of Claes Oldenburg.

THE HUMAN THEME

Very often it is the *way* in which an image is communicated through modern media that has made it compelling for Hamilton as the source for a work. His intense engagement with what one might describe as the poetry of means is always integral to the work's subject. But where the human theme dominates an additonal kind of intensity comes into play, as further examples such as 'Swingeing London 67', 1968–9 (nos.48–54), 'Treatment room', 1983–4 (no.83), 'The citizen', 1982–3 (no.82) and 'War games', 1991–2 (no.106) show. Detachment is to that extent unsettled. It is interesting, though, how even here, where Hamilton's feelings are more exposed, another kind of balance is often at work – a Labour leader is attacked and then a Conservative; a Republican 'martyr' is paired with a Unionist 'knight'.[16]

When Pop art emerged, many commentators objected to the use of source material in which they felt that human values had been debased. It is true that in some degree, whatever the collaboration, the women whose images appear in every work from 'Just what is it . . . ?', 1956 (no.13) to 'AAH!', 1962 (no.19) and again from 'Interior I', 1964 (no.29) to 'My Marilyn', 1965 (no.31) had earlier been used, perhaps even exploited, by the media. Correspondingly, almost any image enters a Hamilton painting only after something has been *done* to it, by an earlier process. Yet in an image developed from such a source the vivacity, even the mystery of the human presence, is renewed or remade in Hamilton's work. The context from which he derived such an image is acknowledged, even re-emphasised, but in the same act it is transmuted through his art.

Hamilton develops a painting by devoting enormous attention to fashioning its surface. He thus reiterates the theme of the transmission of an image through successive stages, which in his art is a major subject in itself. Yet it is not technical characteristics which first engage Hamilton's interest in an image; something else is more important. For all the programmatic aspect of his enterprise and his interest in addressing categories of subject, it is on the level of intuition that Hamilton first responds to a particular image among the hundreds of thousands that he, like everyone else, encounters in the continuous image-flow of contemporary life. He has often picked out an image without at first understanding why it has engaged him. Later – often when absorbed in working on the image at the technical level – he comes to realise that it has a more significant meaning, both in general human terms and for him personally, than at first he suspected. Reviewing Hamilton's works in this sense, one is driven to the conclusion that always to be found at their centre is not only the mind but also the heart.

Art, for Hamilton, is not just transmission but, more importantly, transformation. It is a process which he has likened to alchemy (a link, again, with Duchamp, as well as with Beuys), and he has stated that the artists he admires most are those who *reveal* something to us. The context and the materials employed can be perfectly mundane – Hamilton always insists on reference to verifiable reality – but the result should be an insight which goes beyond the level simply of fact. It is clear that however important to Hamilton in his initial identification of a source image its technical interest may be, there is already some level on which he identifies it as the vehicle for the epiphany or sudden manifestation of insight which, transformed by his art, it also becomes for the viewer.[17] Against the background of postwar despair, out of an examination first of perspective and motion, next of the 'degraded' world of admass imagery and more recently of the political world of the recent past, Hamilton seeks to create a 'white magic'[18] and to draw myths as authentic for our own day as those of earlier art were for theirs. He sees this as the central purpose of art. In a discussion at the ICA in 1968 he declared his wish that the spirituality of man should reappear more strongly than seemed to be the case in the art of the present. It was possible, he claimed, for the classical approach to be revived in figurative art without being academic.[19] Hamilton's aim has consistently been to create works which in their final form make a statement possessed of a lasting energy, images which will go on giving out meaning. He is, therefore, not an iconoclast so much as a maker, in our own day, of a kind of icon.

A LONG TRADITION

The way he does this is, above all, by contriving images by applying paint to a flat surface, a traditional act. This needs to be stated because many commentators have written as though Hamilton merely selects an image and reproduces it, untouched, in the form in which he found it. But he has repeatedly asserted his belief in the superiority of painting over technology as a means of making art of lasting power.[20] Moreover, for all the importance he attaches to input from technical discoveries outside art, Hamilton sees the act of painting in a much longer perspective than that of contemporary circumstances. As he stated in 1978: 'The idea that you're competing with Oldenburg or Warhol . . . these . . . judgements are quite absurd. You are really competing with Rembrandt, Velásquez and Poussin . . . That's the kind of time span that art is all about . . . It's very sad that it's now at the stage where everybody's frantically looking for some new gimmick.'[21]

The degree to which Hamilton feels part of tradition is evident from his introduction to the catalogue of the exhibition *The artist's eye* at the National Gallery in 1978, which he selected from the Gallery's collection. He expressed particular admiration for works which, showing independence of patrons, taste, bombast and rhetoric, revealed high

fig.5 **The artist's eye** 1978
Pencil, watercolour and collage
Private Collection

ambition, calm resolution and daring. In van Eyck (fig.5) he saw these qualities as being united with technical mastery, the invention of a medium and the use of arcane symbolism married to profound simplicity (which he described as 'an epiphany, a crystallisation of thought that gives us an instant awareness of life's meaning'). These, rather than the exigencies of today's media, are the standards which Hamilton seeks to follow in his own work. In 1990 he added 'I rather believe in the old tradition of art schools linked to museums. When the Ecole des Beaux-Arts in Paris was set up it was associated with the Louvre . . . This is much better than the present situation, where the tendency seems to be to relate art schools to commerce – to the current fashionable art scene. It's a complete reversal of what should happen'.[22]

Hamilton's work abounds in references to great art from the past, for example by van Eyck, Velásquez, Zurbarán, Seghers, Watteau, David, Seurat and Picasso. At the same time it constitutes an examination in contemporary terms of many of the genres familiar from art over the centuries, including portraiture, landscape, still-life, religious art, history painting, political satire, interiors and paintings of architecture. It can equally be seen as a meditation on some of the principal themes of human existence, for example birth and death, war and peace, love and justice. Hamilton uses his art as both narrative and symbol, as well as to reflect on art itself, its materials, processes, operation and role in society.

CONTEMPORARY AFFINITIES

fig.6 Rita Donagh **Counterpane**
1987–8 Oil on canvas *Tate Gallery*

In considering affinities between Hamilton's art and that of his contemporaries, there is therefore no reason to seek these in the field of Pop art in particular. While his work shows many points of contact with that of other Pop artists it is to those, such as Oldenburg and Warhol, who show the greatest complexity of thought in combination with originality of form and universality of theme, that his work is closest. Of artists often associated with Pop but who are not properly Pop artists, he shares many preoccupations with Johns. It would be possible to cite many aspects of the enterprise of making figurative images on themes of concern to society and of autobiography, which link Hamilton's work with that of such British artists as Kitaj and Colin Self, despite substantial differences in detail. There is a strong sympathy between Hamilton's vision and that of Rita Donagh, whose meticulously crafted, many-layered, multi-referential paintings condense and transmit intense thought and feeling in a personal genre of marked outward restraint (fig.6). More widely, there is a parallel between Hamilton's work and that of a number of artists, many of them not painters, in terms of an interest in accentuating the effect of a socio-political allegory through the nature of the form within which it is presented, at the same time directing attention to exactly what is going on, both in the work itself and in the area of human affairs under examination.

But it would be a mistake to seek Hamilton's close links as an artist simply in terms of specific categories of art, as his friendship with and admiration for such dissimilar artists as Francis Bacon, Dieter Roth, the Boyle family, Nam June Paik, Gerhard Richter, Marcel Broodthaers and Emmett Williams suggests. Hamilton tends particularly to engage with another artist's work the more it examines both art and life simultaneously, insists on a social context for art, surprises us by its form and combines complexity of idea with simplicity of expression. There is, not surprisingly, an overlap here with the qualities he admires in great artists of the past, but no less significantly there is a striking dissimilarity in idiom between their works and those of most of the contemporaries he admires. A quality which he commends repeatedly in others is that of absence of concern that their work as a whole should show consistency in terms of style; this unites a range of artists as wide as Picasso, Joyce, Stravinsky, Broodthaers, Cage, Beuys and Roth.

Of all other artists it is, however, with Marcel Duchamp that Hamilton's work, in a kaleidoscope of aspects, shows the closest affinity (fig.7). Both artists were thought to have produced little, but produced much. Their early mature careers were marked by works, involving wit, irony and eroticism, which were widely misunderstood but later seen to be of pioneering significance. Both produced extraordinary environments. Each renounced style as a determinant for the development of his work, but showed continuing interest in chance, reversal, perspective projections and time, as well as in human traces (moulds, substances produced by the body). Both made many works which operated like small theatres. In one sense or another they selected objects designed by others and made them their own, using them for another purpose. While concerned above all with the operation of the mind, both made works of great beauty of design and touch, marked by a distinctive tonal subtlety and accompanied by complex texts. Without the precedent of Duchamp it is inconceivable that Hamilton's work would have taken the course or the forms that it has. At the same time it has an entirely personal internal logic and self-sufficiency. Moreover, one of its debts to Duchamp is Hamilton's determination repeatedly to do the opposite of what Duchamp's example would most logically suggest.

fig.7 Marcel Duchamp **Etant Donnés 1° la chute d'eau 2° le gaz d'éclairage** 1946–66 Mixed media assemblage (detail) *Philadelphia Museum of Art: Gift of the Cassandra Foundation*

PRESENTING A WORLD

There is virtually no work by Hamilton in which the 'front' subject is not strongly related (or subjected) to some kind of structure, for example a systematic physical process or a clear intellectual programme. Chance and instinct have important parts to play, but always this is within or against such a framework. In a work by Hamilton, the interaction between motif and structure is an integral part of the 'subject'.

This interplay within a work by Hamilton mirrors his alertness to the significance that is added to an image by the nature of the act of presentation through which, via the media, it originally reached him and millions of others. It further reflects Hamilton's unusually strong interest in how *anything* is presented; this interest drives his design of technological artefacts, the presentation of his written words (both in typeface and on the page), the design of his catalogues and the installation of his exhibitions. Lecturing on Duchamp's 'Large Glass' in 1971,[23] he remarked: 'What the picture is is *where* it is'. While this observation has a special relevance when a work is transparent, it reflects significantly on Hamilton's view both of his own works and on images in general.

These issues relate to Hamilton's concern with the property of containment – with the limits which enclose (and therefore present) a given activity, and with the focus thus accorded to that activity and to its own internal relationships. It is as though he feels that the more the content of a work can be focused by a clear containing device, the more fully that content can be animated and opened up to examination. This explains his interest in the conventions of the book, the frame, the rectangle of the board or canvas and, at opposite extremes, both the postcard and the computer. As Hamilton has pointed out eloquently,[24] other such conventions with which he has been persistently involved are those of the house/home and the room, and it is striking how many of his works represent interiors. All of these, either visibly or by implication, are occupied by people, and on this analogy one can go further and see the great majority of Hamilton's works, whether interiors or not, not merely as containers but as little theatres, animated almost as if by a magician. In each, he opens up a complex world, proposing both an arena of human interaction and a theatre of the mind.

Among those of Hamilton's works in which one has explicitly the sense of watching an action unfolding are such contrasting examples as the Ulysses series, 'Chromatic Spiral' (no.6), 're Nude' (no.11), 'Just what is it...?' (no.13), '$he' (no.16), 'AAH!' (no.19), the 'Interior' paintings (nos.29,30), 'My Marilyn' (no.31), 'I'm dreaming of a white Christmas' (no.46), 'Swingeing London' (nos.48–54), the 'Fashion-plate' series (nos.57–68), the 'Soft landscapes' (nos.70,77), 'Picasso's meninas', 'The citizen' (no.82), 'Treatment room' (no.83), 'Lobby' (no.85), 'The subject' (no.87), 'Northend I' (no.91) and 'War games' (no.106)(which in military terminology represents a 'theatre' of war). In 'La Scala Milano' (no.90), the only work to represent an actual theatre, the cast (in a typical Hamilton reversal) is the audience. Hamilton has pointed to the expressive adoption of particular types of clothing by 'The citizen' and 'The subject' as a theatrical link between these two images. This interest in the self-conscious act of display is prefigured in Hamilton's examinations of women's and men's fashions and in the 'Fashion-plate' series. An implicit theme of Hamilton's self portraits over the decades is the change in the reading of a subject that can be wrought by its mode of presentation, and his three volumes of *Polaroid Portraits* (fig.8) can be read in terms of the contrasting interpretations of a given 'text' as if, again in the theatre, by an extraordinary register of directors. It cannot be without significance for Hamilton's own work that Duchamp's two outstanding versions of his central theme, the 'Large Glass' and 'Etant Donnés', each present a compelling action within an unusually defined enclosure.

Hamilton has been concerned to integrate the viewer into the operation of each work by devices of many kinds, ranging from the magnetism of perspective to the work's literal intrusion into the spectator's own space. But of course a central means of integration is to engage the viewer in the full content of the action which unfolds within the work. In the post-war period, the ideas of the work of art as an arena for actions and of the integration of the spectator into the work were common to a wide range of quite dissimilar-seeming tendencies in art. However odd it may seem, one can speak in these terms of a work by Hamilton just as one might about Abstract Expressionism, against which he was reacting. One can do so still more readily about the Happenings movement, which came out of Abstract Expressionism (among other sources) even as it reacted against it, for Hamilton's work has many points in common with it. As this affinity suggests, an important aspect of Hamilton's means of integrating the viewer was his open return to the *comédie humaine* as the centre of art. He did this primarily through painting and, as so often did such predecessors as Hogarth, Ford Madox Brown (fig.9) and Sickert, he cast his theme in contemporary terms.

One of Hamilton's devices for integrating the viewer is the mirror. The notion of reflection encompasses that of reversing the given, which has repeatedly sparked developments in Hamilton's art. Just as importantly, the mirror reflects at once both the viewer and the space which he and the work occupy. This association is a useful metaphor for the relationship Hamilton sees between work and viewer. His works not only reflect the viewer but they provoke him into reflecting on the many aspects of human behaviour which they themselves reflect.

fig.8 Brigid Polk: Richard Hamilton and Andy Warhol, 16 September 1969, Polaroid photograph (reproduced in Richard Hamilton (ed.), *Polaroid Portraits*, vol.1, 1972)

fig.9 Ford Madox Brown **The Last of England** 1852–5 Oil on panel *Birmingham Museums and Art Gallery*

Hamilton, therefore, sees the viewer very much as an active participant in the life of the work. Richard S. Field has gone so far as to say that 'If Hamilton may be faulted, it is for the burden of effort and cognition he imposes on the spectator. The suspended and fragmented meanings of his images must be detected, synthesised and interpreted before the richness of idea and sensuousness of surface may be fully appreciated.'[25] At the same time, even if one sets on one side Hamilton's crucial activity as a printmaker, which involves working closely with master printers in many techniques, a large number of his activities in art involve detailed collaboration with fellow professionals. Prominent examples include the exhibitions *This is Tomorrow* and *an Exhibit*, the typographical version of the *Green Box* and the reconstruction of the 'Large Glass', the design of the 'Lux 50' amplifier (no.80) and of the Diab DS–101 computer (no.88), and perhaps most all-encompassingly the many collaborations on individual paintings with Dieter Roth. Awareness of this aspect of Hamilton's work should not be allowed to obscure the facts that it is difficult to think of a painter who is more resourceful, unassisted (as he was till as recently as 1989) across a wide range of practical tasks and that it is when he is working alone in his studio that he feels he is most effective. Indeed, Hamilton does not search for opportunities of working with other artists or with professionals in technical disciplines. Collaboration tends to be the result either of his being pressed and finally succumbing because of the interest of the proposal, or of his belief in using every available resource. Its recurrence is, nevertheless, an index of the openness of his art in many directions.

LOCATION AND IDENTITY

These two types of collaboration – with the viewer and with colleagues – are evidence of an obsession which runs through Hamilton's whole oeuvre, namely with the merging of things normally considered distinct. He delights in merging one technique with another and one style with another; in employing figuration and abstraction at once; in merging one artist's work with another (not only Roth with Hamilton, but Hamilton into Bacon) and one being with another (Gaitskell and monster, no.26), but also one thing with another (telephone with record player in 'Pin-up', no.17, toaster and vacuum cleaner in '$he' (no.16) = 'toastuum') and one discipline with another (art with advertising, with design, with the Quantel 'Paintbox', with computer technology). He merges art with life, but does so in such a way as not only to demonstrate their complete interdependence but also, paradoxically, to reiterate their distinctness, celebrating the very artifice in which the making of art consists. He also demonstrates that while life is a process of continuous growth (as brought out by his early mature paintings and by *Growth and Form*) and of change (see *Man, Machine & Motion* and Hamilton's subsequent insistence on embracing new developments in the wider culture as they have occurred), the artist makes order out of this flux. The work of art is a point of concentration and of illumination.

Paradoxically, Hamilton's instinct towards the fusion of distinct elements goes hand in hand with an interest in extremes. With very many of the artists he admires most, their willingness to go to some extreme of form or expression is a key factor in his admiration. But in his own work, too, extremity of subject or of approach is common – as, for example, in the themes of human annihilation and intractable conflict which underlie such works as 'Portrait of Hugh Gaitskell . . .' (no.26), 'The citizen' (no.82), 'The sub-

fig.10 **People multiple (1/1)** 1968
Photographs *Private Collection*

fig.11a (above) and 11b
(overleaf) Sir John Tenniel, two
illustrations to Lewis Carroll, *Through
the Looking-Glass and What Alice
Found There*, 1872

fig.12a (above) and 12b (overleaf)
After Marcel Duchamp? 1969
Colour photographs *The artist*

ject' (no.87) and 'War games' (no.106); of marked purity and impurity respectively, in 'Lux 50' (no.80) and 'Sunset' (no.75); or of substantial physical detachment in a work like 'Still-life' (no.32), by contrast with extended physical engagement in the painting process in 'Lobby' (no.85). Again, one could contrast the minimal interference, the sense of the realisation of an idea in a flash, in a work such as 'Sign' (no.74) with the extreme patience called for in the reconstruction of the 'Large Glass' – an embracing of extremes which, of course, recalls Duchamp. Hamilton has also been concerned, as in 'People' (no.34), with taking an image to the extreme limit of viability, the knife edge between recognition and the abstraction to which this extremely figurative painter repeatedly gives such prominence.

With so strong an interest both in the concept of opposites/complementaries and in the sense of continuity which his obsession with merging seems to imply, it is not surprising that a further persistent subject of Hamilton's work should be the very process of passing from one condition or location to another. Again, his early exhibitions, *Growth and Form* and *Man, Machine & Motion*, address this theme, while paintings such as the 'Trainsitions' (nos.9,10) and 're Nude' (no.11) mark out successive stages in a prescribed movement. In the zoom-in theme of works such as the screenprint 'A little bit of Roy Lichtenstein for . . .', 1964 and the painting 'People' (no.34) (its concept demonstrated, step by step, in 'People multiple', 1968, fig.10) this single-track trajectory takes on the sense of extreme elongation. In other works, the viewer's sense is of a bewildering multiplicity of possible positions and directions. This experience, offered by Hamilton's environmental work *an Exhibit*, is repeated in a different guise in his painting 'Lobby' – only one of the more overt examples of a propensity in all his works to compel the viewer to ask (and on more than one level of meaning) 'Where am I?' A continuous theme of Hamilton's is the relationship between the specific point and infinity.

A change in condition or location implies the crossing of one or a succession of thresholds. Hamilton's works tend to signal the points at which these are being crossed. As the catalogue introduction to *Man, Machine & Motion* pointed out, 'The atmosphere of the photographs [in the exhibition] is a strange one. No human being before was ever portrayed in quite this situation: no contraption made by man before had the unique potentialities of this materialisation of an historic dream. The photographs in fact discover man in a new relationship'. In the complete theatre that each of his works conjures for the viewer, Hamilton often marks the boundary between that depicted world and the space outside it (for example, by the space bars in 'Hommage à Chrysler Corp.' (no.14), the curtain in the 'Interior' paintings (nos.29,30), the slicing-off of the image in 'Mother and child' (no.84), the vertical dividers in 'The citizen' (no.82) and 'The subject' (no.87)). This frontier is, however, boundary rather than barrier, for by as many devices as are introduced in this way to give the viewer pause, Hamilton provides others to ensure that each work actively draws the viewer in.

Entering the particular world of a work by Hamilton has the character as much of an induction as of an act of physical transition. The sense of change involved is that of a mystery. It is perhaps no accident that the world – so very near to us and yet so other – depicted in 'I'm dreaming of a white Christmas' (no.46) recalls the moment when, extraordinarily, Alice *passes through* the Looking Glass (fig.11). Hamilton's 'After Marcel Duchamp?', 1969 (fig.12) invites the eye to move through the image of fifty parallel sheets of glass. But in *all* Hamilton's paintings, however distinct the image, there is a sense of a number of veils (not all of them visible), lying between us and the original motif, which have successively to be drawn back in the mind. His work makes clear that in order for a veil to enhance imaginative experience in this sense it does not have to be of ancient origin. Hamilton shows that if, for one set of reasons, modern devices of communication interpose layers between the original motif and the way we experience it, art can take advantage of these devices for reasons of its own.

As strong in Hamilton's work as the sense of passing from one location or one condition to another is the sense of the passage of time. This, too, can on occasion be shown by means of visible notation, as in 're Nude' (no.11), but more pervasive is the feeling the works give of time extending over a far longer period than that simply of their own process of execution. In 'The citizen' and 'The subject' Hamilton uses this capacity as a metaphor for the depth of the entrenchment of two opposed beliefs. The mysterious 'Langan's' (no.76) elides past with present (itself now, in turn, past) and in the 'North-end' paintings (nos.91,104) Hamilton seems to direct our awareness at once far back into the past and forward into the future. Part of his delight in reconstructing the 'Large Glass' lay in the mystery of seeing this shattered work, with its aged beauty, fresh and clear again, for a time, as in its youth.

All artists enrich their art by referring back to earlier aspects of their own work. A lifeblood of Hamilton's, on which he draws continuously, is the unpredictable unfolding of events in the world, but it is into the theatre of his own actions as an artist that he brings these materials, and it is in *its* terms that he re-presents them in his work. In this way Hamilton's source images, though already charged with the significance of their origin, become in addition the vehicles for that complex range of preoccupations of Hamilton's own which, taken together, identify his personal view of life. This constant reference back and forth, across an oeuvre now of more than fifty years' duration, is perhaps more pronounced in Hamilton's case than in most. It is undertaken not as a game, but rather as a means of affirming a standpoint – one which can be located, ultimately, not on the surface of the work but, *through* it, in the domain of thought and of feeling.

A PARTICULAR PERSPECTIVE

What, then, is the atmosphere of Hamilton's work and vision? They reflect an attitude of intense curiosity – a determination to understand what is happening and to know *how* things work, yet also continually to ask whether things *have* to be as they are. Hamilton does not come up with dogmatic answers; indeed, both his initial choice of image and his treatment of it are directed, among other aims, towards the provoking of questions. He asserts that, in many aspects of life, to question is itself as responsible an approach as to insist on a fixed viewpoint. He also demonstrates that the role of the individual need not be one of passive acceptance, and that life is a matter of taking decisions. He shows that this is the case in all its aspects, however 'neutral' in import these may be (as in the case of clothes, interiors, etc.), but more far-reachingly when it is a case of decisions which can affect the lives of large numbers of people, or that of an individual to a shattering degree. The responsibility, he implies, is greatest when exercised by those who occupy the seats of power. Just as he approaches the making of a work as a form of problem-solving, so does he see the conduct of life, again from the most trivial to the most epoch-making matters, in the same terms. But in both instances, and however detached or analytical the appropriate processes may need to be, the purpose of solving the problem, in his view, is the enhancement of human life.

fig.11(b)

fig.12(b)

An aspect of Hamilton's lack of dogmatism and of his refusal to see a given work as being limited to a single meaning is the way in which he joins exceptionally clear statements of what he intended in the work with an unusual openness to learning from others what it is that he has in fact done. While he is the sole author of each work, he constructs it in such a way as to place the viewer in the role of active participator, on several levels. The wink which, in '$he' (no. 16), flickers at the spectator who stands engaging with the work is a symbol of the sense of complicity which is a keynote of Hamilton's whole endeavour.

It is also a symbol of human warmth, and this is the quality that lies at the heart of the vision of an artist often so strangely described as being detached, as though his methods were an index of his art's purpose. His work always either represents the human figure or searches out and charts the traces of human existence, that mystery which animates and gives significance to interior, to landscape, to media invention, to the political act, to selection, word, mark, diagram and artistic process – alike, in fact, both to technology and to the dream, to artifice and to the imagination. Hamilton asserts that the artist must be free to harness any means that his own era offers, and that in doing this he may provide a lasting image of human experience in that time and place. But his central subject and his purpose are among the constants of fine art as it has come down to us through the centuries. By its combination of economy with fullness – its concentration – Hamilton's work will continue to engage the senses, the intellect and the feelings when our own era itself is history.

NOTES

1 'Joseph Beuys (1921–1986)', *Art Monthly*, no.94, March 1986, pp.10–11.

2 Paul Tillich, 'A Prefatory Note', in P. Selz (ed.), *New Images of Man*, exh.cat., Museum of Modern Art, New York 1959, pp.9–10.

3 In 1988 Hamilton recalled how when he discovered the writing of James Joyce, in the 1940s, 'I had already come to the notion that maybe there wasn't any point in trying to establish this kind of stylistic identity that most artists feel is the aim. The general pattern for an artist, coming out of art school is that until he's identified himself by the way he works, achieved a style that's recognisable, he's not an artist. I resent all this, I felt I needed more freedom'. 'Hamilton's Progress: Richard Hamilton interviewed by Bill Hare and Andrew Patrizio', *Alba*, no.9, 1988, pp.40–3.

4 In 'concept:technology〉artwork' in *teknologi〈ide〉konstwerk : Richard Hamilton*, exh.cat., Moderna Museet, Stockholm 1989, pp.22–4.

5 Lecture given in the Botany Theatre, University of London, 17 February 1971 (tape courtesy of Institute of Contemporary Arts, London.)

6 'Glorious Technicolor, Breathtaking CinemaScope and Stereophonic Sound', lecture of 1959 published in Richard Hamilton, *Collected Words*, 1982, pp.112–32.

7 'Dogma and Talent', *The New Yorker*, 15 Oct. 1973, pp.115–19.

8 'For the Finest Art try – POP', *Gazette*, no.1, 1961.

9 Conversely, just as the 1960s were getting into full swing, Hamilton began to sound a note of pessimism and warning about the forces which threatened liberty and about the dark underside of contemporary culture, a theme which he and increasing numbers of artists would develop in the decades ahead. It is a curious fact that while the catalogue of *New Images of Man*, with which Hamilton's work was in such contrast, was introduced by the well-known quotation from Goya, 'The sleep of reason begets monsters', one of the first of Hamilton's works to signal his own changing outlook, post-Pop, was an image of a political leader turning into a monster in what seemed to Hamilton to be an abandonment of reason. This gives added interest to David Mellor's exploration of the underlying imagery of Hamilton's first Pop painting, on pp.34–5 of this catalogue.

10 cf. two texts by Hamilton on the subject of Conceptual art, 'Propositions' and 'A conceptual exhibition', reprinted in *Collected Words*, pp.266–7.

11 See James Hall, 'Richard Hamilton', *Apollo*, no.336, February 1990, pp.101–4.

12 Hamilton associated Herbert Read with the advocacy along too prescriptive lines of concepts such as 'truth to materials' and 'form follows function'. In different ways, Hamilton himself thought there was much truth in these notions, but it seemed to him that in Read's interpretation they led only to an idealising purity or 'innocence' of form. To Hamilton, the belief that modes of expression should be governed by an ideal was deadening. He sought not a narrowing down but an opening up of possibilities.

13 cf. David Robbins, 'The Independent Group: Forerunners of Postmodernism?', in *The Independent Group: Postwar Britain and the Aesthetics of Plenty*, exh.cat., ICA, London 1990, pp.237–48.

14 Marcel Duchamp believed that each thing should contain its own opposite.

15 See also Hamilton's observation about life being a compound of the beautiful and the grim, in entry on no.72, para.2.

16 This kind of complementarism operates at all levels of Hamilton's work, for example when an examination of female modes of adornment was followed by one of male, or an examination of convexity in the 'Guggenheim' reliefs (nos.37–42) by one of concavity in 'La Scala Milano' (no.90).

17 See entry on no.27 for the relationship between this idea and the writings of James Joyce.

18 See entry on no.10 for Hamilton's view on the relationship between this and the vision of Francis Bacon.

19 15 May 1968, author's notes at the time.

20 e.g. 'The Quantel machine is a wonderful device for sketching and formulating ideas but I feel a certain relief in returning to the practice of painting to "output" "The Apprentice Boy" ['The subject'] in a permanent form' (in 'concept:technology〉artwork', 1989). Also: 'I have yet to be convinced that it will, some day, be possible to build a computer dedicated to image processing that can equal the brain of Velàsquez, or to make a printer that can output hard copy to equal the sensory experience of his great painting "Las Meninas".' (In William Townsend Memorial Lecture, *The Hard Copy Problem*, given at University College London, 18 November 1991 [not yet published]).

21 'The Distant Involvement of Richard Hamilton. An Interview', in *Vanguard*, Journal of Vancouver Art Gallery, September 1978, pp.12–14.

22 'My love of art came from museums', Hamilton interviewed by Jonathan Watkins, *Art International*, no.10, Spring 1990, pp.51–2.

23 See n.5, above.

24 In 'Rooms', in *Four Rooms*, exh. cat., Arts Council of Great Britain, shown at Liberty's, London, February–March 1984 and tour.

25 Introduction to *Richard Hamilton, Image and Process*, exh.cat., Tate Gallery, London 1983, p.9.

THE PLEASURES AND SORROWS OF MODERNITY: VISION, SPACE AND THE SOCIAL BODY IN RICHARD HAMILTON

David Mellor

MAPPING AND DISPLAYING THE NEW BRITAIN

fig. 1 Overseeing a New Britain: Map-model of Harlow New Town, 1951

Richard Hamilton made his earliest mature paintings in the early 1950s, at that watershed moment in British culture when the Welfare State was newly fabricated and the post-war settlement of British society seemed secure. (He was, in fact, personally acquainted with its architect, the Labour politician Aneurin Bevan, through the milieu of the Socialist playwright and patron Benn Levy.) Hamilton can be initially imagined as an artist-technician, an artificer at the crossroads of commercial display design and traditional Renaissance perspective drawing skills; but in the context of a welfareist, communitarian culture which was poised on the threshold of a consumer society. Here was the prospect of a new Britain where deferred utopias from the international modernist 1920s might be enacted. While he studied at the Slade he helped to support his family by making models for exhibitions, in particular by building large 'map-models' of the designated New Towns – Harlow, Basildon and Speke – for the Festival of Britain *Exhibition of Architecture, Town Planning and Building Research* at Poplar (fig. 1). This panoptic rendering of a section of British landscape in all its topography and habitation recurs for Hamilton in the mid-1960s with 'Landscape', 1965–6 (no. 35) – but this time processed by a self-reflexive, game-playing switching of representational codes, rather than as a mimetic, miniaturised simulation of the new Socialist Britain. His planifying aerial view maps groups of humans ('Trafalgar Square', 1965–7, no. 36, 'People', 1965–6, no. 34), while he perspectively dissects social interiors – both are indicators of a constant strategy for him of all-encompassing scrutiny and cultural surveillance.

His interest in technical drawing was first aroused through lectures on perspective given by Walter Bayes at the Royal Academy Schools in the late 1930s. 'This', Hamilton has said, 'was an opportunity to learn a classical tradition. Bayes would start by making a blind, backhanded stab with his chalk at a giant blackboard saying: "You are here" (bang). Then he'd drag his chalk along a parallel beam: "This is the horizon", and then a mark was made bisecting the horizon immediately above his first dot; "This is your centre of vision" (bang). It was really magical'.[1] Classical perspective order in Hamilton's hands, like those of Duchamp, was a clarifying authority, a sure and certain guide but also – paradoxically – a high road to 'magical' excess and the fantastic, as in the delirious rationalism of 'Lobby', 1985–7 (no.85). His wartime 'reserved occupation' employment as an engineering jig and tool draughtsman, which 'required drawing unambiguous descriptions of form to within a thousandth of an inch',[2] permanently disposed him towards certain spatial schemas, one in particular: 'I do tend to work with frontal views . . . with parallel perspective you can even measure up from the drawing.'[3] He has preferred these scrupulous technical gazes, learned both at the Royal Academy and at the Ealing Training Centre; planified over-views, isometric projections, parallel perspectives and front elevations: they have, we might say, helped make him an artist.

Hamilton can be glimpsed encountering modernism in its most oblique and commercial forms when he was an adolescent. In 1937, aged fifteen, he was earning twenty-five shillings a week in the newly opened German emigré design school, the Reimann School of Art, in Regency Street. There he met distinguished German refugee designers in the commercial context of work on money-making projects – Hamilton was employed, for example, cutting out plywood lettering for British Federation of Industries exhibitions, but when business was slack he was allowed to go into the purer realm of the life drawing classes.

Hamilton was introduced to the manufacture of what would become another key site in his visual imagination: the seductive promotional world of display stands. In the late 1940s, he realised that the great modernist expositions constituted a genre of modernist artefacts in their own right, places where the disposition of information and products could be combined with the pleasures of a temporary installation space. The irruption of these promotional places into his output, marking him as a hybrid artisan as well as an artificer, is visible in the series of exhibitions he mounted through the 1950s – *Growth and Form* (1951); *Man, Machine & Motion* (1955); *an Exhibit* (1957–8) – and up to the present with 'Treatment room', 1983–4 (no.83) and 'Lobby', 1985–7 (no.85). From that early experience onwards, 'installation is part of what I've been doing ever since'.[4] More than that, it overlays – literally with his systematic technical drawing techniques – his paintings as well, evident in flat, false perspective constructions such as 'Interior I', 1964 (no.29) and 'Interior II', 1964 (no.30), where walls and screens explode about the figure of the fatal woman, building a display space for guilt.

Taken altogether, Hamilton's drive for space and systems of perspective has a strong and peculiar metaphysic: it begins in affirming strict rationality by a modernist civic optic, which moves from celebrations of the joys of a mixed welfareist/consumer economy in the late 1950s, to mourning the decline of that civic entity in the 1980s.

SCIENCE AND PHANTASY

When Tomas Maldonado lectured at the ICA in April 1957 on automation and the implications of the technological revolution, he dwelt on Britain's European lead in the 1940s in developing 'scientific manpower' with its native virtues of 'courage, phantasy and realism'.[5] Hamilton, in the audience as an admirer of Maldonado's pedagogy, was in fact an exemplary standard bearer for this new constituency of technicians in post-war British social life. In 1943, he had left the rackety eight-man Design Unit team in New Oxford Street, for the vast EMI complex at Hayes. Under the conditions of total war the most rapid developments in electronics were being pioneered in the research block where Hamilton, as a jig and tool draughtsman, worked. He participated in the design team for the manufacture of the first British transistors in 1944–5: he acknowledges that he was 'at the cutting edge of technology'.[6] It was a workplace where Hamilton learnt the skills of scrounging parts and services, improvising a sophisticated state-of-the-art audio system – before the dawn of hi-fi – on a DIY basis. He recognised that this *bricoleur* approach to science and technology unlocked crucial areas of the imagination: as he was to say in 1960, 'contact with the fantasy world is made all the more memorable when the bridge is a newly experienced technological marvel'.[7]

fig.2 The triumph of technotronic culture: 'EMI The Electronic Heart of Britain', advertisement, 1951

fig. 3 The enigmas of perception and buried biomorphism: Perceptual illusion, Group 2, *This is Tomorrow*, exhibition catalogue, 1956

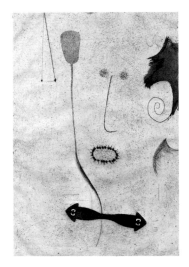

fig.4 The artist's face as carnival site, **Self-portrait b** 1951 Hard and soft-ground etching, engraving, drypoint, aquatint and punch

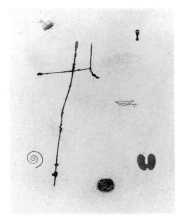

fig.5 Diversity and difference in organic mixity: **Heteromorphism** 1951 Hard and soft-ground etching, drypoint and aquatint

Hamilton has sought to bridge the gap between what C.P. Snow had dubbed *The Two Cultures* (1959); of science and technology on the one hand and the liberal humanities on the other. It was a project he shared with determined ICA Independent Group colleagues, Reyner Banham, John McHale and Lawrence Alloway, throughout the 1950s. Theirs was an attempt to account for the massive post-war proliferation of scientific and technical discourses, perceived as originating mainly in the United States. This effort could be said to have begun with Hamilton's initiation and arrangement of the ICA's Festival of Britain exhibition, *Growth and Form*, in 1951. The inspiration for this installation was the outlook and discoveries of the late Victorian morphologist D'Arcy Wentworth Thompson; Hamilton had found that his fellow students – Henderson, Paolozzi and Turnbull – were spending hours in the Natural History Museum examining fantastic biological forms from the fossil collection, re-accessing Surrealist biomorphism at its root: 'the reason was that D'Arcy Thompson had become part of their visual vocabulary while they were at The Slade'.[8] For Hamilton, Thompson's two-volume *On Growth and Form* (1917) was a poetic text – revealed by Henderson to him at the same time as Duchamp's *Green Box*: Thompson, like Duchamp, possessed a 'cool, godlike understanding'.[9] Again, as with Duchamp, a process of discipleship followed for Hamilton to the 'beautiful theory and beautiful mathematics'[10] (even Hamilton's characterisation echoes Duchamp) of Thompson's magisterial book.

The biomorphic flourishes through the pictorial productions of Hamilton's career: in the lowly specimens in 'Particular System', 1951 (no.7); in the claw or three digited positive/negative visual illusion in the *This is Tomorrow* catalogue in 1956 (fig. 3); in the de-focused aggregate humanoids in 'People', 1965–6 (no.34); and in the body cavity horrors that peep out of the darkness in the right panel of 'The subject', 1988–90 (no.87). We might speak of displaced representations of the human body here; when he painted one of his mid-1950s car pictures he called it 'Carapace' (1954), imagining soft creatures, mollusc-like humanoids, inside the shell of the car, a technicised twist to that Neo-Romantic motif in Sutherland and Vaughan of curled human body and organic shell. But Hamilton's strategy was to drastically relocate the organic: to remove it far from the 'romantic fallacy' and to mix it with the contaminated networks of automotive technologies and the 'low', vulgar commercial genre of science fiction. This switching of the organic from its customary associations, to making it keep strange, possibly even bad, company, distinguishes works by Hamilton from the early 1950s. A carnivalesque slipping of meaning where flat-worms – with eyes, Hamilton observes, like the silent cinema comedian Ben Turpin – figure as Hamilton's bow-tie, organises the etching 'Self-portrait b', 1951 (fig.4), for example.

How far Hamilton recognised the radical heterogeneity of his pictures can be indicated by his title for an etching for the cover of the *Growth and Form* catalogue, 'Heteromorphism', 1951 (fig.5). Where Darwin's conventionalised notion of evolution (it formed the centrepiece display of the 'Living World' section in the Festival of Britain's main site) stressed unified lines of biological descent, Thompson had asserted a revisionist, entirely opposed framework of irreducible difference between certain species and forms. In the conclusion to *On Growth and Form* he called this 'A "Principle of Discontinuity" that is inherent in all our classifications, whether mathematical, physical or biological.'[11] In other words, heterogeneity seemed to order the universe, not an 'oceanic' homogeneity. It was this latter 'oceanic', undifferentiated, cosmic vision that swung into a kind of mysticism which motivated the parallel 1951 exhibition to *Growth and Form* in the United States, Gyorgy Kepes's *The New Landscape in Science and Art* at the

Massachusetts Institute of Technology (MIT). Hamilton contacted Kepes during the course of their projects, but he thought poorly of the ideology and routinised design of the MIT show.

At this point the theories of Thompson and Hamilton's concurrent fascination with James Joyce coincide. As Hamilton has said, 'Joyce wanted to be all-inclusive',[12] but it was an inclusiveness which acknowledged different modes and styles, an aesthetic strategy of differences. The recurrent turning by Hamilton to the motley, to the discontinuous and carnivalesque – the serious buffoonery in 'Self-portrait', 1969 (fig.6) from the 'Cosmetic studies' series, for example, demonstrates a splicing of bodies and gender in the complicit wink of Hamilton's own version of Duchamp's Rrose Selavy. This recalls Joyce's declared principle of 're-embodying': that was to reweave intermittent and opposite fragments of language. Thompson's 'Principle of Discontinuity' rhymed with Joyce's: analogues of a composite world vision with which Hamilton was to proceed, heteromorphically.

In the two years researching *Growth and Form* for the ICA, Hamilton had drawn in J.D. Bernal (personification of a certain Leftist scientific rationality) and the resources of the National Physical Laboratory. At the Slade School, Reg Butler helped build the armature of the skeletal sight screen for the exhibition, while on the three dimensional grid constructed by Hamilton – an open frame and panel structure – stood models of minute organisms, radiolaria and sponges illustrated in Thompson's book (fig.7).[13] These organisms were complemented by a wall-sized blow-up of an x-ray diffraction pattern of a crystal, appropriated by Hamilton from the research scientist Kathleen Lonsdale: a scientific document which became crucial to the genesis of the centre of vision in his painting 'Particular System', 1951 (no.7). The image of a radiating stream of particles was placed by Hamilton onto a lenticular stand that acted as a housing for strobe and other optical displays: a pun on the overall eye shape of the stand that was projecting a world as well as being the gazed-at target. The spectacular diffraction emissions, blown-up, combined the sublime scale of an off-planetary vision of dispersed galactic matter while also anticipating the consumer-graphics trajectories of the (Duchampian) path of the toast from the vacuum cleaner, in '$he', 1958–61 (no.16). As Le Corbusier (a longstanding admirer of Thompson) said at the opening of the exhibition, this ensemble of scientific samplings was the work of a poet. Across on the other side of the narrowed gap between the 'two cultures' the crystallographer Professor Kathleen Lonsdale declared: 'Scientists . . . derive not only useful information but great aesthetic satisfaction from their studies.'[14]

fig.6 The artist's face as carnival site, **Fashion-plate (a) self-portrait** 1969 Collage, enamel and cosmetics on paper *Rita Donagh*

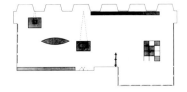

fig.7 Exhibiting the eye of science: plan and elevation of *Growth and Form* 1951

THE MOVING EYE

While D'Arcy Thompson's magnificent system of plural organisms offered one model of a 'beautiful science', Hamilton was to find an equal inspiration in the writing of the contemporary US scientist, James J. Gibson. Gibson's influence brought the question of vision in motion to the forefront of Hamilton's concerns. If Thompson had indicated a multitude of teeming inhabitants for Hamilton's pictures, Gibson's *The Perception of the Visual World* (1950) donated a new kind of space, based on wartime research into human visual perception. Gibson's pragmatic, empirically verified space was opened up by USAAF and US Navy experiments that would, in the hands of Hamilton, extend the pictorial researches of Cézanne.[15] Alerted to it by Lawrence Alloway – who subscribed

fig.8 Swooping, serial schemas of military flight as cue for Hamilton's 're Nude', 1954 (no.11) and 'Still-life?', 1954 (no.12): 'A landing field during an approach . . .' J.J. Gibson, *The Perception of the Visual World*, Boston, 1950, fig.59

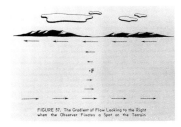

fig.9 The landscape passes in paradoxical motion: the source for 'Trainsition IIII', 1954 (no.10): 'The gradient of flow looking to the right . . .' J.J. Gibson, *The Perception of the Visual World*, Boston, 1950, fig.57

to *Scientific American* – Hamilton found what he called 'Gibson's wonderful book'.[16] In it was a stress upon the visual reading of the entire environment, what Gibson called 'the totality of cues',[17] often from an aerial vantage point, scanning organic and manmade textures for depth and meaning. A richly differentiated, complex world is spread out in an exhilarating pilot's view by Gibson (fig.8) as it surges to meet the eye (pulsing in, like Hamilton's 'Still-life?', 1954 (no.12) and to race away from it. (Two of Hamilton's Independent Group colleagues, Henderson and Turnbull, had both been bomber pilots in the recent world war.) Here was an overview similar to that constructed by Hamilton across the projected new Britain of modern towns and roads, or like a fantastically empowered, technically rationalised, jet-engined version of Bayes' perspectivised renaissance of little worlds in umber wash.

In 'd'Orientation', 1952 (no.8), Hamilton mixed and multiplied such traditional perspectives with Gibson's dynamic viewpoints, while floating a medusa jelly-fish's dangling manubrium across the limpid overview space. In this way the round generative 'buds' on the tentacle – like the nodes in Duchamp's 'Network of Stoppages' 1914 – were morphologically punned with the black circled centres of vision. The painting's narrative looks forward to Gibson's elaborate discussion of how organisms orientate themselves in their environments; 'from the highest to the lowest . . . The human species has a still more differentiated environment'.[18] Gibson's conception of human orientation made a deep impression on Hamilton; summoning up the image of a species negotiating a dense envelope of information – the profane, crowded, heteromorphic universe of Joyce – 'the human habitat consists of millions of things to which a man can find his way'.[19] This was, perhaps, a pre-vision of that packed room in 'Just what is it . . .?', 1956 (no.13), saturated with information. To Gibson, Hamilton added Norbert Wiener's epochal *Human Use of Human Beings* (1954), which saw the human machine cybernetically using feedback in the orienting task of 'adjusting to the contingencies of the outer environment'.[20]

In Gibson the human oriented itself in a topographical schema and locomoted with intent. Hamilton recycled Muybridge's walking man whose contours – in 'After Muybridge' (1953) – resembled the jellyfish's manubrium. Human vision was mobile and in his painting 'Trainsition IIII', 1954 (no.10), Hamilton appropriated Gibson's own diagrams of an 'active observer' in a speeding train with spots of fixation and velocities of flow marked with arrows (fig.9).[21] Hamilton re-did for himself, on the King's Cross to Newcastle train, Gibson's experiments on the relative motion of objects in the visual field of a speeding spectator: objects moved in different directions, the world blurred. In the foreground of the painting, matter has disintegrated, since 'there is no terrain surface on which to anchor the visual world',[22] and depth perception – life and death to a pilot landing on an aircraft carrier or to a trapeze artist – had become ambiguous.

Hamilton would spend much time, from the mid-1950s to the present, pictorially investigating what Gibson called 'the perspective of blur', but re-finding it in the mass media universe. This was in the cueless unfocused haze of narrow depth of field colour photographs: his first wife, Terry, called it 'phloo'. In this unstable zone photography lost its factuality; it fell into Wiener's realm of the contingent and entropic, it drifted, too, towards the erotic. Hamilton rhapsodised this aspect of visual instability in his extraordinary essay, 'Urbane Image', in 1963. 'Definition swings in and out along a lip length. A world of fantasy with unique erotic overtones. Intimacy, trespass yet, on a purely visual plane . . . a dizzy drop into a swoon-like coloured fuzz'.[23] Into his systems the incommensurable had arrived, dissolving bounded vision, being welcomed playfully, finding there the sense of desire, an 'otherness' which eluded mapping. At the borders of rationality and science Hamilton continually runs into the fantastic: it's near at hand in the alien installation of *Growth and Form*. In 'Trainsition IIII' the speeding car just might be being observed not from a prosaic train, but from that favoured point of view of mid-1950s science fiction films; off-planet but proximate, tracking a desert road and a solitary automobile, the alien gaze from a flying saucer, as in *Earth versus the Flying Saucers* or Hamilton's preferred *This Island Earth*. To come under such alien scrutiny launches us out towards Hamilton's more pessimistic civic vistas of the 1980s, particularly the cold wastes and the bug-eyed TV-monitor in 'Treatment room' (no.83).

Perhaps it is within this range of symbolising vision and finding metaphors for the eye that some of his most fascinating pictorial fictions are to be found. All through the era of high-formalist flatness as an imperative of painting in the later 1950s and 1960s, Hamilton conserved traditional concerns with depth (we see him consolidating this through his engagement with Gibson's analyses). Stereometry was a prime priority for him – symptomatically, in his writings on the 3-D and CinemaScope cinema of the 1950s, it was the issue of the audience's illusion of depth and their bonus of satisfaction gained which preoccupied him. The relief format regularly patterns his work: the abstract bodywork of Sophia Loren's '57 Buick rises up from the picture surface in 'Hers is a lush situation', 1958 (no.15); the breasts of 'Pin-up', 1961 (no.17) are padded out in cellulose and the 'Solomon R Guggenheim', 1965–6 (nos.37–42) swells up, flying saucer-like or like the over-weening eye of Odilon Redon's balloon: proximity, depth and desire are conjoined in these bulging sights.

Spectators of Hamilton's paintings plunge towards those centres of vision that Bayes emphatically studded into a compulsively perspectivised world of plentitude and depth. Hamilton has referred to them in 'd'Orientation' (no.8) as targets: 'These centres fix your vision like a bulls-eye'.[24] These black suns are active spots, catching and fixing our gaze and in the process implicating us in our exterior position – here was the radiating dark-pupilled eye embellished by Lonsdale's diffraction patterns and situated to be looked at in *Growth and Form*: here, too, is the infant's veiled look to the paternal photographer elided with the painting's spectator in 'Mother and child', 1984–5 (no.84). With these artefacts Hamilton confirms Jacques Lacan's observations on the meaning of scopophilia, that is, the desire to look: 'the thing looked at is a dark spot that dazzles in the sun . . . it was looking at Lacan . . . Every gaze is like this: it designates and it designates the position of the person who is looking'.[25] And sometimes a gleam rises, *repoussoir*, out of his pictures, a reflection in the chrome in 'Hommage à Chrysler Corp.', 1957 (no.14); the implicating highlit blobs in 'La Scala Milano', 1989 (no.90); the mirror behind Patricia Knight in 'Interior I', 1964 (no.29) – (compare his paradigm of the convex mirror in 'The Arnolfini Marriage') or the reflecting silvered body of 'Toaster', 1966–7 (no.43): as Lacan himself said 'that which is light looks at me and by means of that light in the depths of my eye something is painted . . . it is always that gleam of light'.[26]

CONSUMPTION, OPTIMISM AND ITS LIMITS

There is a long moment of enchantment with the spectacle of the modern world in Hamilton's art. Artificer of a renewed modernity, he reforged the Futurist contract with the transformative powers of technology and its consumer products. Retrospecting, from the vantage point of 1990 and a very different, bleaker, cultural sensibility, he wrote: 'We seemed to be taking a course towards a rosy future and our changing Hi-Tech world was embraced with a starry eyed confidence; a surge of optimism which took us into the 1960's.'[27] Here Hamilton may be almost too harsh with himself: his intoxication with the infinite expansionism of the 'Fabulous Fifties' was never unquali-fied; his American car and 'white goods' paintings, his women consumers and male astronauts of this idyllic moment of technics and pleasure, from 1957 to 1963, were serious, sonorous and occasionally conflicted.

Aiming for a Baudelairean register of celebration for the heroic and mythic in social modernity, he was instead read as being a satirist, specifically on the delights of American consumption. This can be illustrated by the words of the US Cultural Attaché to Britain, Stefan Munsing, when he visited Hamilton's Highgate house around 1960, asking him why he was 'always mocking America in his pictures'.[28] There was a split in Hamilton's attitude towards the United States and it marked a fissure between his overt politics and his cultural politics. A veteran of dissent on the Left through the 1950s – present at the turbulent Whitehall protest during the Suez crisis – he and Terry Hamilton were early members of the Campaign for Nuclear Disarmament and were jailed for a weekend during the mass arrests over demonstrations against the stationing of US Polaris submarines at the Holy Loch in April 1961. Among London avant-garde artists his stand was virtually a solitary one, a matter noticed by the Situation and RCA painters who knew of his staunch radicalism.[29]

fig.10 Making corporate signs, I: Churchill Gear Machines logo, designed by Richard Hamilton c.1956

His was a complex cultural optimism, grounded in direct experience of the pleasures of consuming technical goods: a discerning consumer himself, Dick Smith recalled him taking great pains to import a Braun radio with a rare combination of white casing and grey buttons, about 1959.[30] Most crucially, Hamilton was aware of contemporary industrial procedures, not just, as we have seen, as a draughtsman in the 1930s and 1940s, but also as a design consultant, in the mid and late 1950s, when his clients included firms such as Churchill Gear Machines (fig.10), an engineering works where he felt at home. In Hamilton's milieu in the late 1950s the patronage of the manufac-turer E.J. Power was vital; for example, Lawrence Alloway, beside his ICA job, was financially supported by consultancy work for Power's electronics company, Murphy Radio and Television in Welwyn Garden City. Power amassed the single most import-ant collection of contemporary American and British art, while producing television sets for Britain's suburbs.

fig.11 Making corporate signs, II: Granada TV logo, designed by Richard Hamilton c.1956

Power eventually purchased Hamilton's first US car painting, 'Hommage à Chrysler Corp.' 1957 (no.14), in 1963. If Hamilton had been long integrated with electronics, the same was certainly true of motorcar technology. His father had worked as a driver for Henley's, the prestige car showroom in the West End, and from the end of the 1920s Hamilton junior would often accompany him 'running in' the engine of a top of the range Jaguar or Bentley: 'It was rather glamorous to sit in the front of the car with my father',[31] and this mobile vision would be replayed in paintings such as 'Carapace', 1954. 'Hommage à Chrysler Corp.', conserving the glamour, is in the alternative child-hood space of motorcar associations, the showroom; a place that joins those other crisp and tense stages for display in Hamilton's iconography. An example was his stand at the March 1958 Ideal Home Exhibition, *A Gallery for a Collector* where a blown-up photo of the new Citroen DS entered the domestic space (Hamilton hung 'Hommage à Chrysler Corp.' on the wall in this installation, repeating and wittily insetting a painted showroom within a showroom-cum-gallery) (fig.12). As with 'Interior I' (no.29) and

'Interior II', (no. 30), a near but filmily disembodied scene is framed in 'Hommage à Chrysler Corp.' – conditions of display, of framing are invariably stressed in Hamilton: here, internally, a horizontal bar, with connotations of a Mies van der Rohe steel beam, while in 'The citizen' (no. 82) a vertical metallic strap thematises the prisoner's separation: externally, Hamilton was probably the first British artist to use overall aluminium frames for his paintings.

fig. 12 A showroom for glamour, cars and art: Terry Hamilton in *A Gallery for a Collector* 1958, Ideal Home Exhibition

'Mechnical evolution is comparable with the law of natural selection . . . Motors bear witness to incontestable artistic taste.' So wrote Amédée Ozenfant in *Foundations of Modern Art* (1931),[32] which Hamilton regarded as a bible from the time when he regularly borrowed it from the Buckingham Palace Road Art Library, aged 15. This citation of Darwin in the context of Ozenfant's discussion of motorcars in 'The Engineer's Aesthetic' re-ignites in the presence of the impacted car in the foreground of 'Hommage à Chrysler Corp.' For part of D'Arcy Thompson's argument contra Darwin, in *On Growth and Form*, depends upon the mustering of co-ordinate geometry versions of animal skulls. Mapped by projected webs in the illustrations (fig. 13), they provide a dramatic close to the book and the striking similarity between an eocene rhinoceros skull in squared-up side elevation[33] and the telescoped car might indicate Hamilton's continued use of Thompson into the second half of the 1950s. This has been generally read as part-car, part-bug-eyed monster, but Ozenfant's comparison of evolutionary biology and motor car might have still reverberated for Hamilton. 'The ambiguous insistence on the jawbone lower right', wrote the critic R.C. Kenedy of 'Hommage à Chrysler Corp.' in 1970, 'quotes Dr. Leakey's prize exhibits – the longest lasting unit of the skeleton.'[34]

fig. 13 Scientific talisman and a reminder of death (compare 'Hommage à Chrysler Corp.', no. 14): 'Skull of Hyranchus agragrius', D'Arcy Wentworth Thompson, *On Growth and Form*, 1917 (1942), fig. 538

The visual metaphor of the skull destabilises any assumption of a simply affirmative narrative of consumption by moralising it, so that even here, in the Arcadia of the motor showroom, the viewer is reminded of mortality. After 1963 Hamilton would repeatedly stage such moral tableaux: most obviously in 'Interior I' (no. 29) and 'Interior II' (no. 30), but also in pictures he has described as outright *memento mori* such as the 'Flower-pieces' of the early 1970s (nos. 71–3): finally, by the 1980s, with 'Lobby', 1985–7 (no. 85) and 'War games', 1991–2 (no. 106), severely staged, almost Davidian, civic imperatives of public space draw him closer to the *topos* of death. While we can trace Hamilton's trajectory in the 1970s and 1980s towards an explicitly melancholic standpoint, it is significant that, even here, as early as 1957, at the outset of his epic affirmations of consumption, there may be a complicating trace of human limits.

If 'Hommage à Chrysler Corp.' is, perversely, a tale of terror,[35] perhaps Hamilton mastered it through the power of vision and, perhaps, the genre of the science fiction cinema, where the fear of human extinction was figured and met. The right headlight mutates into the eye of a Zahgon, that hydrocephalic alien who, from its flying saucer platform, observed and 'buzzed' cars, possessing a fearsome alien stare in the film *This Island Earth*. Mid-1950s science fiction cinema regularly turned to the thematics of alien sight and the spectacle of threatened humans perceived through an alien optic – this is best seen in George Pal's *The War of the Worlds* (1953), where tinted paraboloid distortions on a television screen render the point-of-view of a captured cyclopean Martian (fig. 14). The power of sight is staked in the painting: the headlamps/skull's eye sockets, recall the skulls of late Cézanne in their disjointedness, also the anamorphically perspectivised death's head in Holbein's 'The Ambassadors', 1533. Spectators before 'Hommage à Chrysler Corp.', like those before 'The Ambassadors', 'look at this phantom, but see nothing, pass over it'.[36] Hamilton, the Renaissance perspectivist, pursued those sights which could not be rationally projected and mapped: as Lacan has written

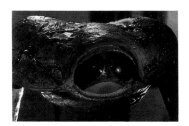

fig.14 A Martian's gaze: Film still from *War of the Worlds*, 1953

of anamorphoses, 'this fascination complements what geometral researches into perspective allow to escape from vision'.[37] For Hamilton these were amorphous 'phloo', the dissolving power of eroticism and maybe Thanatos, too. Thus the sightless, disembodied girl, her lips like a bicellular organism from Thompson, her breast a geometrically contoured target, the glamorous living prop of the glamorous motor showroom, caresses the car-monster with, in the words of the contemporary Doris Day song, 'A Woman's Touch',[38] affirming and displaying this carnival mix of Death and the Maiden.

ENTROPY, SURVEILLANCE, AND THE CIVIC VOID

An acute social and political artist, Hamilton has – over the last two decades – developed and intensified a critical moral vision: the world has been transformed into a fundamentally inhospitable place and more than any other British artist of our time he has charted and railed against our slide into what he has called 'the consciousness of a depressed society'.[39] The promising dawn of a just, welfareist-consumerism of the late 1950s and early 1960s, precisely matched and hymned in his paintings, became clouded. (The incline is evident in the 1960s, even; the baleful 'Hugh Gaitskell as a Famous Monster of Filmland', 1964 (no.26); the scapegoated Jagger and Fraser in 'Swingeing London', 1968–9 (nos.48–54). And then, for Hamilton: 'There was a personal dividing line after 1973 and the petrol crisis, there was a change, because the structures of the world began to break down.'[40] Economic and social dislocation, terrorism and the loss of horizons of expectation came in its wake. Whereas his former pictures were once inhabited by oriented and affirming beings in a rich and complex information environment, they now became abject creatures, like the inane 'idiotic couple',[41] in the deadened modernist interior of 'Hotel Europa', 1986–91 (no.86). Our sorrows are the sorrows of a rundown, soured modernity.

Norbert Wiener's book on the implications of cybernetics, *The Human Use of Human Beings*, one of the key texts circulating amongst Hamilton's circle in the mid-1950s, proposed a probablistic universe. For William Turnbull and for Alloway, as much for Hamilton, this view was supplemented by Von Neumann and Morgenstern's *Theory of Games and Economic Behavior* (1944) which also suggested the contingent as a basis of life and the systems and strategies that could be adopted in the face of this. Such an outlook underlined, for Hamilton, the notion of Alfred Korzybski's 'non-Aristotelian logic': who could say what was wrong or right in a chance-ridden world where a tossed coin seemed the key metaphor? Hamilton has explained that at a certain time in the 1960s he abandoned this guiding principle of non-Aristotelian moral agnosticism: it could be said that by the 1970s he had reached what Wiener had called a tragic view of the universe. Parallel to Freud's concept of the Death Drive,[42] Wiener imagined an entropic drift to be found in a universe that was inevitably destructuring itself: 'from a state of organisation and differentiation in which distinctions and forms exist, to a state of chaos and sameness . . . But while the universe as a whole tends to run down, there are local enclaves . . . fighting nature's tendency to degrade the organised and the meaningful.'[43] Wiener's conclusions were simultaneously apocalyptic and optimistic – chiming well with science fiction's outlook and a civilisation living under the threat of nuclear weaponry. The activities of 'control and communication', the exchanging and study of human communications and communications between man and machine, could stand as a (temporary) bulwark against this all-devouring entropy.

Possibly Hamilton has staked himself to this project, playing (in Huizinger and Von Neumann's ludic spirit) and affirming at the edges of entropy. Nowhere can this tragic, yet affirming, sense be better seen than in his recent 'Self-portrait' series of 1990 (nos.92–103), where Hamilton grapples with intimations of self-annihilation to confirm his photographically obscured and disappearing features. Far from the gestural rhetoric of Arnulf Rainer, these pictures find Hamilton switching and mapping the aggressive paint marks he has permutated across his perplexed but enquiring face. The doubting, spectral aspect of this experimenting and performing body, a poignant self made up of paint and photograph, recapitulates 'My Marilyn', 1965 (no.31) and 'Palindrome', 1974 (fig.25 on p.173), and entropy is held back, from moment to moment, through the renewed structure of indexical signs of corporeality. From the mess of narcissistic boundaryless abjection, depth cues re-emerge and a kind of incarnate perspective: meaning is restored.

Surveillance emerged as a dominant issue, not just in Hamilton's work but all across the imagination of Western social experience in these years of disillusionment. From the position of the 1970s, Michel Foucault felt able to rebuke Situationists and those others who had represented 1950s and 1960s everyday life as a manipulative pop-consumer spectacle: 'Our society is not one of spectacle but of surveillance ... under the surface of images one invests bodies in depth.'[44] As early as 1964, in 'Interior II' (no.30), a body is being searched for in the depths of the false-perspectivised set, denied as a mess of bloodied paint or slyly cued as an enigmatic, displaced, humped outline. Patricia Knight, the suspect, is under our scrutiny, a filed photograph, spectral. 'People', 1965–6 (no.34) predates and shadows Antonioni's *Blow-Up*, 1967, in its slides and progressions of the desire to see and to find the virtually illegible body in an overseen crowd. According to Foucault surveillance could refer to a number of ways in which civil institutions – schools, hospitals as well as prisons and police authorities – monitored the population, gathering information in the rationalised world of the industrialised era – Max Weber's *verwaltete welt* of civic administration. The literal and overt signs of surveillance seemed to Hamilton in the early 1980s to be as oppressive as the scene in 'Interior I' (no.29) and 'Interior II' (no.30). 'One way mirrors and closed circuit TV are the ubiquitous overseers of public spaces.'[45]

'Treatment room' (no.83) is his most sustained meditation of this topic – abject plastic buckets and a pathetic blanket, a remnant of the body, compromise the hygienic set, where the almost toxic power of x-rays ironises Hamilton's previous use of Lonsdale's x-rays with their positive connotations of science, aesthetic pleasure and well-being, back with *Growth and Form*, in 1951. 'This treatment', meted out to the vacant and hapless subject beneath the screen, 'need not be medical' Hamilton has observed.[46] The set looks like an updated electronic version of Kafka's ferocious satire on the imposition of authority onto the body of a wrongdoer, *In the Penal Colony*. On the screen Mrs Thatcher beams an exposition of Conservative Party policy to be inscribed onto the unfortunate being examined in an NHS hospital at the time of public health expenditure cuts. Nye Bevan's emancipatory and caring project has come to this: 'The future we once felt so bright', wrote Hamilton, 'includes the vision of Mrs Thatcher patronising a victim of the National Health Service.'[47] When 'Treatment room' was first shown in Liberty's shop in 1984, in the high days of the cult of 'body maintenance' (that 1980s efflorescence of Jane Fonda 'working out', of gymnasia for financial services operatives, etc.), it read against the way a resurgent neo-capitalism had refocused attention on the body's vitality, energy and limitless capacity to labour. The installation appeared as a macabre portent, a counter-image of the actual deterioration of the civic body politic under the discipline of reformatory monetarist remedies.

Through the 1980s, Hamilton re-presented this Triumph of Disorder in contemporary civic life; by the time of the collage for the Winterthur exhibition catalogue cover in 1990 he showed a showroom panorama of social disease and political abjection in Britain. There stood the unspeakable Irish dimension, centre, with the ragged figure of 'The citizen' (no.82), flanked by 'Treatment room' (no.83) and the organic soup and colour fog of 'phloo' from 'Lux 50', 1979 (no.80); while the scatological idyll of 'Soft pink landscape', 1971–2 (no.70) formed an exterior window view set over an ominous negative heap, the site for a missing body, that elusive body in the vacant post-human spaces of neo-capitalism and post-modernity. Hamilton has figured his absent body in the less hectic group of paintings around banalised lobby spaces – 'Europhotel Berlin', 1974–5, 'Hotel Europa', 1986–91 (no.86) and 'Lobby', 1985–7 (no.85). These projected rooms have a peculiar pathos.

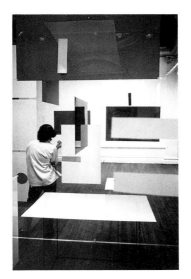

fig.15 The well-ordered environment of modernity: *an Exhibit* 1957, Hatton Gallery, Newcastle-upon-Tyne and Institute of Contemporary Arts, London

The young couple have disappeared and the clerk is missing from the hotel desk; there is only the reflection of a distant blank and bisected male, a vague presence in 'Lobby', where the mysteries of Hamilton's virtuoso geometry – following de Chirico's depopulation – empty out a social space. Hamilton's strategies of staging manage the space filled by flat, rectangular plane geometry and mirrors, making it resemble a profane version of the intersecting, partly transparent Perspex planes of *an Exhibit* in 1957 (fig.15). The unearthly light-blue light that floods from the fictive horizon is like an emitted television light, towards which, in one of the postcard sources, the 'idiot couple' have oriented themselves; here, in 'Lobby', it functions as a sign of an appalling after-life, a limbo. In the late 1940s Hamilton attended the first English production of J.-P. Sartre's *Huis Clos*, with Alec Guinness cast as the solitary male, stranded with two women in a hotel setting which turns out to be the spiritual zone of Purgatory. 'Lobby', he feels, is a reflux of *Huis Clos*; and it has other reference points in the theatrical and literary imagination – to the unyielding surfaces of Robbe-Grillet's *Nouveau Roman* or the 'compressionist'[48] spaces of British post-war drama – where the incestuous boy–girl dyads aimlessly inhabit the deserted shopping centres of Stephen Poliakoff, for example.[49] Robbed of their television set, they are deracinated in 'Hotel Europa', an inauthentic, fallen, version of the 'Arnolfini' *bridalpaar*: winsome, with epicene glances, they have withdrawn from the world and the limits of their world are the lobby – they fail to rise up against the frame like the ambivalently heroic 'citizen' – embalmed dolls, they are sequestered in a childlike narcissism encouraged by the larger play of reflections around them.

BEYOND MELANCHOLIA

The framing of death and life preoccupies his most recent paintings; the looming television image of a crass simulation of the Gulf war in 'War games', 1991–2 (no.106) and the tottering family snapshot of an infant in 'Mother and child', 1984–5 (no.84). Life and death is mediated here through the chief communication channels of modernity and post-modernity, those devices of technology which Heidegger characterised as flat, instrumental modes of enframing,[50] and which Hamilton has set out, contrarily, to redeem through painting. For almost thirty years Hamilton has taken still photographs from the television, initially asking himself, in the guise of the good consumer, 'What image makes my day?',[51] amongst all the other channels of mass-imagery that claimed attention in the 1960s. 'A revolution has happened, a turning point in history . . . The great leap, accomplished by thousands of anonymous technicians making pictorial imagery available to vast audiences has been achieved without purpose in a moral sense.'[52] Looking through his archive of three decades of snatched television photographs there is a change from the harsh black and white, 405 line-scan of jazz musicians (fig.16) and US culture heroes of the early 1960s, to the moment of colour television's introduction into Britain at the end of that decade and into the 1970s: a grim comedy unfolds – the ironies of the Black and White Minstrels prancing in colour, Nixon and Agnew with faces like Otto Dix physiognomies, footballers game-playing against the geometry of pitch markings.

fig.16 Snatched, screened and scanned: 'What image makes my day?': Jazz Musician on TV, photograph by Richard Hamilton, 1962–3

Hamilton's 'War games' recalls Norbert Wiener's 1954 observation that Von Neumann and Morgenstern's cult book, *The Theory of Games* 'has made a profound impression . . . not least in Washington. When Mr Shannon talks of the development of military tactics he is not talking moonshine, but is discussing a most imminent and dangerous contingency.'[53] Just as Hamilton's masterpieces of the early and mid-1950s derived directly from J.J. Gibson's military research spin-offs, 'War games' alludes to this context. 'Is this a game or is it for real?', the young hacker types into a US military WOPR (War Operations Plan Response) computer program in the 1983 film called *War Games*. 'What's the difference?' responds the game-playing computer, blithely. Hamilton's 'War games' grounds his concerns with surveillance, the technotronic ways of organising information – computers, electronic image-scanning and the interactions between them – with that moral sense he found detached in the past. Simulation, that post-modern social bogey of Jean Baudrillard,[54] is frontally addressed by Hamilton in 'War games' (and in the hallucinatory spaces of 'Lobby', too). The bloodied, stepped, impervious blocks (a kind of 'Death of Marat' with the protagonist vanished) of the television monitor, VCR and speakers, have been electronically scanned from Hamilton's original photograph and then deposited on the surface of the final picture: but by a brilliant inversion, the television screen, the enthroned site of electronic imagery, has been painstakingly painted by him to double the BBC 'Newsnight' 'Sandpit' model of the war zone. It is a painting of anachronisms – the toy tanks and balsawood models as an image of the Gulf war rather than those off-planet video games of remote targeted destruction which became the general visual currency of the war. Proximate, front stage rather than remote sensing, Hamilton decided to emphasise organic presence and a mortal sign: the viscous enamel paint drops of blood 'oozing out from under the screen',[55] that break the immaculate boundary and disturb the prevailing system of imagining the war. This is Hamilton as master of the territory of abjection[56] – as he was in 'Treatment room' (no.83) and the miasmas of 'Soft pink landscape' (no.70) redeeming through paint (here transubstantiatory blood) the death of feeling and subjectivity.

NOTES

1 Richard Hamilton in conversation with the author, 7 July 1991.
2 Ibid.
3 Ibid.
4 Ibid.
5 T. Maldonado, *The Pedagogic Implications of Automation*, typescript, Robyn Denny Archives, London.
6 Richard Hamilton in conversation with the author, 27 November 1991.
7 'Glorious Technicolour, Breathtaking CinemaScope and Stereophonic Sound' 1960, in R. Hamilton, *Collected Words*, 1982, p.113.
8 Richard Hamilton in conversation with the author, 27 November 1991.
9 Ibid.
10 Ibid.
11 D'Arcy Wentworth Thompson, *On Growth and Form*, 1917 (1942), p.1094.
12 Richard Hamilton in conversation with the author, 7 July 1991.
13 Thompson 1917 (1942). cf. Prismatium tripodium, p.716, fig.337 and the spicule of a tetractinellid sponge, anatriaene, p.686, fig.314e.
14 K. Lonsdale, 'Art and Crystallography', in G. Kepes (ed) *The New Landscape in Art and Science*, Cambridge, Mass. 1956, p. 359.
15 US Navy funding was extended to Gibson's research in order to gauge the problems of landing fast combat aircraft on aircraft carriers pitching and rolling at sea.
16 Richard Hamilton in conversation with the author, 27 November 1991.

17 Ibid.
18 J.J. Gibson, *The Perception of the Visual World*, Boston 1950, p.229.
19 Ibid.
20 N. Wiener, *The Human Use of Human Beings*, 1954, p.18.
21 cf. Gibson 1950, fig.57.
22 Gibson 1950, p.127.
23 *Collected Words*, p.50.
24 Richard Hamilton in conversation with the author, 18 December 1991.
25 Catherine Clément, *The Lives and Legends of Jacques Lacan*, 1983. pp.194–5. cf. J. Lacan, *The Four Fundamental Concepts of Pyschoanalysis*, 1979, chap.8.
26 J. Lacan 1979, p.94.
27 R. Hamilton, 'An inside view', *Richard Hamilton*, Kunstmuseum Winterthur 1990, p.44.
28 Richard Hamilton, Royal Academy Pop Symposium, 12 September 1991.
29 Roger Coleman in conversation with the author, 2 September 1991. David Hockney was also a supporter of CND.
30 Richard Smith in conversation with the author, 2 November 1991.
31 Richard Hamilton in conversation with the author, 18 December 1991.
32 A. Ozenfant, *The Foundations of Modern Art*, 1931, p.151.
33 Thompson 1917 (1942), p.1074, fig.538.
34 R.C. Kenedy, 'Richard Hamilton' *Art International*, March 1970, p.50.
35 As R.C. Kenedy insists, p.46.

36 H. Rapaport, 'Gazing in Wonderland' *Enclitic*, vol.6, no.2, p.69.
37 J. Lacan 1979, p.87.
38 Included in the musical *Calamity Jane*.
39 R. Hamilton, 'An inside view', p.44.
40 R. Hamilton, RCA Seminar, 28 October 1991.
41 R. Hamilton in conversation with the author, 12 December 1991.
42 S. Freud, *Beyond the Pleasure Principle*, 1920.
43 N. Wiener 1954, pp.12 and 17.
44 M. Foucault, *Discipline and Punish*, 1975, p.217.
45 R. Hamilton, 'An inside view', p.46.
46 R. Hamilton in conversation with the author, 27 November 1991.
47 R. Hamilton, 'An inside view', p.46.
48 cf. Laurence Kitchen, *Drama in the Sixties*, 1968.
49 e.g. *Hitting Town* (1975) and *City Sugar* (1976).
50 M. Heidegger, *The Question Concerning Technology*, 1954.
51 R. Hamilton, 'Supermarket', *Ark*, no.34, July 1963, p.37.
52 Ibid.
53 N. Wiener 1954, p.178.
54 cf. J. Baudrillard, *Simulations*, New York 1983 and *The Ecstasy of Communication*, New York 1988.
55 R. Hamilton in conversation with the author, 7 July 1991.
56 Julia Kristeva, *Powers of Horror*, 1982, p.4.

'A LIQUID, ELEMENTAL SCATTERING': MARCEL DUCHAMP AND RICHARD HAMILTON

Sarat Maharaj

'Lits et ratures' – 'beds and erasures' – Duchamp's pun on 'littérature' sets off a mad-hatter, speeded-up unhinging of meanings, signs, images. To render it as 'litter erasure', as 'rubbing out rubbish' – not forgetting that a bed is also a litter – is to give it a sharp-tongued, iconoclastic Dada inflection.[1] It plays on the idea of wiping the belles-lettres slate clean, of sweeping away tasteful expression and its debris no less than it suggests a drive beyond art's 'littoral edge'.

The more the pun races away from everyday sense and its echoless, brittle norms, the more we are obliged to keep them in mind – if we are to grasp the pun's adventures at all, its detours and derailings. What it seeks to shake off it pulls along in its wake. In one move it both affirms and annuls. It is in terms of this chameleon force that we might map Hamilton's relationship with Duchamp – a double-turn in which something is cited even as it is crossed out, not unlike what Derrida calls thinking 'under erasure' and signals thus (sous rature).[2]

A not dissimilar scene of deletions and 'doubletakes', to use Hamilton's word, greeted him as he glanced through Duchamp's *Green Box* notes on *The Bride Stripped Bare by her Bachelors, Even*, 1915–23.[3] Little in it does not bristle with tension between lines that have been struck out and those that have not. Crossed-out passages have not so much been expunged or indeed excised from the text as left in for attention. Phrases ringed in red for transposing elsewhere on the sheet, inserts, effacings, words scribbled over with variants – ploys for what Duchamp called a 'delay in glass' – all thwart any attempt to pin down meaning in a narrow, single-coded way.

Few texts would seem to be written as 'sous rature', as strung out between inscribing and erasing. What strikes up in the play off between these poles is, to use a Duchamp word, an 'extra-rapid' shuttle between terms – the text's sense taking on a flittering, vaporising quality. Jotted down elements and those blotted out shadow each other, the one shaping and subverting the other – a plain-speaking and double-dealing thrust, not unlike the pun, in one breath.

We might imagine Hamilton at that mythic first moment in 1948–9 with the *Green Box*. It is his Slade days. He's out walking with Nigel Henderson who suggests that as they are near the Penroses' they might drop in for tea. There he makes free of Roland Penrose's library for Hamilton's benefit.[4] Chance, daring surprise, forethought – the scenario approaches Duchamp's own 'specifications for a ready-made'. To use his words, 'a snapshot effect'; the moment had arrived to 'inscribe' Hamilton's 'rendezvous' with the legendary *Green Box*.[5]

It led in 1960 to his recasting its handwritten notes into typographic form (fig.2) – an erasing of Duchamp's script only to put its effects into print.[6] For even as he makes the text more legible, its 'unreadability' – Duchamp's ruses for waylaying easy reading – surfaces in pronounced fashion. If he gives the notes a book's linear sequence he leaves

fig.1 Group of sheets from Duchamp's *Green Box*

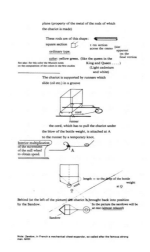

fig.2 Page from Richard Hamilton's typographic version of Marcel Duchamp's *Green Box*

fig.3 Marcel Duchamp **Door: 11 rue Larrey** *Galerie Schmela, Düsseldorf*

its pages unnumbered – reclaiming its random dispersal. He irons out the text only to make us more aware of the Duchampian crumpling up of meanings, its unending semantic littering.

A task both against the 'letter' of the *Green Box* and for it? We meet this double-turn as we see Hamilton quoting Duchampian elements and excerpts only to undercut them – as if starkly spotlighting and blacking them out in one move. Duchamp had drama-tised something of this in 'Door: 11 Rue Larrey' (fig.3) which he designed for his Paris studio. To swing it open to get into the bedroom was to close off the bathroom; opened to enter the latter it closed off the studio.[7] Shut and open at the same time – the idea flew in the face of common sense and logic.

It touches on what Hamilton has in mind in describing his use of elements from both sides of fine art/popular culture divide as non-Aristotelian.[8] The phrase signalled a non-hierarchical approach to elements drawn from opposing worlds of representation – fine art/advertising, avant-garde/kitsch, modernism/mass-media, painting/photography – a flattening out of high/low distinctions between them. It's a stance where each ele-ment should count in its own right – a refusal to prejudge them in terms of handed-down notions of value and taste, or at least, to keep such judgements at bay for as long as possible, to 'delay' them.

It parallels what he notes of Duchamp – a capacity to play off colliding oppositions and contraries without always wanting to dissolve them.[9] If they blend into a 'fine art/Pop soup' Hamilton's idea is to stop short of total synthesis.[10] The opposing terms are not so much taken under the wing of some 'higher' third term, subsumed by it, as sug-gested in dialectical thinking. They throw each other into relief, speak about and against each other – a mode which inflects itself differently in his classic Pop artworks (1957–64) from his later pieces' apparently less discontinuous, seamless air.

To comprehend his relationship with Duchamp, therefore, in art historical notions of influence would be to miss its about-turns and inversions, in a Duchamp phrase, its 'mirrorical returns'. For as Hamilton observes, what stamped itself on his thinking was Duchamp's iconoclasm.[11] The very principle demanded that it be turned against itself, the idea of an authoritative source, the master. Not, however, in an anti-Duchamp spirit but as a matter of being at one with his work only to be at odds with it. A relation-ship 'sous rature', perhaps best summed up, to use one of his own *Green Box* typo-graphic devices, thus – (Duchamp).

'LUBRICIOUS' DESIRING MACHINES: 1957–64

Shot through with traces of 'The Bride Stripped Bare by her Bachelors, Even'[12] – some less effaced than others – Hamilton's Pop artworks strikingly play off Duchamp's reflec-tions on the chimerical nature of the Bride/Bachelor machine's erotic desire against advertising/mass culture myths of consumerist desire.

Hamilton's musings on how these myths come to be scripted and staged[13] had been signposted by 'Just what is it . . .?', 1956 (no.13). It pictured the world of objects and things as the mirror of human desire – putting on show that yearned-for but elusive 'mythic' moment of absolute gratification promised by commodities. We see him cast-ing an admiring, quizzical eye over the scene. He probes its 'design for living' as spun out by advertising in its shift from 'bloodless description' to 'poetic interpretation'[14] – towards evoking products through fantasy, reverie, spectacle.[15] The shift is towards relating to commodities as if from within the stormy intensities of bodily appetites and passions – towards the feeling that one was responding to their seductive call freely, without any manipulating hand behind it. It's a move 'from propaganda towards persuasion' – the forging of the period's 'strategy of desire'.[16]

The scene reads as a vanitas, an essay on the styling of the five senses by consumer goods and gadgetry. What Hamilton is scanning is the 'persuading image', the 'look of things'[17] how objects, bodies, the micro-texture of everyday life not only take on an irresistible erotic charge, but also serve as a system of signs, symbols and representations through which desires and needs come to be interpreted and voiced.

But in such a strategy what is consumed, Baudrillard notes, is not so much the commodities themselves but the myths they stand for, the styles and symbols of consumption. He alerts us to the paradox of 'consommation' in which desire is at once 'consummated/consumed', an attaining which is a burning out, a fulfilling which is no less an emptying. Its effect is the ever more fierce reawakening of desire as the compulsive, restless chase after gratification expressed through this or that commodity-sign starts up afresh.[18]

Hamilton links the commodity-sign's 'ever-deferred' promise of bliss to Duchamp's 'delay' of an absolute union of the Bride with the Bachelors. Both are start/stop dramas about the obsessive, fumbling search for satisfaction, about not dissimilar cycles of promise, fulfilment, frustrating hold-ups in the grand consummation that never quite comes. The link devolves on the arrestingly similar automobile/female body/orgasm metaphor he encountered in Duchamp and in motor car design/advertising.

'Hommage à Chrysler Corp.', 1957 (no.14) and 'Hers is a lush situation', 1958 (no.15) are eulogies to the 'vehicle of desire' metaphor, on advertising's clever, allusive play on it.[19] They are no less a stripping bare of it, an exposé on its rhetorics of persuasion – featured as it was in design parlance as the 'mechanical bride' or 'dreamboat'[20] Symbol of erotic bliss, the automobile was described as an 'orgasm in chrome'.[21] It's an association Hamilton grafts on to the 'Large Glass' drama in which the Bride's 'intense desire for orgasm' expresses itself in 'three cinematic blossomings'. Duchamp depicts its 'crowning goal' as a flesh-colour Milky Way, an 'orgasmic cloud' which explodes and spreads across the top part of the 'Large Glass'.[22]

Hamilton first quoted the image in a study for 'Hommage à Chrysler Corp.' Later we see it in a looser rendering – a penumbra of smeary brushwork intimating body surface, organs, orifices. As in 'Hers is a lush situation' it suggests a spreading stain, trace of some overflowing emotional excitation. It serves what storyline there is of the 1957 Buick/Sophia Loren Bride-machine's electrifying sweep through the cityscape dissolving inner yearning and the outer-world into a turbulent flood of desire.[23]

The 'orgasmic cloud' takes on many guises – the Bride's 'splendid vibrations', a mimicking of Abstract Expressionist gesture or soft focus photography. Hamilton's note on 'Hommage à Chrysler Corp.' that 'one quotation from Duchamp remains from a number of rather more direct references which were tried',[24] reaffirms this effacing/inscribing. Earlier studies show the Bride's 'wasp cylinder' (fig.4) as a source for '$he', 1958–61 (fig.5 and no.16), just as the bride's veil and 'washing machine/butterfly pump' imagery in 'Glorious Techniculture', 1961–4 (no.18) recall the *Green Box* – muffled or full-voiced, such allusions echo through the Pop pieces.

'A national immorality in three orgasms' – Joyce's topsy-turvy summing up of *Ulysses*[26] startlingly recalls Duchamp's three cinematic blossomings. It seems from Hamilton's drawing 'Bronze by gold', 1949 (fig.6), that it might have been in the

fig.4 'Sex cylinder (Wasp)' from Richard Hamilton's version of Marcel Duchamp's *Green Box*

fig.5 **Study for '$he' III** 1958 Ink and gouache on paper *Private Collection*

fig.6 **Bronze by gold (Sirens)** 1949 Pencil and watercolour on paper *Ulster Museum, Belfast*

fig.7 Sandow Developer for use in chest-expanding exercises

fig.8 Original source for 'Adonis in Y-fronts': from an advertisement in *Mr Universo* magazine, 1960

'Sirens' section of *Ulysses* that he first stumbled across something like the 'Large Glass' saga of the Bachelor-machine.[27] Duchamp had spoken of a 'tormented gearing' that had led the lust-crazed Bachelor to make his coarse, abrupt advances towards the Bride. Rebuffed, he is driven to auto-eroticism – the 'Bachelor grinds his chocolate himself'.[28]

Hamilton's drawing depicts Miss Kennedy and Miss Douce – listening entranced to the 'croppy boy' song, caressing the erect and phallic beer pumps. They are in the Ormond Bar, which Joyce evokes as a scene of flirtatious exchange and arousing sexual innuendo. The refrain throughout is 'to and fro' – a masturbatory movement akin to the Bachelor-machine sleigh-glider's comings and goings. Joyce's scene of 'beerfroth splash, stacks of empties' and Duchamp's 'litanies of the chariot' – 'beer professor, ona-nism, junk of life' – mirror each other remarkably.[29]

They conjure that muscular maleness Hamilton came to explore in 'Towards a defini-tive statement on the coming trends in mens' wear and accessories', 1962 (nos.20–23) – four portraits of the masculine, based on the male energies represented by the nine malic moulds central to Duchamp's Bachelor-apparatus. In the 'stretch-tumescence' figure of 'Adonis in Y-fronts' (no.22) – do we see Joyce's 'twang it snapped' elastic garter,[30] the Bachelor-machine's Sandow Chest expander (figs.2,7)[31] as much as body-building magazines (fig.8)? Sources proliferate – we cannot hold back the semantic littering.

The 'fat, lubricious Bachelor-Machine', well-oiled, heavy-breathing, throbbing, stands poised to perform in 'AAH!', 1962 (no.19). The car's dashboard, the sparking tension between finger and gear, recall the 'tormented gearing' at its base. The title puns on ejaculation, on gasps of delight at the sight of consumer goods. Hamilton is gently deflating advertising's grand promise and double-entendre – showing up the anti-climax of what it actually delivers. The potent 'Isher weapon' turns out to be little more than a flaccid penis, the inferno of passion the weak flicker of a cigarette lighter – the consumerist myth fizzles out as a 'comically-dribbled sigh of ecstasy'.[32]

CONCEPTUAL/VISUAL: 'NEIGHBOURING METALS'

'What a drip', exclaims Duchamp, marvelling at the Bachelors' spectacular splash and tittering at its ludicrous excess, the racket created by the 'crash splash'.[33] The pun sums up the 'extra-rapid' shuttle in the 'Large Glass' between a serious metaphysics of desire and a hilarious account of its cumbersome, spluttering mechanics. Hamilton matches it by playing up advertising's contraptions of wit and irony even as he strips bare its 'new ideology'.[34]

The switch-overs between the serious and comic connect with the crossover figure Marcel Duchamp/Rrose Selavy. For Duchamp/ 'Eros c'est la vie', as the pun suggests, eroticism was a 'dear subject'. It touched on the life-force itself, coming closer 'than philosophy or anything like it to this animal thing'. As the underlying element of the 'Large Glass' it served as a strategy for 'delaying' traditional approaches to art, as a pleasurable stand-in for painterly visualism.[35] In a telling image Duchamp speaks of using it 'as you would a tube of paint to inject into your production.[36]

The 'orgasmic' Duchamp, scrupulously teased out in Hamilton's readings, thus signals a far more intertwined play between the conceptual/visual than later tendencies towards an abstemious conceptualism cared to note. The recoil from painterly abstrac-tion's retinalism encouraged an overly mentalist, 'grey matter' view of Duchamp. It

fig.9 'Illuminating Gas' in Richard Hamilton's typographic version of Duchamp's *Green Box* gained ground in the 'death of art' ambience of the 1970s as a drive towards the purely textual. Without feeling for their ambiguities, Duchamp phrases such as 'pictorial nominalism' or 'illuminatistic scribism' were sometimes taken as slogans for an unbending discursivity.[37]

It's an extreme edge probed by Hamilton in the late 1960s.[38] In 'After Marcel Duchamp?', 1969, he reflects on Duchamp's death and its import – the fate of art against conceptualism's rising tide? It's a spectral erasing/inscribing of the phrase 'd'après Marcel Duchamp' – 'in his manner and footsteps'. But it heralds Hamilton's swing away from him towards an engagement with a sheer, though not mindless, visualism. For his 'Flower-pieces', 'Landscapes' and 'Collaborations' of the 1970s, no less than his history paintings of the 1980s, remain as demandingly conceptual as they are retinal. An iconoclastic move 'the way Duchamp would like it' – it signalled a subverting turn against the all-too-conceptual and its institutionalised face.

The shift marks one of Hamilton's outstanding insights into and contributions to Duchamp's post-war reception. In conceptualism's wake, his turn towards the retinal mirrors post-structuralist hesitations over the conceptual and its brisk, dominating rationality. Against the 'death of art' thesis – which sees art's absorption into the 'higher' life of concepts and discursive ideas – Adorno was to stress the distinction between the 'wordless syntax' of the visual and the repressive grammar of conceptual thought. He saw the former as a way of resisting the conceptual machine which ground down everything into its one-dimensional terms.[39]

Duchamp's desiring-machines thus crop up, somewhat surprisingly, with Deleuze's/Guatarri's view that the grip of conceptual structures can only be undone by a radical libidinal force.[40] Lyotard seems to reflect this in distinguishing between Duchamp's idea-work and Barnett Newman's painterly work.[41] But he also calls for a Duchampian 'delay' in thinking the relations between them and seeks to stave off a simple counterpoising of the conceptual as something 'imprisoning' against the visual as 'liberating'.[42] His focus is on the 'figural', a force which appears from within the discursive-conceptual regime of representation itself and disrupts it.[43]

There are perhaps few places where the figural is as vividly dramatised as in the 'Large Glass'. Duchamp conceived its upper section as the 'top inscription' made up of 'triple cipher nets' which orient the Bride's 'authorizations and commands' in the link-up with the Bachelors. It operates as a rebus: letters metamorphose into images, pictures into words in 'extra-rapid' flow. Duchamp sees it as a 'moving inscription', an unstable alphabet. With typical clarity Hamilton compares it to the flashing screen of picture-word bulletins on Times Square[44] – a telescoping of graphic and plastic forces. The verbal and visual thus do not simply translate and decipher into each other's terms: we are called upon to elaborate something from between them – the figural – which adds up to more than their sum.

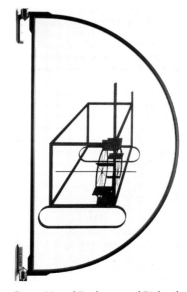

fig.10 Marcel Duchamp and Richard Hamilton **Glider containing a water mill (in neighbouring metals)** 1913–15, replica 1965 Mixed media on glass *Richard Hamilton*

Is this force perhaps best illustrated by Duchamp's answer to the question about the materials that went into making 'Glider containing a water mill (in neighbouring metals)', 1913–15 (fig.10)? His reply 'I do not know what these metals are but I know they are neighbours'[45] brings us up short against the pointedly redundant. What flashes up is a startling text-image we cannot quite render into discursive coherence. But if elements of the phrase 'neighbouring metals' do not square conceptually they 'configure' a disturbing intensity, a transgressive force which leaves everyday sense tongue-tied.

With Duchamp, Hamilton stresses, 'reasoned concepts' are articulated as 'aesthetic experience', 'abstract and non-visual' projections as 'visual poetry'.[46] Hence his reservations about Schwarz's interpretation, not so much because of its heavy-handedness, but because it so completely misses the visual dimension.[47] He simply decodes the Duchampian conceptual into discursive ideas – a semantic literalism rather than the littering it suggests for Hamilton.

If 'Epiphany', 1964 (no.27) signposts Hamilton's more conceptual phase it also leaves us with a split-second, dazzling emblem of desire which slips through the discursive net. We witness what Joyce calls 'the ineluctable modality of the visible' – a phrase which almost sums up for Hamilton the 'unspeakable dimension' of the conceptual and which he uses in his moving essay on John Latham, a fellow Duchamp transformateur.[48] Across 'The citizen', 1982–3 (no.82) the excremental smears read as signs of protest, rage, humiliation despite their 'retinal' immediacy. But they also scribble out a free-ranging, incontinent force which seems to approach what Duchamp calls the visceral.[49] We see not an overflow of meaning but an excess over it – the figural etches out itself, stubborn and sticky.

'LUBRICITOUS CONJUGATION'

'Lubricious, lubricous, lubricitous': the word's variant spellings in Duchamp and Joyce[50] add to the slipperiness of what it signals – a well-oiled, wanton creativity that cuts across rules and laws and flouts them. Both are describing a transgressive force not unlike their own work's effects. These are so widespread and pervasive that to speak of followers seems meaningless – at odds with their ever-changing strategies, in a Joyce phrase, their 'lubricitous conjugation'.

fig.11 Marcel Duchamp **Wedge of Chastity** 1951–2 Galvanised plaster and dental plastic *Private Collection*

Hamilton notes that 'all branches put out by Duchamp have borne fruit' yet 'no individual may lay claim to be his heir. He can have no true progeny because his wisdom has led ultimately to neutrality'. The point is pictured through Duchamp pieces of the 1950s: 'he made Man (*Object Dart*), Woman (*Female Fig Leaf*) and symbol of their union (*Wedge of Chastity* [fig.11]). Strangely, the conjunction is not to be fruitful: the nesting wedge fits its mould with a sure finality, polarity is brought to negation by their intercourse, master is lost in matrix.'[51]

Paradox of fruitfulness without issue – Duchamp as master and mentor even as the idea is undercut? With Hamilton, a spare, quiet observation not infrequently has a more demanding theoretical drift. We move from the patriarchal metaphor of creativity centred on the founding father and his heirs towards the notion of a sportive, aleatory force. Duchamp's phrase 'a liquid elemental scattering, seeking no direction'[52] captures something of this rather more postmodern sense of creativity: not a systematic sowing but a random spilling, not an inseminating activity but a dispersing of effects and influences, what Derrida calls a 'scattering abroad' or 'dissemination'.[53]

It makes us hesitate over the label Father of Pop used of Hamilton, since it tends to straitjacket his work's proliferating involvements and its transgressive drive. For with his work we see the everyday commodity both for its own sake and as object of aesthetic transfiguration; our attention shuttles between the worlds of popular culture and fine art; we see elements of modernism played off against those of mass culture, the canonical and colloquial against each other. It would be hard to imagine the postwar art world outside these perspectives. Yet such is his grain of voice that none might latch on it without striking a false note.

'We have to do some erasure', Hamilton remarked in the 1960s of students' precon-
ceptions about art which had to be put into question during the first year of the fine art
course on which he taught. It was an essential prelude to getting them to inscribe them-
selves as individual sensibilities.[54] The course contributed decisively to revising
approaches to art studies in Britain – producing followers only in the sense that they
might have learnt to follow themselves.[55]

But the open-endedness is not so much a doctrine as a way of thinking and making
tied up with assemblage and its modes. In Duchamp's hands, Hamilton saw it as 'tinker-
ing'[56] – like the bricoleur's strategy of creating not from scratch but from already-there
material stored against use at the right moment.[57] He fuses the approach with Joyce's
view of artwork as 'work in progress' to which there no finality[58] – an echo of the 'unfi-
nished business' of the 'Large Glass'. It entails constructing meaning rather than un-
covering it as if it were a pre-existing thing. Hence a disseminating movement at odds
with the idea of heading towards a goal, a teleological vision which seemed to hold the
period's painterly practices in its grip.

The movement dramatises itself in Hamilton's 'Interior' series, 1964–5 (nos.29,30)
and in the air of extravaganza of the 'Fashion-plate' variations, 1969 (nos.57–68) – a
flood of signs and meanings that goes with excerpting consumerist representations, tak-
ing them apart even as they are put together into fresh statement. It's a double
commentary – on the manufacturing of consumerist taste and its texture and on the
activity of fabricating as such.

From 'Toaster', 1966–9 (no.43) and 'The critic laughs' 1971–2 (no.69) on to 'Treat-
ment room', 1983–4 (no.83) Hamilton pushes the mode of assemblage to its farthest
limits. As the art object audaciously tests the thinnest of lines between itself and high-
style consumer goods we sense Duchamp's notion of 'inframince' at play. Hamilton is
toying with the 'indeterminate object' and its unnerving ambivalence as it demands to
be looked at both as undressed commodity and as fine art object, as critique of the con-
sumerist object-system and as one of its glamorous products.

But by the 1980s a rather different conception of assemblage is afoot with Hamilton.
It evolves steadily out of his probing the boundaries between original/copy/definitive
version. 'Towards a definitive statement . . .' was a stalling for time – none of its four
pieces is the 'final word' – not unlike the way the Pop multiple sidesteps the sense of
finality associated with the unique piece. Hamilton touches on this further in tackling
the idea of the impossibility of 'definitive style' in 'Picasso's meninas', 1973, and 'My
Marilyn', 1965 (no.31).

The tendency prefigures Hamilton's play on the original/copy relationship which
ends up blurring the distinctions between them and turning them inside out. For in
'Collaborations' 1976 (fig.12), Hamilton and Dieter Roth quote and misquote each
other in a fast-moving, hilarious mix-up of styles which does not leave authorship itself
unscathed. Each of its thirty-seven pairs of work involves an 'original' and a 'certifi-
cate'. To authenticate the former and its wayward conceits, one would have to refer to
the latter, a 'fair copy' of it in a 'comprehensible' style. It vouches for the original's bona
fides. The upshot is that we begin to see the original as something propped up by the
certificate – hardly the free-standing entity we expect.

Scandalous inversions – the original dependent on the copy, object on its image, 'the
real world out there' on its representations – these themes, however, stretch back to
Hamilton's readings of Joyce and Duchamp. Both had rendered 'the real' a derivative of
something else. For Joyce it was fashioned out of language and style as explored in the

fig.12 Richard Hamilton and Dieter
Roth, No.12 from 'The Collabor-
ations of Ch. Rotham' Enamel on
plastic, ceramic tile

'Oxen of the Sun' section of *Ulysses* where he does not hesitate to render 'copied passages' of literature as 'original expression'. Both versions of Hamilton's 'In Horne's house', 1948–82, were inspired by this – the second a tour de force 'assemblage' of styles and representations.[59] For Duchamp, too, the everyday world seemed to be little more than a projected copy, a dependent version of a more ideal, fourth-dimensional model beyond it.[60] We see Hamilton getting to grips with its back-to-front mapping of things, especially the key notion of appearance/apparition.[61]

But if these ideas seem strange, they were to meet up, through Hamilton's growing involvement, reaching back to the 1950s, with information theory and its even stranger notions of assembled, artificial worlds, models, virtual realties. By the 1980s we see him moving towards a 'high-tech' mode of assemblage – possibilities for fabricating new image-realities through advanced photography and image-making computer technology. As studies for 'The citizen' (no.82) and 'The subject' (no.87) show, he was to shift around clips and excerpts of stills to assemble the final, seamless image – a 'graft which rings more true than the original'?

Through the mode he both mirrors a world where 'the real' increasingly disappears into media-constructed versions of it and comments on the phenomenon – something signposted by the echoless atmosphere of 'Lobby', 1985–7 (no.85) and its synthetic, hallucinated quality. We touch on Baudrillard's world of simulations and simulacra – artificial realities conjured out of media-projected images which 'mould and model' the world.[62] Perhaps 'War games', 1991–2 (no.106), Hamilton's most recent work – based on a television model of the Gulf war-zone – is a metaphor for the fateful side of this drive towards the scripting and staging of 'the real'. In the 1950s we see Hamilton scanning consumerist myths and spectacle: in the 1990s he is looking at how spectacle runs away with itself, spinning out a world of simulations and representations with no 'original'. With these weird, wanton assemblages, 'lubricitous conjugations' indeed, Hamilton remains, as ever, ahead of things.

A literal translation of the word 'Duchamp' gives us something as banal as 'of the field'. Perhaps none other than the field of representation ploughed up in the 'Large Glass' by what he calls an 'instrument for farming' – an 'Agricultural Machine' for staging its orgasmic drama. Hard on its heels chugs along Hamilton's 'Reaper' series, 1950–1 (fig.13). A scatter of signs, ideas, images in its wake, a 'bedding and littering' of the postwar art world throughout which we sense Hamilton's touch without quite seeing his hand – a presence–absence we might picture as (Hamilton).

fig.13 **Reaper (e)** 1949 Etched line and roulette *Rita Donagh*

NOTES

[1] Marcel Duchamp, *Rrose Selavy*, Paris 1939, unpag. Francis Picabia used the pun in his cover design for Andre Breton's *Litterature*, no.7, 1922. E. Peterson transliterates it as 'litter erasure' in *The Writings of Marcel Duchamp*, ed. M. Sanouillet & E. Peterson, New York 1989, p.115.

[2] J. Derrida, *Of Grammatology*, London 1977, pp.23–4.

[3] Marcel Duchamp, *Notes and Projects for the Large Glass*, London 1969.

[4] Richard Hamilton, *Collected Words*, London 1982, p. 10.

[5] *Notes and Projects*, p.90 Note 54.

[6] *The Bride Stripped Bare By Her Bachelors, Even*, a typographic version by R. Hamilton, trans. G.H. Hamilton, London 1960.

[7] For the status of this work in the Duchamp canon see A. Schwarz, *The Complete Works of Marcel Duchamp*, London 1969, pp.496–7.

[8] *Collected Words*, p.52 ('Urbane Image', *Living Arts 2*, 1963, pp.44–59).

[9] *Collected Words*, p.223 ('The Large Glass', *Marcel Duchamp*, exh.cat., Museum of Modern Art, New York 1973).

[10] *Collected Words*, p.31 and *Richard Hamilton, Paintings etc. '56–66*, exh.cat., Hanover Gallery, 1964.

[11] *Collected Words*, pp.206, 238 ('Duchamp', *Art International*, January 1964, pp.22–8 and 'Whom do you admire?' *ARTnews*, November 1977.)

[12] Between 1957 and 1959 he was working on the typographic version. *Richard Hamilton*, exh. cat., Hanover Gallery 1964, p.11.

[13] R. Hamilton, *Man, Machine & Motion*, exh.cat., Newcastle-upon-Tyne/London 1955. For his more theoretical reflections see *Collected Words*, pp.28, 49–53,150–60.

[14] H. Scheleyer, 'The Power of the Image', *Advertising Review*, vol.1, no.1, Summer 1954, p.35.

[15] G. Debord, *Society of the Spectacle*, Detroit 1970, theses 1–22 and his *Comments on the Society of the Spectacle*, 1990, pp.2–8.

[16] *Persuasion*, vol.1, no.1, 1939, p.43 and E. Dichter, *The Strategy of Desire*, New York 1960. He touches on Dichter's ideas in *Collected Words*, pp.50 and 140.

[17] *Collected Words*, pp.135–43 (shortened version first published as 'Persuading Image', *Design*, February 1960, pp. 28–32).

[18] J. Baudrillard, *Le Systeme des objets*, Paris 1968, pp. 275–83.

[19] R. Banham, 'Vehicle of Desire', *Art*, no.1, September 1955.

[20] M. McLuhan, *The Mechanical Bride*, 1951, revised 1967, pp.93–7 and R. Banham, *Man, Machine & Motion*, exh.cat., Hatton Gallery 1955, p.14.

[21] G. Gammage and S. Jones, '"Orgasm in Chrome": Rise and Fall of the Automobile Tail Fin', *Journal of Popular Culture*, vol.8, no.1, 1974.

[22] *Notes and Projects*, pp.22–30 Notes 4–10. In a celebrated remark he compares the 'Large Glass' to 'an automobile hood covering a motor' in J. Schuster, 'Marcel Duchamp, vite', *le surrealisme, meme*, no.2, Spring 1957, p.144.

[23] *Collected Words*, pp.49–52 ('Urbane Image', *Living Arts 2*, 1963, pp.44–59).

[24] *Richard Hamilton*, exh.cat., Hanover Gallery, 1964, p.7.

[25] *Notes and Projects*, p.110 Note 70 and p.156 Note 101.

[26] James Joyce, *Ulysses*, 1922, 1983 ed., p.216.

[27] His reading of *Ulysses* and the drawings based on it go back to 1946–7.

[28] *Notes and Projects*, p.210 Note 140.

[29] *Ulysses*, p.285 and *Notes and Projects*, p.192 Notes 131–2.

[30] *Ulysses*, p.276.

[31] *Notes and Projects*, p.196 Note 132.

[32] *Collected Words*, p.50 ('Urbane Image', *Living Arts 2*, 1963, pp.44–59).

[33] *Notes and Projects*, p.156 Note 101 and p.168 Notes 111–13.

[34] *R. Hamilton*, exh.cat., Hanover Gallery 1964, p.1.

[35] P. Cabanne, *Dialogues with Marcel Duchamp*, London 1979, pp.88–9.

[36] Marcel Duchamp interviewed by G.H. Hamilton and R. Hamilton, BBC Third Programme 1959, recording published by *Audio Arts Magazine*, vol. 2, no.4.

[37] Marcel Duchamp, 'The White Box', in M. Sanouillet and E. Peterson, New York and 1989, p.78.

[38] See 'Composition (Chicago Project)' (1969), 'A Conceptual Exhibition' (1970) and 'Propositions' (1971) in *Collected Words*, pp.266–8.

[39] T.W. Adorno, *Aesthetic Theory*, 1984, pp.263, 323, 453–79.

[40] G. Deleuze and F. Guattari, *Anti-Oedipus*, 1984, p.18.

[41] J.L. Lyotard, *The Lyotard Reader*, ed. A. Benjamin, Oxford 1989, pp.240–9.

[42] J.L. Lyotard, *Les Transformateurs Duchamp*, Paris 1977, p.20. Also *Machines celibataires*, Venice 1975, pp.98–102 and 'Etants Donnés' in *Marcel Duchamp: abecedaire*, Paris 1977, pp.86–109.

[43] J.L. Lyotard, *Discourse, Figure*, Paris 1971, pp.298, 303–4.

[44] *Collected Words*, p.229 ('The Large Glass', *Marcel Duchamp*, exh.cat., Museum of Modern Art, New York 1973).

[45] Marcel Duchamp/Marcel Jean, *Correspondence*, Munich 1987, p.74.

[46] *Collected Words*, p.205 ('Duchamp', *Art International*, January 1964, pp.22–8).

[47] *Collected Words*, p.235 (Review of A. Schwarz, 'The Complete Works of Marcel Duchamp, *Sunday Times*, 22 February 1970).

[48] R. Hamilton, *John Latham, Early Works 1954–72*, exh.cat., Lisson Gallery 1987, pp.7–16.

[49] P. Cabanne, London 1987, p.43.

[50] *Notes and Projects*, p.20 Note 2. Duchamp's word is 'lubrique' which G.H. Hamilton renders in the first two forms. The third is Joyce's in *Finnegan's Wake*, 1975, pp.115 and 121.

[51] *Collected Words*, pp.209 and 217. (Respectively in *NOT SEEN and/or LESS SEEN of/by MARCEL DUCHAMP/RROSE SELAVY 1904–1964*, exh.cat., Mary Sisler Collection, Cordier & Ekstrom Inc., New York and *Marcel Duchamp*, exh.cat., Tate Gallery 1966). Whereas P. Cabanne, *London 1979*, p.95 presses Duchamp into the role of father of the younger generation of artists. Duchamp quietly resists.

[52] *Notes and Projects*, p.156 Note 101.

[53] J. Derrida, *Dissemination*, 1981, pp.355–8.

[54] *Collected Words*, p.179 ('What kind of art education?' *Studio International*, September 1966).

[55] D. Thistlewood, *A Continuing Process: The New Creativity in British Art Education 1955–61*, exh.cat., ICA 1980, p.10.

[56] *Collected Words*, p.219 ('The Large Glass', *Marcel Duchamp*, exh.cat., Museum of Modern Art, New York 1973).

[57] C. Levi-Strauss, *The Savage Mind*, Chicago 1966, p.17.

[58] R. Hamilton, *Work in Progress*, exh.cat., Orchard Gallery 1988.

[59] *Ulysses*, pp.380–425.

[60] *Notes and Projects*, pp.210–16 Notes 141–4.

[61] *Collected Words*, pp.203–5 ('Duchamp', *Art International*, January 1964, pp.22–8).

[62] J. Baudrillard, 'The Precession of Simulacra', *Art & Text*, no.11, September 1983, pp.3–47.

'YES' & ... NO ...[1]

Stephen Snoddy

fig. 1 **Leopold Bloom** 1983 Soft-ground, roulette, engraving and aquatint

Ireland is a place where people are born with charm as a central characteristic; time is judged as a convenience and not as a burden, and conversation is a form of entertainment. The Irish identity is associated with the outrageous and with the poetic soul capable of wild and impractical gestures. It is colourful in speech, song and literature, yet with the turn of an eye it can also be moody and rebellious. In Ireland, the future is clouded with regret and it is the past that is full of promise.

A sense of the nostalgic is inseparable from the Irish experience and it was a fanciful view of the Emerald Isle which was imparted to Richard Hamilton as a child. His father had joined the British army early in his teens to escape the horrors of labour in the Staffordshire coal mines; he was sent to serve in Ireland, where he was billeted with an Irish family. Compared with Stoke-on-Trent at the turn of the century, Ireland was a fairyland. For Hamilton, the salt-pork barrel by the peat fire, the characters in the pubs, the songs, the tales of heroic exploits were all part of the repertoire of childhood bedtime stories in his English childhood.[2] In the context of his work, the romantic Irish culture symbolises Hamilton's sense of a modern 'high' culture restoring itself through contact with a 'primitive' tradition and from time to time he duels with this mythological monster called Ireland. As an artist he did so first by responding to a great Irish novel, James Joyce's *Ulysses* (fig. 1).

Ulysses is a book that offers promises and pleasures of diverse kinds to its readers, but through Joyce's endless perambulations we learn and sense the ebb and flow of language and life. He celebrates the fact that the written word is not 'owned' by a literary hierarchy which insists on separating the 'nod and a wink' of everyday mundane reality from the intellectual bombast of the ivory tower. Each reader of *Ulysses* therefore cherishes his or her own visualisation of the written text and it becomes a collaboration between the individual's own memory, life and experience and the changing rhythms and metres of language. The building blocks for this act of visual reconstruction emanate from a distinctive and age-old Irish tradition of the verbal. That is, that language is spoken, that language is alive, and that language is free.

It is just this understanding of the transformability of language that Richard Hamilton received from his reading of *Ulysses* during his period of National Service. Almost at once, in 1947, he began to think about the possibility of interpreting James Joyce's epic novel and the drawings and prints that followed were his first considered exploration of a subject in multiple ways. Joyce's mastery of styles, his virtuosity, his 'polyphony of tongues, codes, ideolects'[3] was 'the exemplar that later freed me to try some implausible associations in paint'.[4]

Although each of the episodes of *Ulysses* is treated differently, all eighteen are tautly bound together by a common schema. The narrative becomes a labyrinth, in which it is possible to explore in many different directions. Through the novel's series of devices, both stylistic (stream of consciousness, symbolism, onomatopoeias, phonic analogies, etc.) and technical (each episode corresponds to an hour of the day, a scene, an organ in the body, an art, a colour, a symbolic figure and a technique)[5] Joyce and Hamilton meet on common ground. Their shared analytical approach to the creative process is not only a means to an end but also, in the pleasure of the experience, a reward in itself. Hamilton accepts and recognises these different models and systems in order to enter into the world of *Ulysses* and to make images that are 'free to speak for themselves about the experience of learning ways to make images from the master of language'.[6]

In 1981, Hamilton returned to *Ulysses* after a thirty year pause because the centenary of James Joyce (1882–1941) was approaching. 'None of the episodes of *Ulysses* is more complex than "Oxen of the Sun", in which the birth of a child in Horne's house, a lying-in hospital, is echoed in the text by the birth of language, and its historic progress, in a procession of English prose styles, from Latin incantation through Anglo-Saxon, Mandeville, *Morte d'Arthur*, Milton, Bunyan, Pepys, "and so on through Defoe-Swift, and Steele-Addison, in a frightful jumble of Pidgin English, nigger English, Cockney, Irish, Bowery slang, and broken doggerel" as Joyce himself describes it.'[7]

From what he called his 'unworthy solution', the original 'In Horne's house' study of 1949 (fig.2), Hamilton progressed to a complete reworking in 1981 of an unfinished second drawing of 1949 (fig.3), to reflect Joyce's series of brilliant parodies (or pastiches) of English prose style, from Anglo-Saxon to the twentieth century. This metamorphosis of language corresponds to Hamilton's own belief that he can adopt any technique which co-exists with his innate sense of a visual tradition, in order to answer pictorial questions. In 'In Horne's house, study III' (fig.4) Hamilton assigned different styles to each of the participants and their setting – stepping from Easter Island through Egypt, Bellini, Rembrandt, Baron Gros, Cézanne, Cubism, Futurism, and abstraction. The visual form of the studies is fragmentary, line and plane are in flux and they become the visual equivalent of the linguistic complexity of the episode. Hamilton's response to Joyce was to institute 'the principle that media and messages have equal rights and that everything has to give some sort of logical account for its presence'.[8]

Between 1949 and 1981 events both in Hamilton's personal life and in Ireland itself had developed so as to give his interest in Irish themes a more disturbing emphasis. It is for this reason that a particular character in *Ulysses* whom Hamilton had represented in 1949 now takes on a special significance. The subject of Hamilton's 'Finn MacCool – first study', 1949 (fig.5) is a semi-legendary figure, an Irish poet and Chieftain leader of the warrior force the *Fianna*, from which the Fenian Society (Irish Republican Brotherhood) took their name. Organised in 1858 by James Stephens, the IRB was committed to the achievement of Irish independence through terrorist tactics and violent revolution, rather than through parliamentary or constitutional reform.

'Cyclops', the twelfth episode of *Ulysses*: Time, 5.00pm; Scene, Barney Kiernan's pub, 8–10 Little Britain Street; Organ, muscle; Art, politics; Colour, none; Symbol, nationalism; Technique, parody of literary styles.[9]

This episode's narrative technique shifts between Bloom's easy going and gentle manner and a series of commentaries in vastly different styles (each style is a gross caricature of the legal, the epic, the scientific, the journalistic, etc.). At the centre of the episode is the discussion in Barney Kiernan's pub, which is concerned throughout with aggression, but this theme is manifest in two distinct ways. In one, language itself masks or ritualises the violence of the event; in the other, language itself is the violent act. In the 'Cyclops' episode, Joyce identifies the 'citizen' with Finn MacCool. The Homeric parallel to MacCool's appearing at this point in the narrative is Odysseus's encounter with the one-eyed Cyclop, Polyphemus. The citizen personifies Polyphemus's one-eyed crudity. He can see no point of view other than his own and Polyphemus's

fig.2 **In Horne's house, first study** 1949 Ink and watercolour over pencil grid on paper

fig.3 **In Horne's house, study II** 1949–81 Ink over pencil grid on paper, reworked in 1981 with pencil and grey and white washes

fig.4 **In Horne's house, study III** 1981 Pencil and wash on paper

fig.5 **Finn MacCool – first study**
1949 Ink and pencil on paper

fig.6 **Of the tribe of Finn** 1982–3
Soft-ground, aquatint, open bite and
dry point

fig.7 **Finn MacCool – working
drawing** 1983 Gouache and
retouching inks on photograph *The
artist*

gigantic stature is reflected in the citizen's grossly inflated ego and greatly exaggerated claims. 'We'll put force against force' says the citizen, 'We'll have our greater Ireland beyond the sea'.[10] A picture emerges of Bloom in lonely opposition to a hostile environment, an individual in isolation, in a world of extremes and excesses.

Hamilton returned to the subject of Finn MacCool in 1982 (fig.6) and the source of 'Finn MacCool – working drawing', 1983 (fig.7) 'became identified in my renewed consideration of the mythic character with a photograph of a nationalist detainee, Raymond Pius McCartney, on hunger strike in the Maze prison in Northern Ireland'.[11] The trigger for this review of his subject had an element of chance with precedents in Hamilton's work – 'Kent State' (fig.30 on p.185) had also offered itself with an involuntary insistence. His sources derive from his preoccupation with all things modern and his acute awareness of contemporary culture and society. Looking back to 1970 he recalled 'It had been on my mind that there might be a subject staring me in the face from the TV screen. I set up a camera in front of the TV for a week. Every night I sat watching with a shutter release in my hand. If something interesting happened I snapped it up. During that week in May 1970, many possibilities emerged, from the Black and White Minstrel Show to Match of the Day; I also had a good many news items. In the middle of the week the shooting of students by National Guardsmen occurred at Kent State University. This tragic event produced some of the most powerful images that emerged from the camera, yet I felt a reluctance to use any of them. It was too terrible an incident in American history to submit to arty treatment. Yet there it was in my hand by chance – I didn't really choose the subject, it offered itself.'[12]

Ten years later, Hamilton again discovered a compelling image in a random manner via the television screen. 'By chance in 1980, I was struck by a scene in a TV documentary about republican prisoners in the H blocks. To the surprise of the British public film was shown of men "on the blanket", a term used to describe action taken by detainees in defiance of prison regulations. It was a strange image of human dignity in the midst of self-created squalor and it was endowed with a mythic power most often associated with art. It manifested the noble spirit of Irish patriotism having retreated (or was it pushed?) into its own excreta.'[13]

Hamilton also spoke of the 'dirty' protest when in conversation with Richard Cork: 'it's a question of jumping in when a chance offers itself, when the image itself is so compelling. You can't go out and find it.'[14]

Yet, however detached Hamilton appears to be from the realities of Northern Ireland he makes clear his position as a viewer of 'the troubles' in *A Cellular Maze*. 'Being with Rita Donagh keeps me close to the troubles. She was born of Irish parents in the Industrial Midlands of England. I was born in London. Our home is now in an ideal English country landscape. To be haunted by Ireland's problems may seem a little artificial. But our experience is not a rare condition: most British people feel Ireland's difficulties as a constant intrusion.'

Since the early 1970s, Rita Donagh's work has explored Ireland through the device of the map. The works are constructed around a network of complex grids and contour lines, projections and aerial views that plot an inner feeling and a deeply felt state of emotion. Ireland is seen as a particular place, a place of physical beauty and historical tragedy. The works juxtapose violent incidents with a personal searching for truth, a quest for a new perspective of picturing Ireland. Donagh's work consistently deals with how the media communicate such incidents and how they disclose or cover up the facts. As the media were the catalyst for Donagh's 'Evening Papers' work of the early

1970s, so Hamilton recognises his own use of the media. He also owes a debt to Donagh's first hand experience of the human conflict of Northern Ireland through her teaching at Belfast College of Art from 1974 onwards.

Hamilton has stated his own abhorrence of the IRA's campaign of terror, but at the same time he acknowledges the human sacrifice of the hunger strikers in the extremity of suffering they inflicted upon themselves for their principles. This dichotomy of feeling – a respect for the dignity of the protest, counterbalanced by horror at the terrible crimes committed – is a potent element in the meaning of 'The citizen'. Hamilton and Donagh use the media, factually and emotionally, to construct their work, yet the distinction between their work is one of mood: it could be compared to that between different pitches of sound. Donagh's is a quiet, measured, self-reflective approach, like the softness of an echo compared to Hamilton's big bang, raw and direct style of 'The citizen', 1982–3 (no.82) and 'The subject', 1988–90 (no.87). As Samuel Beckett once remarked, 'Alone together so much shared', Hamilton and Donagh strike a lyrical chord and a double sense of being at once intimately close to and at a distance from their powerfully charged motifs. Hamilton's identification with Ireland can therefore be seen in terms of the broad subjects of his work – contemporary history; media, technology and communication; mass culture; the iconography of modern society – but along with these he refers us to his sense of an ancient and primitive self, whereby the contemporary is interwoven with the mythic past and the public 'secondary' media experience with the private human emotion.

In wall murals across Northern Ireland, William III still rides into battle at the Boyne (fig.8). These are associated with the commemorative summer parades by Orangemen, while the Republican wall murals often centre on notions of Mother Ireland and of a new Ireland. It is easy to dismiss both as mindless sectarian graffiti, but perhaps it is much more accurate to describe the wall mural tradition in Northern Ireland as a folk art that is omnipresent. Just as the kerbstones are painted red, white and blue or green, white and gold to mark out a territory, so the murals are part of the street iconography of Northern Ireland. Hamilton, again through the media, was to respond to the many indigenous street images he saw on television and in a letter to the author, 13 November 1991, he recalled the circumstances of his embarking on painting 'The subject'. Having completed the painting "The citizen", I remembered all the exposure given to the other faction. Orangeman seemed the natural complement to Blanketman so I began to research material for a companion painting. The project was given some impetus when I was invited to make a contribution to the TV series of Paintbox programmes called "Painting with Light". Having used traditional collage materials for "The citizen", I had the opportunity to collage with electronic means. I carried the source material to the Quantel machine and made the composition in the two days allocated to the programme' (fig.9).

fig.8 'King William III', gable end mural in Rockland Street, Belfast, 1985 (photograph by Belinda Loftus)

The contrast between this dispassionate report and the expressive force of 'The subject' and its companion is so great that in order to understand these works one must appreciate on the one hand the political backdrop in Northern Ireland and on the other the personal and emotional ties which underlie and bind these images.

The sectarian struggle in Northern Ireland has been going on not just since 1969 but for generations before that year. Yet, at the time of writing, the death of defenceless people, misery for thousands of families and households, destruction of private and public property and the continuing communal hatreds look as if they will continue well into the twenty-first century.

fig.9 Source photograph, 'The subject'

The roots of conflict in Ireland can be traced back to the year 1170, when with the approval of King Henry II French Norman warriors crossed the Irish Sea. For the next four hundred years, the English rule of Ireland was confined to a thirty mile radius around Dublin. However, the defeat of the Gaelic chiefs at the Battle of Kinsale in 1601 signalled the end of the old Gaelic order and with the 'Flight of the Earls' this gave James I the opportunity to colonise Ulster with mainly Presbyterian Scots. From the beginning, land and religion were inextricably linked and religion remained the barrier to assimilation because the settlements took place in the wider context of the Counter-Reformation. Oliver Cromwell, in 1649, was to despatch the native Irish to the west of Ireland, leaving three-quarters of the land in the hands of the Protestant minority. In 1690, the Catholic Irish, with James II, the Catholic monarch, were decisively crushed by the army of King William III at the Battle of the Boyne. For the better part of the next hundred years, the Protestant ascendancy ruled and the penal laws of 1695 banned Catholics from public office, the legal profession and the army, nor could they vote, teach or own land. The conquest of Ireland seemed complete.

fig. 10 Source photograph, 'The subject'

The Orange Order dates back to 1795 when the first Orange Lodges were set up after a particularly fierce sectarian clash, the Battle of the Diamond, near Loughall, Co. Armagh. According to S.E. Long, a prominent modern Orange clergyman, these lodges were formed as defensive organisations because of 'Protestant reactions to the attacks of Roman Catholics on their persons and properties'.[15] Orangemen are continually urged to 'Remember 1690' (the Battle of the Boyne). The defeat then of the English Catholic monarch James II by William III, Prince of Orange saved the Protestants of Ireland, as an old saying goes, from 'popery, wooden shoes and brass money' – in other words from *superstition, oppression and poverty*.

The Act of Union of 1800 abolished the Irish Parliament, uniting Britain and Ireland in one kingdom with one parliament. The history of the next 120 years is the history of attempts to undo the Act of Union and to give Ireland a parliament of its own. The granting of Catholic emancipation in 1829 was felt by some Irish Protestants to threaten their status. The Home Rule crisis of 1886 was to give Orangeism the political impetus which has carried it forward to the present day. Protestant politicians who, in increasing numbers, began to fear that Home Rule might mean Rome Rule, saw in the Orange order, with its network of local lodges, an organisational framework upon which they would establish a popular Protestant party, the Unionist party. From those days 'the principles of Orangeism were clearly stated and have been consistently followed: defence of the Protestant religion; defence of the Protestant ascendancy in Ireland; maintaining the constitutional links with Britain, and loyalty to the crown, *so long as the monarchy remains Protestant*'.[16] The Home Rule movement was to create vociferous, widespread and militant Protestant opposition, to the extent that the Ulster Volunteer Force was formed in 1912, an army of some 100,000 who were prepared to resist Britain by force of arms to prevent implementation of Home Rule. The third Home Rule Bill of 1912 was passed in 1913 but its realisation was delayed by the outbreak of the First World War. It was clear, however, that Home Rule would not be for the whole of Ireland, but that parts of Ulster would be granted exemption.

The Government of Ireland Act of 1920 partitioned Ireland, creating Northern Ireland from the six counties of Antrim, Armagh, Derry, Down, Fermanagh and Tyrone. Westminster devised the parliamentary convention which blocked discussion of Northern Ireland's internal affairs in the House of Commons. Northern Ireland therefore became a semi-autonomous part of the United Kingdom. As a consequence, Unionist politicians were able to protect their positions of power, their social privileges and their economic and professional interests. They were immune from outside scrutiny and criticism and when violence erupted in 1969 through the civil rights demonstrations, it was against a background of over fifty years of injustice and political persecution, religious discrimination in housing and employment and electoral disenfranchisement. Reforms had to happen. However, while the diagnosis was easy, the cure seemed impossible to achieve.

By early 1970 the civil rights movement had achieved most of its major objectives, but the army's presence had become a symbol of old hatreds. By the middle of 1972 violence in Northern Ireland was escalating at an unprecedented rate. The IRA responded to the government's introduction of internment in August 1971 with a military campaign of unparalleled ferocity. One hundred and thirty-four people died in the following five months. The Abercorn Restaurant bombing; Smithfield Bus Station; the Shankill Butcher murders; the 'Bermuda Triangle' sectarian killings; La Mon House Hotel; the Miami Showband murders; the Lisburn train fireball bombing; Warrenpoint; this despairing list of carnage littered the 1970s, with the only attempt at a political solution during those years being the 1974 Sunningdale Agreement. The 1980s approached with no real prospect of an end to the violence.

On behalf of the Republican prisoners at the Maze/Long Kesh[17] prison outside Belfast (fig.11), Bobby Sands went on hunger strike on 1 March 1981,[18] the fifth anniversary of the date on which the government had started to phase out special status, which had existed between 1971 (when internment without trial was introduced) and 1976. Special status meant that those prisoners who were interned (under the Special Powers Act) were treated as political prisoners and not as common criminals. The hunger strike would peak at Easter of 1981, the anniversary of the 1916 Uprising and symbol of Republican resurrection. It was to be the climax in the prisoners' four year campaign for political status. This campaign had begun with the 'blanket' protest, in which prisoners convicted of what would, in other times, be described as politically motivated offences refused to wear prison uniform, the badge of a common criminal, and covered themselves with the only clothing at hand – their blankets. The 'blanket' protest became the 'no wash' protest, then the 'no slop out' protest, and finally the 'dirty' protest, in which Republican prisoners smeared their own excrement on the walls, floors and ceilings of their cells. Their vow to fast to death if necessary was made in order to attain their five demands: to refrain from prison work; to associate freely with one another; to organise recreational facilities; to have one letter, visit and parcel a week; and to have lost remission time restored.

fig.11 Aerial photograph of H Blocks

Both the government and the hunger strikers maintained their respective positions rigidly. There were few real efforts to negotiate a solution. On the one side was a simple refusal to consider concessions on any of the demands; on the other a simple refusal to consider anything other than concessions on all five. As a consequence, the hunger strikes polarised Northern Ireland to an extent that no single event since 1969 had, or has since. Within the Catholic community the ambiguous relationship between militant Republicanism and the Catholic Church was unveiled, between ancient mythologies of blood sacrifice and the statement of Pope John Paul II, on his visit to Ireland in 1981, 'murder is murder and must not be called by any other name'. Within the Orange community, responses to the hunger strikes exposed the depth and intensity of a hatred of Republicanism, a deep rooted fear of Catholicism, and the extent to which these factors were thought to be fused. Both communities were caged inside traditional

fig.12 **Study for 'The citizen'** 1982
Acrylic underpainting and oil on
canvas *Artistes du monde contre
l'Apartheid, Paris*

fig.13 Source photograph,
'The citizen'

fig.14 Source photograph,
'The citizen'

fig.15 Source photograph,
'The citizen'

ideologies which could not and will not be unlocked overnight. An historical twist to the situation was that it was the siege of Derry, in 1689, which had provided Protestantism with its enduring slogan, 'No surrender', when their enemies had attempted to starve the Protestant people into submission.

The showing of 'The citizen' (figs.12–15) and 'The subject' side by side in London in summer 1991 evoked in me an immense feeling of personal sorrow. It is important to view 'The citizen' and the 'The subject' as companion paintings (this is the only the way I have viewed them, literally and symbolically) and thus more fully to understand the convictions, postures, fanaticisms and dualities which these images are about. It was noticeable that an English audience felt somewhat removed from the symbolism of the images and sidestepped the iconography of the paintings, thereby being able to discuss them only in relation to Hamilton's use of technology. It was as if the paintings called for a collective re-examination of a part of history which had become taboo. Such images correspond to a contemporary history and situation and ask questions of the viewer's position towards the subject of these paintings. An Irish showing of the paintings should permit a more direct look and place the work more closely in the context of political and social events. It is the reality of the paintings that can only be the subject of the debate.

The actions of the hunger strikers were beyond Protestant comprehension. They were seen by the world at large to be victims, but to Protestants, victimhood is not self-inflicted. For the ordinary Protestant takes refuge in the reason for the supreme sacrifice (as when, for example, thousands of young Northern Irish Protestants gave their lives in the trenches at the Somme during the First World War), rather than in the process of the sacrifice itself. A Protestant would justify and find ways of contributing to and living for a country (the work ethic), while the hunger strikers chose ancient Gaelic laws of self-denial and sacrifice. It is what the historian A.T.Q. Stewart calls a 'nightmarish juxtaposition of the folk memory of Jungian psychology'; not only were the hunger strikers asserting claims to Protestants' physical territory but they were invading the loyalist psyche.[19]

To keep the nationalist cause at the top of the political agenda and in touch with international consciousness Republican prisoners carry on the fight by resisting the prison regime. Maintaining the struggle within the prison is part of the psychology of 'the long war'.[20] This claustrophobic tension exists alongside the celebratory triumphalism of the Orangeman stating his claim to march the route of his forefathers.[21] 'The citizen' and 'The subject' are opposing images of incarceration and freedom, yet their conjunction evokes the survival of the species syndrome. Each opposing side is a closed world with an unchangeable internal code of its own, impervious to the passage of time. The inflexible, no-compromise stance is so deeply rooted in both communities that everything conforms to an action-response pattern that endlessly repeats itself.

'The citizen' and 'The subject' correctly portray Northern Ireland's politics as a battle between two irreconcilable groups. Conforming to the two sides' intransigent stereotypes, they glare at each other. One evokes a screaming silence, the other a screaming defiance. Both attract a macabre fascination through their military associations and each signals a staunch, devout will, a stubborn intolerance and a fanatacism masquerading as nobility of cause.

The dirty protest crystallised Ulster Loyalist attitudes to the hunger strikes and their sense of isolation was reinforced by the worldwide media coverage of Bobby Sands and his death. It led them to perceive the world outside Northern Ireland as hostile to their position and sympathetic to the Republican cause. The universal association of excrement with things decayed and contaminated, embodied in the minds of Ulster Loyalists perceptions of evil. 'If cleanliness is next to Godliness', asked Peter Robinson, 'to whom are these men close?'[22] For Northern Ireland Protestants, heavily influenced by Calvinistic puritanism, it was anathema for people to live in their own excrement and this aroused their deepest disgust. Yet, during the years of being on the blanket and the dirty protest, of having endured physical deprivation to the point where their reaction to it had become existential, the prisoners' worlds had somehow become deconstructed; the physical self was something that existed outside the real self, and thus the pain and suffering could be deflected. Loyalist prisoners felt a special revulsion for the dirty protest; *Ulster*, the mouthpiece of the UDA,[23] never tired of pointing out that the Loyalist prisoners 'would not lower their dignity and self respect by fouling their own nests'. When six Loyalist prisoners began a hunger strike of their own to draw attention to what *Ulster* called 'their clean, dignified, and unnoticed protest for segregation', it was a cry for attention and of fear lest their public identity should be submerged by the Republican protest.

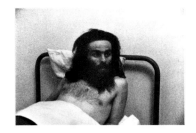

fig.16 Source photograph, 'Finn MacCool' fig.7

In Hamilton's words, 'What we had heard of the blanket protest, mainly through the propaganda agencies of Sinn Fein, could not prepare us for the startling photographic documentation on TV. The picture presented, first by Granada Television and later by the BBC, was shocking less for its scatological content than for its potency. An oft declared British view of the IRA as thugs and hooligans did not match the materialisation of Christian martyrdom so profoundly contained on film. One became acutely aware of the religious conflict that had resulted in civil inequalities that gave a platform for IRA activity. The symbols of Christ's agony were there, not only the crucifix on the neck of the prisoners and the rosary which confirmed the monastic austerity but the self inflicted suffering which has marked Christianity from the earliest times.'[24] The prisoners claimed the high moral ground because their fast to death reinforced their identification as martyrs. By fusing the ancient myth of militant nationalism and of heroic sacrifice with the central characteristics of Irish Catholicism, penitential fasting, atonement for wrong doing and self-denial, we can understand the context of Father Matt Wallace's statement '[They] were almost akin to Christ-like' (figs. 16, 17).[25]

fig.17 'Blessed are those who hunger for justice', gable end mural in Rockmore Street, Belfast, 1981 (photograph by Ciaran McGowan)

A subsequent development forms an appropriate conclusion to Hamilton's intertwining of public sources and personal links in his process of making 'The citizen'. He recalls: 'There was a TV programme on the "H" blocks about a year ago. It showed the Maze under its present regime where good relations exist between warders and prisoners. Each faction, IRA and INLA have their own commanding officer running their men in good military order. Relations with the administration are on what seems to be a prisoner of war footing with due formalities observed. We were shown a discussion between the IRA catering officer and the administration on the subject of sausage rolls. There was an interview with the commanding officer of the IRA group of prisoners; Raymond Pius McCartney, whose face I had used for the Ulysses etching called "Finn MacCool" and with whom I have corresponded. On the wall of his cell was a pin-up that seemed somehow familiar, it looked like my "citizen". A close up of the image on the wall revealed it was indeed a photograph of the painting. It seemed that things had come full circle when a painting of an image derived from a TV presentation of the dirty protest period of the "H" blocks becomes an icon in the very same cells when the cameras return years later to show the calm that resulted from acceptance of the hunger strikers' demands'.[26] There is a curious truth to the fact that 'The citizen' has taken its

fig.18 Orange parade, Shankill Road, Belfast, 16 November 1991. In protest of the sixth anniversary of the Anglo-Irish agreement (photograph by Sean Smith)

fig.19 **Countdown** 1989 Humbrol enamel on Cibachrome on canvas *Hirshhorn Museum and Sculpture Garden, Smithsonian Institution*

logical place in the complex labyrinth and mega-textual world of Joyce and Hamilton. It is part of fact and fiction, art and life.

Nationalism has a power over peoples' minds and hearts. The defence or cause of 'a nation' is one of the few commitments for which people will kill others or voluntarily lay down their lives. The psychology of nationalism is powerfully connected to a sense of self. It is the need for people to belong to a group which is linked by culture, customs, religion and a common history. Only the collective group can give meaning and fulfilment to individuals within the group and it is the pack instinct which is the driving force. The packs have leaders who perpetrate primitive tribal rituals by imposing strongly held convictions that each individual belongs to a certain human grouping. This segregation of human beings into distinct groups can be defined as a 'sense of national identity', when people find it neccessary to identify themselves with a particular tribe. 'The citizen' and 'The subject' (figs.18, 19) have this sense of national identity. They both use history as a weapon against each other. History is defenceless, it can be used and manipulated to maintain the polarisation between the tribes.

Religion in Northern Ireland is a powerful early learning tool in each side's perception of the other. Childhood upbringing and shared family experience make the religious aspect of 'the troubles' reach the deepest levels of the human psyche. 'The citizen' and 'The subject' convey this depth. They give a strong sense that while the individual is grounded in the world of his or her ancestry, his or her power is the collective power of the tribe.

The Orangeman is very much a fact of life in Northern Ireland. Nearly one-third of adult male Protestants belong to an Orange Lodge. 'The subject' in his regalia of an assertive power strides out triumphantly emphasising his supremacy. A dignified gentleman in his Sunday best, he is a staunch defender of Ulster's glorious past. 'The subject' is also a 'citizen'; a citizen who loves his Queen and country; a citizen who would die in its defence; a citizen who is obedient to the forces of law and order; a citizen who believes in the democracy of one man one vote. 'The subject' is as much about nationalism as 'The citizen', they both identify with a strong sense of self and a fanatical devotion to the same cause of defence of 'the nation', 'The subject' proudly commemorating and proclaiming his 'victory' at The Boyne; 'The citizen' symbolising a sacrificial martyrdom recalling a mythological past. Their meeting brings a troubled history up to the present and into the future. History in Ireland replicates itself and in a country where people pride themselves on their memory, the future is therefore weighed down with a sense of the inevitable, that is, there is no hope of compromise. They are mirror images reflecting the human tragedy of using force to settle arguments, as Odysseus, in Book 9 of the *Odyssey* describes his adventures among the one-eyed Cyclopes, who are 'giants, louts, without a law to bless them'.

'The citizen' and 'The subject' are a reflection on the political conditions in which one and a half million people are forced to live in Northern Ireland. It is a situation of the impossibility of consensus. Through generations of political manipulation and intransigence, the communities have been 'misplaced' by history. The younger generations have turned to political violence as a means of escape from the sectarian dilemma in which they have been put by the intolerance of their ancestors. Any interpretation of these paintings cannot dismiss the moral questions they ask; to do so is to ignore the content in favour of the aesthetic considerations. Hamilton has insisted on his right to paint images of such directness that they demand a response, not an averted glance. Although everything in these works is dependent on the 'content', we have become sanitised or practiced at resisting images of raw power. Yet, though we may turn a blind eye, these paintings are located in the mind's eye. They hover between not wanting to remember and not being able to forget.

Whatever judgement posterity may reach, these images grasp a painful and sorrowful reality, a sense of anger and frustration, sadness and grief. They cast shadows upon us; we cannot be oblivious to their presence. They touch a nerve, a trapped nerve, yet by their existence they confirm a future. Regretfully, a predictable future of the zero sum game, a Beckettian game of waiting, 'The light glitters an instant and then it's night once more' (*Waiting for Godot*). An endgame, a game over which the spoils cannot be shared or negotiated, but only won or lost. STOP.

fig.20 'STOP'. More than 2000 campaigners from both sides of the Irish border gathered in the Republic, at Cooley, County Louth, to spell out their protest against the IRA at the murder of a local farmer, 1991

NOTES

1 'Yes' – 'Yes, you're right. The book [*Ulysses*] must end with yes. It must end with the most positive word in the human language.' James Joyce, quoted in Richard Ellmann, *James Joyce* (new and revised edition), Oxford University Press, 1983, p.522.
  . . . No . . . relates to the Ulster loyalist cries of 'Ulster says No' and 'No Surrender'.

2 A sentiment similar to that he felt for Ireland developed later in Hamilton. His early teens saw the Spanish civil war, he was moved by Picasso's 'Guernica' when it was shown in London in 1938, and Catalonia, with its living tradition of anarchism, stood alone against fascism in Europe. He has always regarded the house he has enjoyed in Cadaqués since 1969 as being located in Catalonia rather than in Spain.

3 Richard Hamilton, *Work in Progress*, Orchard Gallery, Londonderry 1988, Terry Eagleton, p.8.

4 Ibid., p.10.

5 For example, 'Oxen of the Sun', the fourteenth episode of *Ulysses*: Time, 10.00pm; Scene, the National Maternity Hospital; Organ, womb; Art, medicine; Colour, white; Symbol, mothers; Technique, embryonic development.

6 *Work In Progress*, p.10.

7 *Work in Progress*, p.40.

8 Anne Seymour, Introduction to Richard Hamilton, *Drawings, Prints and Paintings 1941–1955*, Anthony d'Offay Gallery, London 1980.

9 This schema was first published in

part in Stuart Gilbert's *James Joyce's Ulysses*, New York 1930.

10 James Joyce, *Ulysses*, The Corrected Text, Penguin Books, 1986, p.270.

11 *Work in Progress*, p.36.

12 Richard Hamilton, *Collected Words 1953–1982*, Thames and Hudson, 1982, p.94.

13 Richard Hamilton and Rita Donagh, *A Cellular Maze*, Orchard Gallery, Londonderry 1983 (unpaginated).

14 'Epiphanies', Richard Hamilton in conversation with Richard Cork, BBC Radio 3, 1 April 1985.

15 Information from *Orangeism, A New Historical Appreciation*, 2nd ed., The Grand Orange Lodge of Ireland, Belfast, 1969.

16 Andrew Boyd, *Northern Ireland: Who is to Blame?* Mercier Press, Dublin 1984, p.27.

17 It is Long Kesh to Catholics, the Maze to Protestants; Derry to Catholics, Londonderry to Protestants; the six counties or the North of Ireland to Catholics; Northern Ireland to Protestants. Although both communities share a common first language, they both need what Alasdair MacIntyre describes as 'a second first language'. Padraig O'Malley, *Biting at the Grave*, The Blackstaff Press, Belfast, 1990, p.185.

18 This was the second hunger strike after the first hunger strike broke down during Christmas 1980. Bobby Sands joined the IRA in 1972 and within six months was imprisoned for possession of firearms. He was released in 1976, however in September 1977 he

was sent to the Maze/Long Kesh charged again with possession of firearms. He immediately went 'on the blanket', and from that onto the dirty protest.

19 *Biting at the Grave*, p.165.

20 I am indebted to Declan McGonagle for this information and many other insights through various conversations.

21 In conversation with Richard Hamilton, he recounted how he had seen the Orange marchers clash with the RUC in 1985 on television when their traditional marching route through 'the Tunnel' in Portadown (a Catholic area in a Protestant town) was blocked by the police because of a ban on marches that were likely to cause a breach of the peace.

22 Peter Robinson is the Deputy Leader of the Democratic Unionist Party (DUP), the Rev. Ian Paisley is Leader.

23 The UDA is the Ulster Defence Association. Started in 1971 as a co-ordinating body for a great variety of Loyalist vigilante groups, the UDA is Northern Ireland's largest Protestant paramilitary organisation. It is legal, although its military wing, the UFF (Ulster Freedom Fighters) is proscribed. The UDA advocates independence for Northern Ireland.

24 *A Cellular Maze* (unpaginated).

25 *Biting at the Grave*, p.109. Father Matt Wallace, a priest in the parish of one of the hunger strikers.

26 Letter to the author, 13 November 1991.

COLOUR PLATES

2 **Nude** 1940
61 × 50.8 (24 × 20)

1 **Figure study (Flossie)** 1940
50.8 × 43.1 (20 × 17)

3 Portrait of James Tower 1940
55.8 × 40.7 (22 × 16)

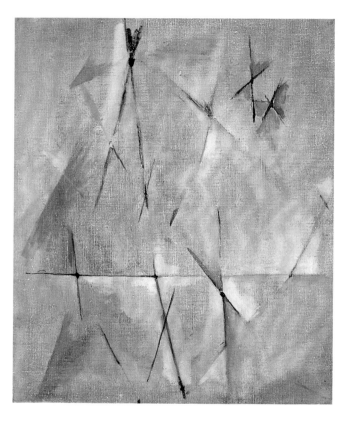

4 Induction 1950
51 × 40.5 (20⅛ × 16)

5 Microcosmos: tangential ovoid 1950
38.2 × 51 (15 × 20⅛)

6 **Chromatic spiral** 1950
53.5 × 47 (21 × 18½)

7 Particular System 1951
101.5 × 127 (40 × 50)

8 d'Orientation 1952
117 × 160 (46 × 63)

9 Trainsition III 1954
76 × 56 (30 × 22)

10 Trainsition IIII 1954
91.5 × 122 (36 × 48)

12 Still-life? 1954
$61 \times 51 \ (24 \times 20\frac{1}{8})$

11 re Nude 1954
122 × 91.5 (48 × 36)

13 Just what is it that makes today's
homes so different, so appealing? 1956
26×25 ($10\frac{1}{4} \times 9\frac{3}{4}$)

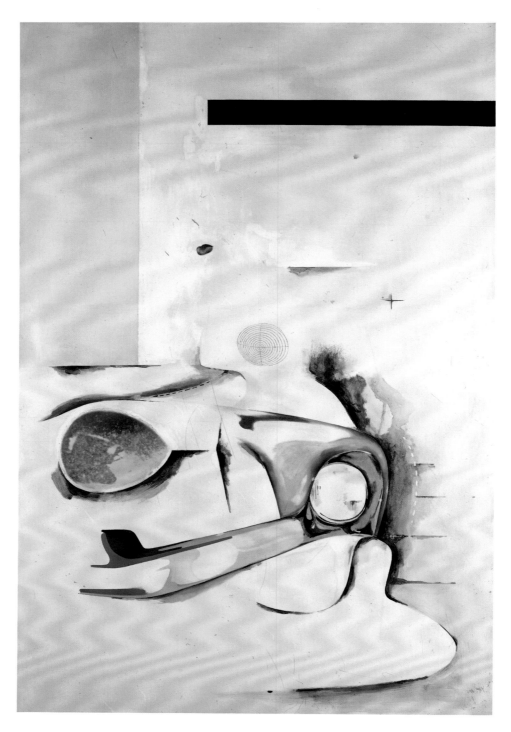

14 Hommage à Chrysler Corp. 1957
122 × 81 (48 × 32)

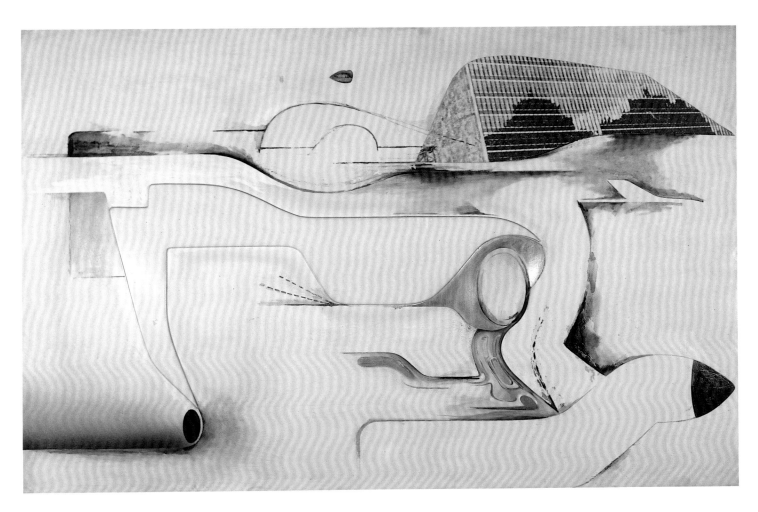

15 Hers is a lush situation 1958
81 × 122 (32 × 48)

16 She 1958–61
122 × 81 (48 × 32)

17 **Pin-up** 1961
122 × 81 (48 × 32)

18 Glorious Techniculture 1961–4
122 × 122 (48 × 48)

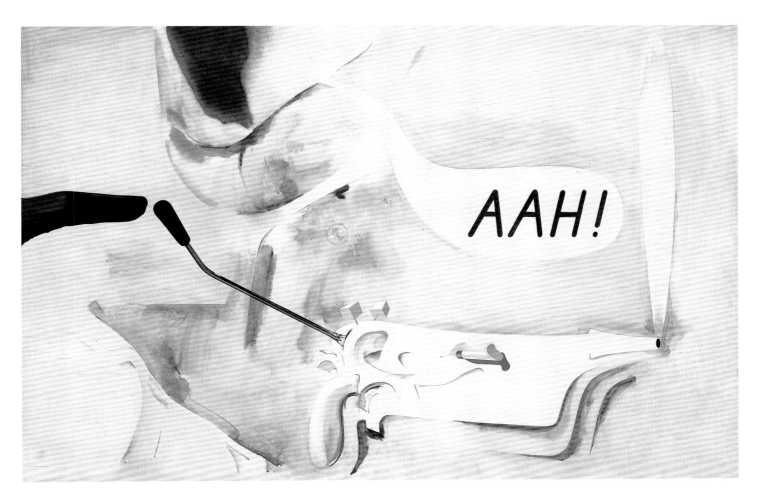

19 AAH! 1962
81 × 122 (32 × 48)

24 AAH! in perspective 1963
(second version, 1973)
26 × 17 (10¼ × 6¾)

20 Towards a definitive statement on the
coming trends in men's wear and accessories (a)
'Together let us explore the stars' 1962
61 × 81 (24 × 32)

21 Towards a definitive statement on the
coming trends in men's wear and accessories (b)
1962 61 × 81 (24 × 32)

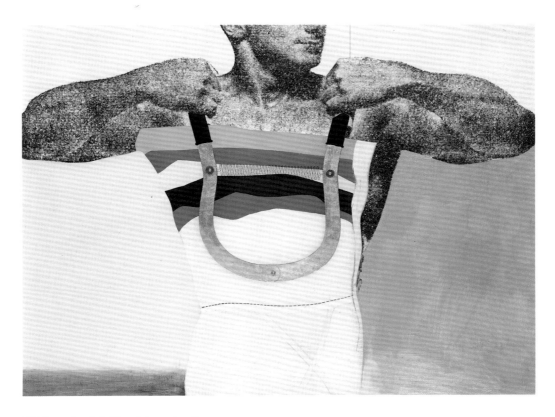

22 Towards a definitive statement on the
coming trends in men's wear and accessories (c)
Adonis in Y-fronts 1962
61 × 81 (24 × 32)

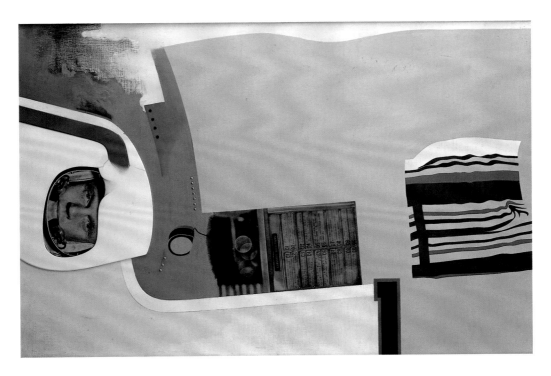

23 Towards a definitive statement on the
coming trends in men's wear and accessories (d)
1963 122 × 81 (48 × 32) or 81 × 122 (32 × 48)

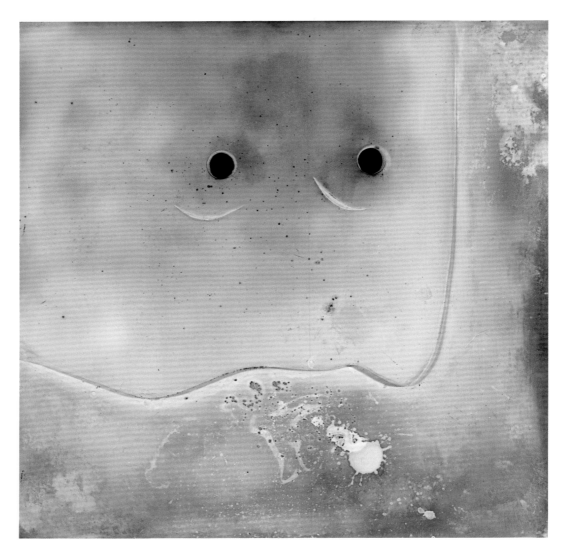

**25 Study for 'Portrait of Hugh Gaitskell
as a Famous Monster of Filmland'** 1963–70
45.5 × 45.5 (18 × 18)

**26 Portrait of Hugh Gaitskell as a
Famous Monster of Filmland** 1964
61 × 61 (24 × 24)

27 Epiphany 1964
122 (48) diameter

28 Desk 1964
61 × 89 (24 × 35)

29 Interior I 1964
122 × 162 (48 × 63¾)

30 Interior II 1964
122 × 162.5 (48 × 64)

31 My Marilyn 1965
102.5 × 122 (40¼ × 48)

32 Still-life 1965
89.5 × 91 (35¼ × 35¾)

33 **Whitley Bay** 1965
81 × 122 (32 × 48)

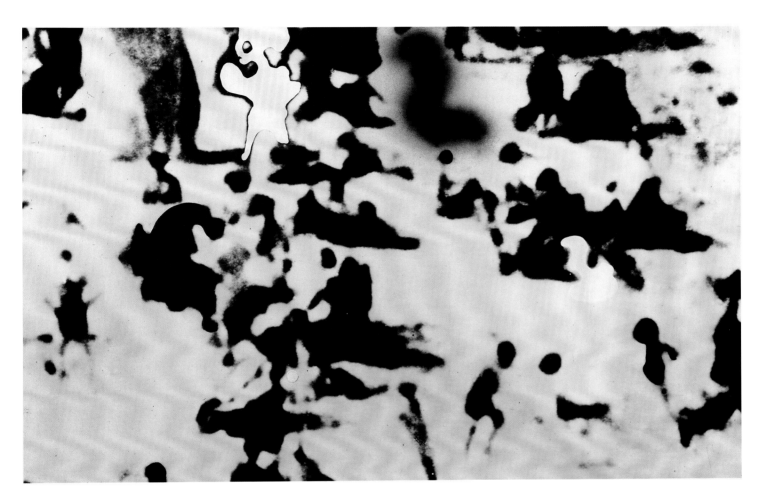

34 People 1965–6
81 × 122 (32 × 48)

35 Landscape 1965–6
81 × 244 (32 × 96)

36 Trafalgar Square 1965–7
81 × 122 (32 × 48)

37 The Solomon R Guggenheim (Black and White) 1965–6
122 × 122 × 18 (48 × 48 × 7¼)

38 The Solomon R Guggenheim (Neapolitan) 1965–6
122 × 122 × 18 (48 × 48 × 7¼)

39 The Solomon R Guggenheim (Black) 1965–6
122 × 122 × 18 (48 × 48 × 7¼)

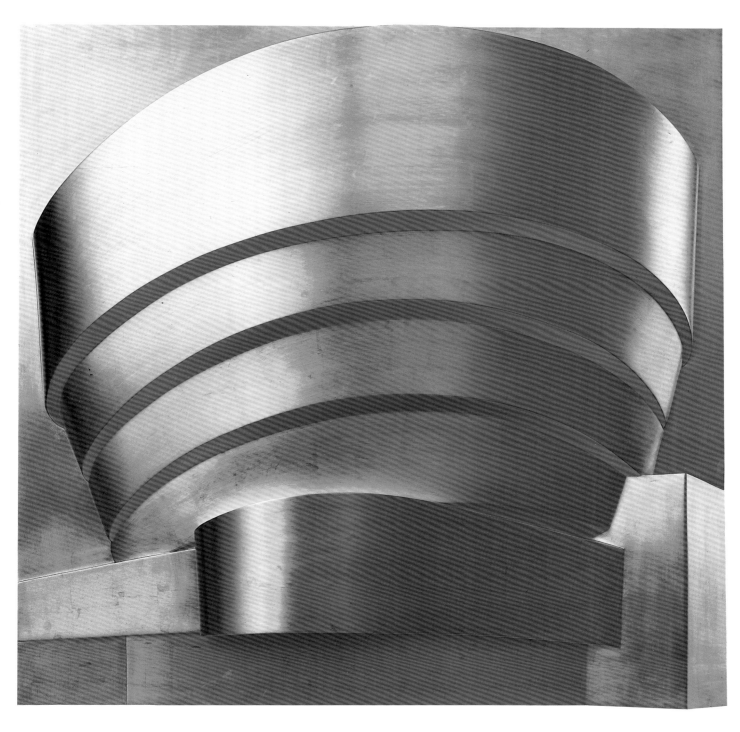

40 The Solomon R Guggenheim (Gold) 1965–6
122 × 122 × 18 (48 × 48 × 7¼)

41 The Solomon R Guggenheim (Metalflake) 1965–6
122 × 122 × 18 (48 × 48 × 7¼)

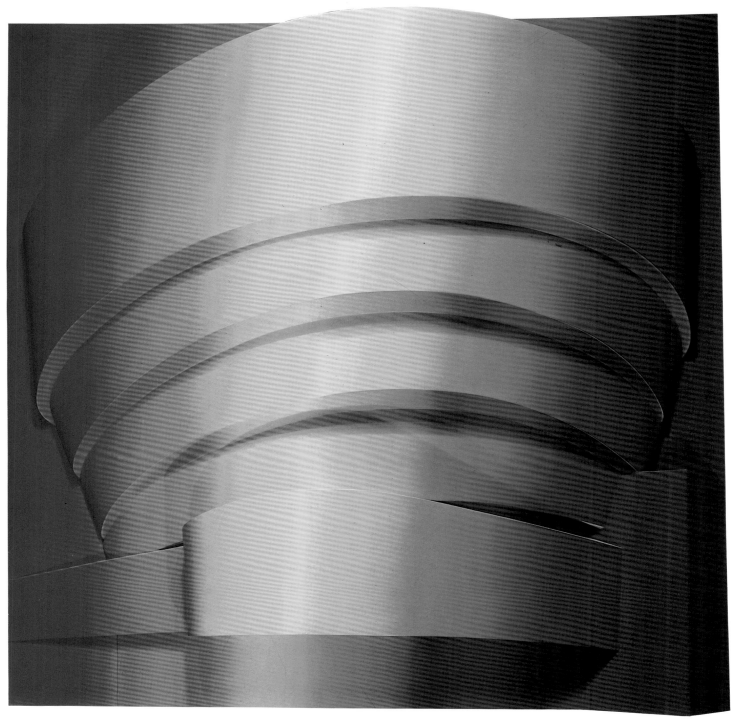

42 The Solomon R Guggenheim (Spectrum) 1965–6
122 × 122 × 18 (48 × 48 × 7¼)

44 Bathers I 1966–7
84 × 117 (33¼ × 46¼)

45 Bathers II 1967
76 × 114.5 (30 × 45)

47 Picturegram 1968
101.5 × 65 (40 × 25½)

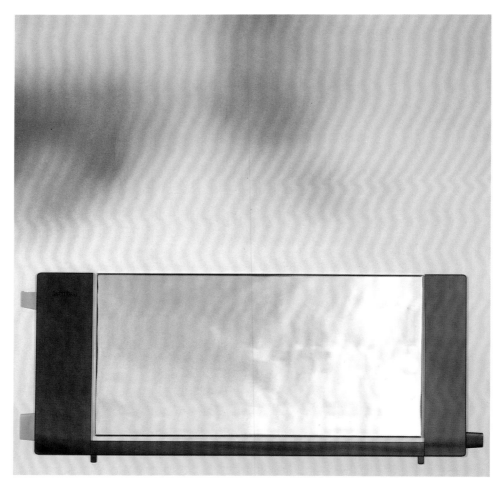

43 Toaster 1966–7 (reconstructed 1969)
81 × 81 (32 × 32)

46 I'm dreaming of a white Christmas 1967–8
106.5 × 160 (42 × 63)

48 Swingeing London 67 (a) 1968–9
$67 \times 85 \ (26\frac{1}{2} \times 33\frac{1}{2})$

49 Swingeing London 67 (b) 1968–9
$67 \times 85 \ (26\frac{1}{2} \times 33\frac{1}{2})$

50 Swingeing London 67 (c) 1968–9
$67 \times 85 \ (26\frac{1}{2} \times 33\frac{1}{2})$

51 Swingeing London 67 (d) 1968–9
$67 \times 85 \ (26\frac{1}{2} \times 33\frac{1}{2})$

52 Swingeing London 67 (e) 1968–9
$67 \times 85 \ (26\frac{1}{2} \times 33\frac{1}{2})$

53 Swingeing London 67 (f) 1968–9
$67 \times 85 \ (26\frac{1}{2} \times 33\frac{1}{2})$

54 Swingeing London 67 1968
58.5 × 79 × 7.5 (23 × 31⅛ × 3)

55 Chicago project I 1969
81 × 122 (32 × 48)

56 Chicago project II 1969
81 × 122 (32 × 48)

57 Fashion-plate (cosmetic study I) 1969
100 × 70 (39⅜ × 27½)

59 Fashion-plate (cosmetic study III) 1969
100 × 70 (39⅜ × 27½)

58 Fashion-plate (cosmetic study II) 1969
100 × 70 (39⅜ × 27½)

60 Fashion-plate (cosmetic study IV) 1969
100 × 70 (39⅜ × 27½)

61 Fashion-plate (cosmetic study V) 1969
100 × 70 (39⅜ × 27½)

63 Fashion-plate (cosmetic study VII) 1969
100 × 70 (39⅜ × 27½)

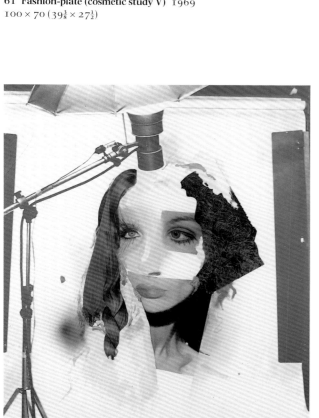

62 Fashion-plate (cosmetic study VI) 1969
100 × 70 (39⅜ × 27½)

64 Fashion-plate (cosmetic study VIII) 1969
100 × 70 (39⅜ × 27½)

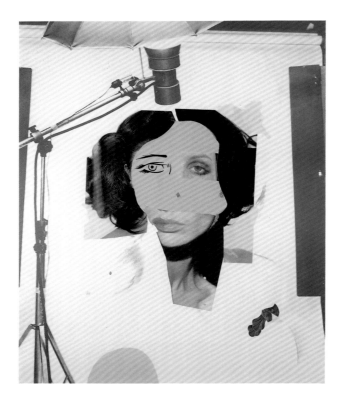

65 Fashion-plate (cosmetic study IX) 1969
100 × 70 (39⅜ × 27½)

67 Fashion-plate (cosmetic study XI) 1969
100 × 70 (39⅜ × 27½)

66 Fashion-plate (cosmetic study X) 1969
100 × 70 (39⅜ × 27½)

68 Fashion-plate (cosmetic study XII) 1969
100 × 70 (39⅜ × 27½)

69 The critic laughs 1971–2
27 × 11 × 6.5 ($10\frac{3}{4} \times 4\frac{1}{4} \times 2\frac{1}{2}$) (cased)

70 Soft pink landscape 1971–2
122 × 162.5 (48 × 64)

77 Soft blue landscape 1976–80
122 × 162.5 (48 × 64)

71 Flower-piece I 1971–4
95 × 72 (37½ × 28⅜)

72 Flower-piece II 1973
$95 \times 72 \, (37\frac{1}{2} \times 28\frac{3}{8})$

73 **Flower-piece III** 1973-4
95 × 72 (37½ × 28⅜)

75 Sunset 1975
61 × 81 (24 × 32)

76 Langan's 1976
92 × 92 ($36\frac{1}{4}$ × $36\frac{1}{4}$)

74 Sign 1975
34.7 × 80 (13¾ × 31½)

78 Carafe 1978
9 × 20 × 6 (3½ × 8 × 2⅜)

79 Ashtray 1979
3.4 × 15.5 × 13.5 (1⅜ × 6⅛ × 5⅜)

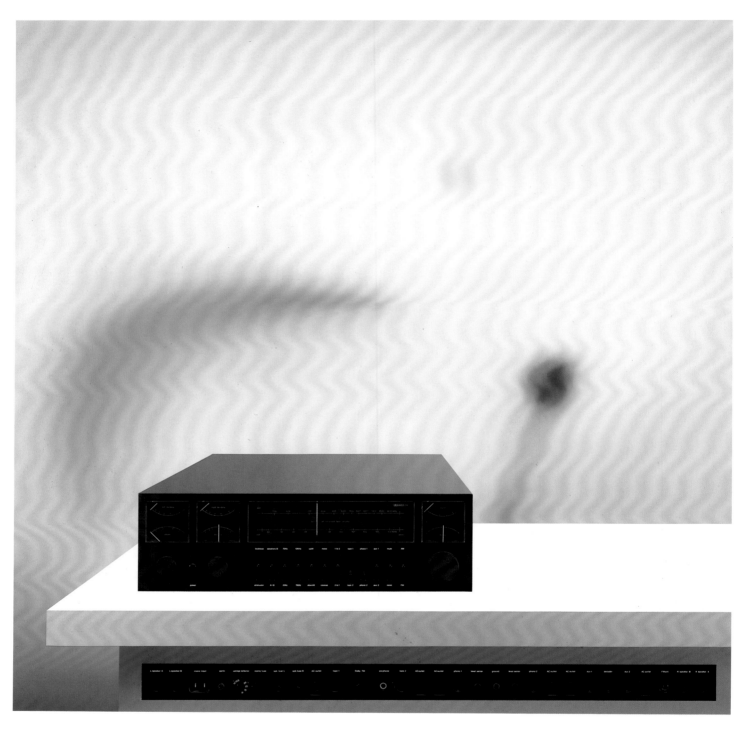

80 Lux 50 – functioning prototype 1979
100 × 100 (39⅜ × 39⅜)

83 Treatment room 1983–4
Installation 275 × 550 × 550
(108 × 216 × 216)

81 Study for 'The citizen' 1982
87.7 × 67.7 (34½ × 26¾)

82 The citizen 1982–3
2 canvases, each 200 × 100 ($78\frac{3}{4}$ × $39\frac{3}{8}$)

86 Hotel Europa 1986–91
100 × 100 (39⅜ × 39⅜)

85 Lobby 1985–7
175 × 250 (69 × 98½)

88 Diab DS-101 computer 1985–9
70 × 50 × 50 (27½ × 19¾ × 19¾)

90 **La Scala Milano** 1989
100 × 144 (39⅜ × 56¼)

89 Countdown 1989
100 × 100 (39⅜ × 39⅜)

87 The subject 1988–90
2 canvases, each 200 × 100 (78¼ × 39⅜)

91 Northend I 1990
100 × 109.5 (39⅜ × 43)

84 Mother and child 1984–5
150 × 150 (59½ × 59½)

92 Self-portrait 12.7.80 a 1990
75 × 75 (29½ × 29½)

94 Self-portrait 13.7.80 a 1990
75 × 75 (29½ × 29½)

93 Self-portrait 12.7.80 b 1990
75 × 75 (29½ × 29½)

95 Self-portrait 13.7.80 b 1990
75 × 75 (29½ × 29½)

96 Self-portrait 04.3.81 a 1990
$75 \times 75 \left(29\frac{1}{2} \times 29\frac{1}{2}\right)$

98 Self-portrait 04.3.81 c 1990
$75 \times 75 \left(29\frac{1}{2} \times 29\frac{1}{2}\right)$

97 Self-portrait 04.3.81 b 1990
$75 \times 75 \left(29\frac{1}{2} \times 29\frac{1}{2}\right)$

99 Self-portrait 05.3.81 a 1990
$75 \times 75 \left(29\frac{1}{2} \times 29\frac{1}{2}\right)$

100 Self-portrait 05.3.81 b 1990
75 × 75 (29½ × 29½)

102 Self-portrait 05.3.81 d 1990
75 × 75 (29½ × 29½)

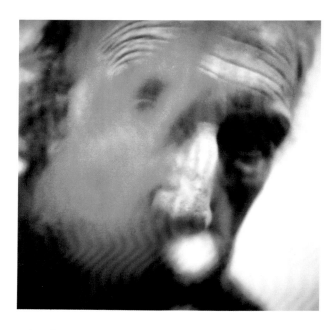

101 Self-portrait 05.3.81 c 1990
75 × 75 (29½ × 29½)

103 Self-portrait 05.3.81 e 1990
75 × 75 (29½ × 29½)

104 Northend II 1991
99.3 × 108.7 (39½ × 42¾)

105 Two gentlemen of Alba 1991
100 × 78 (39⅜ × 30¾)

106 War games 1991–2
200 × 200 ($78\frac{3}{4} \times 78\frac{3}{4}$)

CATALOGUE

Catalogue entries on individual works in the exhibition have been edited by Richard Morphet in close consultation with the artist, by whom they have been approved. The entries were drafted by Jacqueline Darby, using information from a number of sources including earlier catalogues and other publications. The drafts were supplemented by extensive new information from Richard Hamilton.

The entries on works between 1949 and 1969 draw extensively on those in the catalogue of the Tate Gallery's Hamilton retrospective of 1970. Much material in the 1970 catalogue entries has been omitted here for reasons of space, not least that which traces the development of a work in relation to its sketches, studies and related prints. Equally, the present entries on works of 1949–69 contain information not present in the 1970 catalogue.

The entries on the works in this catalogue should be read in conjunction with the chronology of Richard Hamilton's life and work on pp. 186–92. In the sequence of catalogue entries passages have been introduced at appropriate points to summarise Hamilton's activity in a number of areas (such as his thematic exhibitions and his concern with the work of Marcel Duchamp) which have an exceptionally close bearing on his work as a fine artist.

The catalogue entries quote frequently from Hamilton's published writings on his works and on the culture of our time. For the fullest compilation of these texts the reader is referred to Hamilton's *Collected Words* (Thames and Hudson, 1982). The fullest catalogue to date of Hamilton's prints is *Richard Hamilton Prints 1939–83* (Waddington Graphics, 1984). Both these publications are Edition Hansjörg Mayer. References to 'bib.' in the text are to entries in the Bibliography, pp. 193–201.

In the titles of the works, capitalisation follows Richard Hamilton's original designation. Measurements are given in centimetres followed by inches in brackets, height before width.

Student paintings

In 1938 Hamilton became a student at the Royal Academy Schools in London at the age of six-teen, a good deal younger than was usual. Three paintings survive from the period. They exem-plify his preoccupation at that time with the accurate rendering of tonal adjacencies in the motif as observed. The clarity of Hamilton's manner and the precision of the borders of each block of colour were unusual among students of his generation at the Royal Academy Schools. Hamilton was predisposed in this direction through awareness of the work of Wyndham Lewis and through having seen the drawing style of Merlyn Evans and Matvyn Wright at the Reimann Studios where they taught in the life class.

1
Figure study (Flossie)
1940
Oil on canvas
50.8 × 43.1 (20 × 17)
The artist

Students sometimes volunteered the task of modelling if professionals were not available. Flossie, a friend and fel-low student, was the subject in the life-room on this occasion. The sombre tonality of these student oils results from a method of working introduced to the RA Schools by Flos-sie herself. Paint is mixed with a palette knife and a sample of colour held on its tip is compared directly against an area of colour on the model; the process is repeated until a match is made. The technique inevi-tably produced darkly-hued paintings to the despair of Sir Walter Russell, then Keeper of the RA Schools, whose method of teaching was to smear, without comment, each student's canvas in turn with white paint.

2
Nude
1940
Oil on canvas
61 × 50.8 (24 × 20)
The artist

This painting, typical of the art school life-room, shows early signs of Hamil-ton's eclecticism. It is a flirtation with Cubism which follows the pattern of many life-drawings he made at the RA Schools at the same time – they explore different traditional Beaux Arts techniques and styles and also reveal a curiosity about current modernist modes. The painting has more in common with Jacques Vil-lon's approach to Cubism than Picas-so's, yet it is unlikely that Hamilton could have been aware of the work of the brother of Marcel Duchamp, an artist who was to become so import-ant an influence.

3
Portrait of James Tower
1940
Oil on canvas
55.8 × 40.7 (22 × 16)
The artist

James Tower (1919–88), a fellow painting student and later an out-standing artist potter, sat for this por-trait in Hamilton's home. The paint-ing indicates a willingness in the youthful artist to seek for alternative solutions to any problem. Instead of the angular divisions seen in the two previous pictures, there is here an attempt to define a contour around an area of tonal difference. These stepped boundaries of light and shade define form in much the way that contour lines on a map show hills and valleys.

   A larger early portrait, 'Inge' *c.*1941 (untraced) had similarities to the portrait of Tower. After leaving the RA Schools in 1940 Hamilton was substantially prevented from painting by war work.

Ulysses

fig.1 **The Transmogrifications of Bloom** 1984–5 Soft-ground and aquatint

fig.2 **In what posture?** 1986 Heliogravure in 1 colour and 2 blacks from 3 plates

Among the strongest influences on Hamilton's approach to image making was the novelist James Joyce. Hamilton began illustrating *Ulysses* in 1948, for his own pleasure, because he found Joyce's use of language 'demonstrated a stylistic and technical freedom that might be applied to painting'. He determined to modulate form, technique and style in each illustration, echoing the varied treatments of the eighteen chapters of the book, in order to create a visual equivalent to the changing fabric of Joyce's prose.

Complexity is compounded within a single episode known as 'Oxen of the Sun', which moves relentlessly from primitive utterance through to modern colloquial speech parodying, in chronological sequence, paragraph by paragraph, most of the great masters of English literature (figs.2,3,4 on p.50).

Hamilton's parodic prose style in his text 'Urbane Image' (bib. A19), written in 1963 – the verbal equivalent for his painting style of 1957–64 – follows Joyce in the use of a separate literary style for each paragraph. The concept of 'epiphany' (cf. no.27) derives from Joyce's first novel, *Portrait of the Artist as a Young Man*, and the ambition to explore the possibility of an epic narrative poetry expressed in purely visual terms can be traced to his last, *Finnegan's Wake*. The jokey titles of works between 1949 and 1955, in which words are broken into small units of sound and syllable (several separate meanings may be communicated in a single word or phrase), also owe a debt to *Finnegan's Wake*.

Joyce's interest in patterns of the 'quotidian' (contemporary daily life and experience), the complex relationship between image and idea, visual sign and meaning, form and message, kindled Hamilton's contribution to the genesis of Pop art.

Early works 1950–55

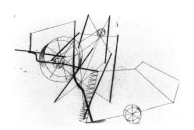

fig.3 **Reaper (a)** 1949 Etching

During his period of studentship at the Slade School of Art (1948–51) Hamilton made few paintings. His first year was spent drawing in the life-room, the second mainly in the etching studio, where he produced, among other prints, twenty engravings of a type of agricultural machine, the reaper (fig.3). These were exhibited under the title 'Variations on the theme of a reaper' at Gimpel Fils in 1950. The third year was spent researching and producing *Growth and Form* (see p.145).

In his first three abstract oils, paralleling similar etchings and also painted at the Slade, the description of form is schematic, so too is the use of colour. The spectator is taken from the essential contrivance of a pictorial system to its physicality as paint on a surface.

Hamilton's approach was always to assess the essential nature of the activity in hand and then to construct a painting from a predominantly intellectual premise. In 1950 he decided to rethink from scratch the process of representing the world through painting. To do this, he had first to consider the nature of image making itself. He therefore started with, as it were, a *tabula rasa*, into which blank arena he first introduced marks, then space, and only then forms of life, beginning with the most primitive. Not until 1954 did the human figure reappear in Hamilton's oils. The crowded Pop compositions which followed were a natural development of this progressive engagement with the surroundings in which Hamilton found himself.

4
Induction

1950
Oil on canvas
$51 \times 40.5 (20\frac{1}{8} \times 16)$
The artist

Three paintings (of which this is the most abstract), a drawing and two prints were first titled 'Microcosmos', to suggest a visual analogy between works of this type and Bartok's piano exercises, simple enough to be played by anyone.

Hamilton's preoccupation at this time is with the use of minimal elements to articulate the picture surface (see also nos.5, 6). His aim was that such articulation should result from relationships naturally developed as one mark leads to another. He deliberately eliminated style, to emphasise that the life of the picture lies within itself as an autonomous, self-explanatory organism and container of ideas.

A white surface is given structure by the use of only the most primitive and fundamental indications, beginning with the simplest, a point, its location determined by what already exists (in this case the size and shape of the canvas). Hamilton concluded that even the simplest mark on a ground tends to suggest space: its relative shape, size, colour, tone, position and direction will all be subconsciously interpreted by the human mind as having three-dimensional implications. Hamilton has indeed stated that 'perspective is the dominant clue in our interpretation of any image'. (bib. D33). In 'Induction', as in 'Chromatic spiral' (no.6), a rudimentary horizon line inevitably implies extension in depth.

The emphasis, here, is on investigating and constructing form rather than on representation. Hamilton was concerned that there be a reason for making each mark in order to form some kind of systematic relationship over the picture surface.

5
Microcosmos: tangential ovoid

1950
Oil on canvas
$38.2 \times 51 (15 \times 20\frac{1}{8})$
Private Collection, England

A simple negative form is generated by a ring of tangential lines.

6
Chromatic spiral

1950
Oil on panel
$53.5 \times 47 (21 \times 18\frac{1}{2})$
Private Collection

Describes a process of systematic increase: around a single point nine further points form a spiral. Each point is part of a group of crisscrossed straight lines which increase in number from group to group, from one to nine. As each line moves across the surface it has an organic life of its own. The line extending upwards from the first point leads the eye to the second point and in each subsequent group one line points to the group that follows. The lines are in the seven colours of the spectrum, plus black and white; one colour is added in each group. Black starts the sequence, white ends it.

Hamilton had become interested in Klee's *Pedagogical Sketchbook* (which from 1952 he would use as a primer in teaching). This painting was influenced by Klee, as were the sculptures of William Turnbull, which interested Hamilton and which simi-

larly involved constructing a work from the simplest elements of point and line. Fundamental to 'Chromatic spiral' was D'Arcy Wentworth Thompson's discussion of the processes of growth in nature (see pp.29,145). The painting symbolises Thompson's appreciation that organic physical structures develop as a result of mathematically definable processes and that they often take a spiral form.

Growth and Form

fig.4 Installation view of *Growth and Form* 1951, Institute of Contemporary Arts, London

Between 1951 and 1958 Hamilton created all or part of five major environmental exhibitions, each described below, which parallel the investigation of the subject matter pursued in his paintings. *Growth and Form*, organised and designed by Hamilton, was a contribution by the ICA to the Festival of Britain in 1951 (fig.4). The exhibition was inspired by D'Arcy Wentworth Thompson's book *On Growth and Form* (first edition 1917). Its theme was the way in which biological function in nature produces its multiplicity of forms. The exhibition was opened by Le Corbusier, whose contributions to international exhibitions Hamilton had admired, particularly in his concern with making a synthesis from disparate sources and with creating a specifically modern environment.

Like much of Hamilton's work since, *Growth and Form* was an investigation into what the world is composed of, the processes which structure it, and the means by which we perceive and understand it. In *Growth and Form* he juxtaposed actual scientific specimens with diagrams and, more importantly, with photographs taken by a wide variety of means. Images were transmitted by cinematic projection onto horizontal surfaces above and below the spectator's eye level, by split-second illumination by high-intensity strobe flashes, and by infinite multiplication by means of mirrors.

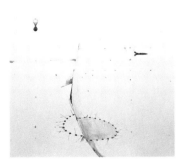

fig.5 **Refraction** 1952 Oil on panel *Mary Banham, London*

fig.6 Terry Hamilton with **Super-Ex-Position** 1953–4 Oil on hardboard *Destroyed*

7
Particular System

1951
Oil on canvas
101.5 × 127 (40 × 50)
The artist

Biological function produces forms many of which are invisible to the naked eye. It is photographic technology which reveals these structures, unseen either through vast distance, microscopic proximity or obstructions overcome only by x-rays or infra-red. 'Particular System' is directly inspired by images from D'Arcy Wentworth Thompson's book on morphology, *On Growth and Form*, witness the sea urchin, lower right, and the micro organism, top right. It also owes a debt to Kathleen Lonsdale's x-ray diffraction patterns, which are produced on a photographic plate by the scattering of electrons beamed at a fragment of crystal (see fig.4, left of photograph).

In this 'particular system', the encircled black spot (a diagrammatic symbol used often in these paintings to mark vanishing points) denotes 'centre of vision'. Its central place as well as its form make it a powerful visual target but its alignment with the eye and its size introduce an ambiguity – is it on the horizon or closer? Perhaps it is as close as the nearest part of the painting, the flat area of colour in the foreground, to which there is a strong link. The painting's punning title refers to the particularity of this central spot, as well as to the image being composed of particles. It is as though the world were being created by deflection from the visual point of focus.

Spatial location is here indicated by simple perceptual clues, such as colour and distribution of non-figurative marks – green and yellow denote proximity (and ground), blue, distance (and sky). The tall, transparent foreground object standing on its own rectangular base has no particular source, though displayed in conjunction with biological organisms it reflects the preoccupation with museums and exhibitions then current in Hamilton's circle. A similar transparent vessel appears in his painting 'Refraction', 1952 (fig.5), in which he examined the distortion produced when something is seen through water.

In 1978 Hamilton wrote of his charted perspective studies 'These empty notations invited habitation and my reaction was to populate the diagrammatic space with token life forms abstracted from primitive orga-

nisms.' (bib. D33) Another painting, 'Super-Ex-Position' (fig.6), concerned with movement in space, for which some studies exist, was completed in 1954. It was destroyed a few years later – storage was becoming a problem.

8
d'Orientation

1952
Oil on hardboard
117 × 160 (46 × 63)
The artist

'd'Orientation' is the most extreme example of Hamilton's preoccupation with systematic representations of space. The rigidity of the Renaissance concept of fixed, idealised viewpoints is confronted by modern ideas of time and flux.

Here, three perspective viewpoints are prescribed with their corresponding vanishing points (one of which is common to all), to postulate an observer moving to three different locations in a notional space. A dual or multiple role is allowed for any mark occurring within more than one of the 90 degree angle viewpoints created. The marks also conform strictly to a two-dimensional grid of squares and golden sections, thus introducing the ambiguity of the possibility that the rectangular grid is a fourth viewpoint looking at the scene from above; a reasonable hypothesis since the three locations, denoting the positions of the viewer, appear as on a map.

Between these perspective systems and the spectator Hamilton interposes an object – part of a jellyfish – which is both natural (organic, in contrast with the artificial device of perspective) and outside the established perspective systems. It is anomalous because it cannot be integrated into any of the possible schema, especially the fourth, since the hanging, suspended, character of the natural form contradicts a vertical view.

9
Trainsition III

1954
Oil on canvas
76 × 56 (30 × 22)
Private Collection

Four pictures titled 'Trainsition', of which 'I' was a preliminary version of 'IIII' and 'II' a trial run for 'III', carry the exploration of schematic treatments of simultaneous movement of spectator and subject into a new area of representation. The study of motion perspective seen in such paintings as 'd'Orientation' emerged from purely conceptual notions into the world of direct visual experience. The paintings were made at the time of Hamilton's frequent travelling by rail between London and Newcastle-upon-Tyne, where he was teaching. The title is a pun on 'Train sit I on', as the typographic of the numbering is a pun on the structure of railway lines, which rest on sleepers. In 'Trainsition III' the observer gazes in the direction of travel.

10
Trainsition IIII

1954
Oil on panel
91.5 × 122 (36 × 48)
Tate Gallery. Purchased 1970

'Trainsition IIII' adopts the viewpoint of an observer looking out of the train at 90 degrees to the direction of travel. The painting investigates the experience of focusing on a middle distance object (a tree) from the right-hand window of a moving vehicle (a train). Everything between train and tree appears to move from left to right (the opposite direction to the movement of the train), while everything behind the tree appears to move from right to left. Diagrammatic arrows (which recall Klee) register this movement. Two other figurative elements in motion are a telegraph pole (seen three times in the instant when it intersects the point of attention) and a car (moving at the same speed in the opposite direction to the train and thus displaced at an interval double that if it had been static).

Hamilton was interested in how, in a mobile situation, the only fixed point is the one on which the observer focuses at any moment. If the focus is changed to another position, closer or further away, the direction of movement of objects and surfaces in front of and behind the point of focus relates to that new visual pivot.

These studies of relative motion are contemporaneous with Hamilton's investigation into Marcel Duchamp's analysis and representation of movement and there are echoes of Duchamp's own 'Sad Young Man in a Train', in which movement is conceived as a metaphor for the fluctuations and transitions of mood and ambience.

The paintings show a growing involvement with subjects peculiar to the accelerating, ever more technically sophisticated pace of life of the 1950s. As Lawrence Alloway pointed out at the time, they are concerned, among other things, with a classic situation of the Hollywood movie of the day – the speeding car seen from a moving train. Hamilton's painting 'Carapace', 1954 (Private Collection)

represents the view looking out through the windscreen of a moving car. At the approach to a crossroad, the word 'Slow' is seen in perspective.

'Trainsition IIII' bears a striking, if fortuitous, resemblance to Francis Bacon's painting 'Landscape', 1952 (repr. in col. Ronald Alley, *Francis Bacon*, 1964, No. 40) and is the first indication of Hamilton's path running parallel with an artist he admires greatly. He sees Bacon's work as having a relation of opposites to his own: anguished rather than cool; black as against white magic; painterly rather than delineated; mysterious instead of lucid. Hamilton's pastiche 'Portrait of the artist by Francis Bacon', 1970 is a friendly homage.

11
re Nude

1954
Oil on panel
122 × 91.5 (48 × 36)
Moderna Museet, Stockholm

The painting is a reflection on the rules of depiction which govern the traditional nude genre (hence the pun on the word 'renewed') and examines the process of movement from and towards the object, comparable to the tracking movement of a movie camera or the motion of a train (see no.10). The title also marks a return to the subject of the female nude after a break of fourteen years.

Here the subject is 'still'. An art school nude model (with a blank white panel destined to become the painting standing behind her) is approached in three stages. Because the unpaid model posed in her limited spare time Hamilton worked on a watercolour study (fig.8) to provide information to be transferred onto the painting in the model's absence. The process has something in common with André Gide's stratagem of writing a diary while writing a novel about an author keeping a diary.

fig.7 **Crossroad** 1954 Pencil and watercolour on paper *The artist*

fig.8 **Study for 'Re nude'** 1954 Watercolour and pencil *British Museum*

When the second session with the model commenced the subject had changed. The notations of the watercolour had been worked into the oil painting, only to find themselves ready to be recycled back into the watercolour during the next period with the model. The painting itself had become part of the image and the subject evolved into a process of continuous feedback. The sessions with the model, moving between three marked positions, are multiplied again by three in the painting, which thus produces a nine times replication of the model as seen in the painting as subject.

Hamilton's interest in the representation of movement was stimulated by the precedents of Futurism and Duchamp, but also by the photography of Marey and Muybridge, who had represented successive stages of movement respectively on a single plate and by breaking it down into multiple images. The influence of Duchamp is strong in 're Nude', but in a negative sense. In Duchamp's 'Nude Descending a Staircase' his nude treads lightly down, watched by the artist locked in contemplation. Hamilton's nude is led back to the life-room and firmly seated on a stool; she sits immobile while scrutinised by the artist from several viewpoints. As distance closes on the subject there is a change of scale, with the increase appearing as an expansion about the central vanishing point (the top of the model's left arm), the only unchanging feature of the painting (see also no.7). 're Nude', like Duchamp's descending nude, represents not only movement through space but also the passage of time.

While all the paint marks in 're Nude' identify the exact location of things seen, they are at the same time tokens for those things' presence. They are necessarily selective in order to avoid the incoherence of image that would result if all facial parts were repeated three times and then three by three. Hamilton omitted most of them, allowing one in particular, a single pair of lips, to stand for the facial features as a whole. After 1954 Hamilton's next seven works would each draw attention to the female body and six of them would highlight specific parts of body or head, three of these again being the lips.

12

Still-life?

1954
Oil on canvas
$61 \times 51 (24 \times 20\frac{1}{8})$
Private Collection

Using the motif of a group of artist's oil and turpentine bottles in his studio, Hamilton here experimented with Cubist-derived overlapping views created by the motions of the observer; hence the question mark in the title. Because the bottles are below eye level on a table there is an apparent progressive tilting of the surface on which they are standing, as the eye moves in three stages towards the subject. Image is superimposed on image so that the linear drawing comes close to the idea of multiple exposures on a single photographic plate, which then produces the serial image.

Not only the subject but also the sober hues of this painting (as of 're Nude', no.11) recall Cubism. Although the world of mass media imagery into which Hamilton would shortly move was reflected by most Pop artists in ways that emphasised its brashness, most of Hamilton's Pop paintings would continue the preference his earlier work had shown for restraint, tonal subtlety and careful compositional construction. His move from pure paint on canvas to the attachment of found materials, starting in 1956, paralleled Cubism's movement from its 'analytical' to its 'synthetic' phases.

While Hamilton was spending time in his studio comparing and contrasting Futurist and Cubist approaches to the problem of representing a mobile object, and the different graphic means adopted to communicate the complexities of an eye moving relative to a subject, he was engaged in a companion project. This was a didactic exhibition on the theme of man's achievements in aiding and controlling his own movement through space.

Man, Machine & Motion

fig.9 Installation view of *Man, Machine & Motion* 1955, Hatton Gallery, Newcastle-upon-Tyne

Designed and organised by Hamilton over a two-year period, *Man, Machine & Motion* was shown in the summer of 1955 at the Hatton Gallery, Newcastle-upon-Tyne and at the ICA in London (fig.9). It was a pictorial review, in over two hundred photographs and photographs of original drawings, of machines which extend the power of the human body and increase man's capacity for autonomous movement. It was assembled in four distinct groups: Aquatic (underwater devices), Terrestrial (surface locomotion), Aerial (aircraft) and Interplanetary (space travel), the images from each group being disposed accordingly below, at or above the spectator's eye level.

Emphasis was predominantly on the seventy years preceding 1955, since photography is more or less coeval with mechanised transport and belongs to the same technological environment. The material was selected so that 'each image should show a machine and a recognizable man' (Reyner Banham, 'Man, Machine & Motion', *Architectural Review* 1955, pp.51–3).

Large photographs were fixed at various levels in a slender, modular framework, thereby producing semi-architectural spaces which were as important to the effect as infill. The arrangement permitted the spectator to see photographs of different subjects and periods in an infinite number of permutations. *Man, Machine & Motion* recalls Duchamp and Picabia in their ironical interpretations of the machine becoming one with human beings, a theme Hamilton was to develop in the coming years.

In writing about the exhibition Hamilton noted that man 'has realised an aspiration which lies deeper than thought, the longing for a power with no natural limits; he finds himself in real life the super-human inhabitant of his dearest fantasy' (bib. D4, preface).

Paralleling the development of Hamilton's painting from 1950 to 1954 *Man, Machine & Motion* represented a more advanced stage of evolution than that dealt with in *Growth and Form*. A theme common to both exhibitions, as to Hamilton's paintings, was the way in which form is determined by function. Precisely this theme also underlies the yet more sophisticated world of mass media imagery which Hamilton would now explore in art. It should further be noted that the theme of bodily appurtenances which was so prominent in *Man, Machine & Motion* would be addressed repeatedly by Hamilton in the years ahead, for example in works as diverse as the 'Cosmetic studies' (nos.57–68) and 'The citizen' (no.82) and 'The subject' (no.87).

This is Tomorrow

Held at the Whitechapel Art Gallery, London, in 1956, *This is Tomorrow* (fig.10) investigated the possibility of collaboration between groups of artists and the integration of different arts. Each of twelve groups, consisting of a painter, a sculptor and an architect, worked to produce an environment. Hamilton worked with the sculptor John McHale and the architect John Voelcker.

fig.10 Installation view of *This is Tomorrow* 1956, Whitechapel Art Gallery, London

This exhibition attempted to summarise the various influences that were beginning to shape post-war Britain. Hamilton's group included a profusion of carefully chosen images from advertising, popular magazines, comics, film, and even fine art, Voelcker's structure of a fun house (for which Hamilton constructed a cut-and-fold diagram reproduced in the catalogue) and John McHale's six-foot high collaged close-up of food. Twenty-two years later Hamilton would again use a colour reproduction of Van Gogh's 'Sunflowers' in an installation, though in the very different setting of the National Gallery.

A feature of Hamilton's section was the involvement of all the senses, including smell and touch. Hearing was engaged by pop music and the loudness of this in combination with the intense colours, the pictorial immediacy and often the scale of the imagery from mass popular culture was controversial and considered by some to be provocative; parallels were drawn with Dada manifestations. The tone of presentation was in marked contrast to that of the other contribution most remarked, both then and now, that of Henderson, Paolozzi and the Smithsons, which was concerned with basic human habitation and dominated by an archaeological ethos. Hamilton viewed the component elements of his 'fun house' as raw material from which new kinds of art might be made. Popular images were disposed in a reverse perspective, moving from a screen of small-scale images merging different modes of visual communication to a robot sixteen feet high.

The tactic of the 'fun house' was to juxtapose popular imagery with a demonstration of the ambiguities of perception. 'Just what is it ...?' (no.13) faced a negative–positive image in black and white on the opposite page of a double spread of the catalogue, in prophetic anticipation of two of the chief preoccupations of art in the 1960s – Pop and Op. Hamilton's catalogue statement reads 'We reject the notion that "tomorrow" can be expressed through the presentation of rigid formal concepts. Tomorrow can only extend the range of the present body of visual experience. What is needed is not a definition of meaningful imagery but the development of our perceptive potentialities to accept and utilize the continual enrichment of visual material.'

13

Just what is it that makes today's homes so different, so appealing?

1956
Collage
$26 \times 25 \ (10\frac{1}{4} \times 9\frac{3}{4})$
Kunsthalle Tübingen, Zundel Collection

The collage was conceived as both catalogue illustration and poster for the exhibition *This is Tomorrow*. Hamilton found the title, a caption to some long-forgotten magazine illustration, among cast-off trimmings while working on his collage. With the caption pasted beside it his picture answered perfectly the question posed.

Thirty-five years later, the scene Hamilton created here 'seems to define the dreams and aspirations of an entire era' (Andrew Graham-Dixon, 'Popping On', *The Independent Magazine*, 15 June 1991, p.59), with its packaged cultural commodities. In this consumer paradise excerpts, quotations and whole passages are 'lifted' from photographic sources and advertising, popular culture and mass-media art, in the spirit of what Hamilton was to call 'self-confessed plagiarism'.

Before scavenging his material Hamilton typed a list of categories as a programme for the collage: 'Man, Woman, Food, History, Newspapers, Cinema, Domestic Appliances, Cars, Space, Comics, TV, Telephone, Information'. It is an inventory which gives not a hint of the rich play of witticisms and dual roles found in this compendium of different ways of communicating information, ranging from words, printing, painting, symbols, photography, film, television and diagram to recorded sound (cf. the tape recorder in the foreground).

Hamilton made this collage at the London home of fellow Independent Group member, the artist Magda Cordell. She and Terry Hamilton searched through piles of magazines, many brought back by John McHale from the United States, extracting illustrations of objects which exemplified Hamilton's categories of subject specified in the previous paragraph. His choice of any particular image to use within each category was determined by its ability to relate convincingly to the perspective space he was building up.

The small picture initiated Hamilton's fascination with the theme he developed in the sixties: the ambiguity of interior/exterior space. In 1990 he wrote of the collage: 'Though clearly an "interior" there are complications that cause us to doubt the categorization. The ceiling of the room is a space-age view of Earth. The carpet is a distant view of people on a beach [cf. no.34, for a review of the same theme]. It is an allegory rather than a representation of a room. My "home" would have been incomplete without its token life-force so Adam and Eve struck a pose along with the rest of the gadgetry.' (bib. D46, p.44).

The 'POP' on the lollipop is possibly the first use anywhere in a corresponding work of art of the word that would come to designate a major new tendency in art. The comic strip image (here framed and hung on a wall) anticipates by some years a theme of Lichtenstein's. 'Just what is it . . .' has been described as 'perhaps the closest that the British side of the [Pop] movement came to producing a work comparable in importance to Picasso's "Demoiselles d'Avignon" in relation to Cubism' (Marco Livingstone, 'In glorious techniculture', in *Pop Art*, exh. cat., Royal Academy of Arts, 1991, pp.12–19).

Works of the Pop art period 1956–62

The subject matter of Hamilton's paintings after 1956 (the cinema, domestic appliances, car styling and clothes) had been explicit topics of discussion for Independent Group members at the ICA, London, in the preceding years. Originally the term 'Pop art' was not a designation of an art movement but a label they applied to an important part of contemporary culture: those entertainment products made by skilled professionals for a mass market.

Duchamp's antipathy towards the sensuous hedonism of Abstract Expressionism sanctioned Hamilton's quest for an art which evenly balanced image and idea, icon and meaning, symbol and concept. By the mid-fifties he had come to feel that pop culture, mass media and the language of advertising offered a web of messages about contemporary patterns of life and feeling out of which he could tease more intellectual kinds of statement, rich in allusion and commentary.

In 1957 Hamilton defined Pop art (in the Independent Group's sense of the term) as: 'Popular (designed for a mass audience), Transient (short-term solution), Expendable (easily forgotten), Low cost, Mass produced, Young (aimed at youth), Witty, Sexy, Gimmicky, Glamorous and Big business'. Ten of these eleven criteria are essential to his paintings from this date on; the issue of expendability is still open to speculation. In his subsequent works Hamilton sought to revive fine art by openly deploying its essential elements in terms relevant to the time. As he was to declare in an article suggestively entitled 'For the Finest Art Try – POP' in 1961: 'If the artist is not to lose much of his ancient purpose he may have to plunder the popular arts to recover the imagery which is his rightful inheritance' (bib. A15). He goes on to say that 'the artist in twentieth century urban life is inevitably a consumer of mass culture and potentially a contributor to it'.

The Pop works which Hamilton would now begin to create were concerned not simply with popular imagery but also with the means by which that imagery was created. Essentially the subject of these paintings is the world of advertising and the mass media. Hamilton explained in 1968: 'One wasn't just concerned with the car and the idea of speed but [with] the way it was presented to us in the mass media . . . presenting a glamorous object by all the devices that glamorous advertising can add' (bib. C8). The Pop paintings are anthologies of the mechanics of visualisation.

Each of Hamilton's Pop works was the result of his carrying through a predetermined programme. First, solving the specific problem addressed in the individual work. Secondly, ensuring that his works as a whole should constitute a solution to the wider problem of how to realise in fine art the fresh insights offered by mass popular culture. From the perspective of the 1990s it is difficult to appreciate just how original were both this endeavour and the forms given by Hamilton to its realisation in his Pop paintings.

A typographic version of Duchamp's Green Box (1957–60)

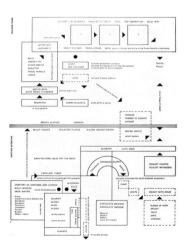

fig. 11 Diagram from Richard Hamilton's typographic version of Duchamp's *Green Box*

Marcel Duchamp's *Green Box*, 'a literary masterpiece having a unique form', supplements his large painting on glass titled 'The Bride Stripped Bare by Her Bachelors, Even', yet it was little known in the 1950s. The neglect of this great text by the art world was probably due to the rarity of the original edition and because so little had been done to assist a clear understanding of what the notes say. Even in French there was no typeset version until 1959.

The *Green Box* was published in 1934 in an edition limited to 300 copies. In what serves as an imprint on the inner spine are the words '*cette boite doit contenir 93 documents (photos, dessins et notes manuscrites des années 1911–15) ainsi qu'une planche en couleurs.*' Each handwritten note is reproduced in exact facsimile, including torn edges, blots, erasures and occasional illegibility. To date there had been four published translations into English of fragments of the documents. Hamilton's aim was that 'the complete typographical translation with its accompanying diagrams, should have very much the appearance of a primer to the Glass' (bib. A6).

Hamilton writes in the appendix to his typographic version that 'Duchamp's intention was that the Large Glass should embody the realization of a written text which had assisted the generation of his plastic ideas, and which also carried layers of meaning beyond the scope of pictorial expression. The text exists beside the Glass as a commentary and within it as a literary component of its structure. Without the notes the painting loses some of its significance and without the monumental presence of the Glass the notes have an air of random irrelevance . . . What the facsimiles present, above all else, is the evidence of a prolonged meditation on art – a conscious probing of the limits of aesthetic creation'. It was almost impossible to project the sporadic nature of much of the writing , so a mixture of type was used to show the changes of hand or change in the writing medium. As Hamilton explained, 'all oddities of phrasing, punctuation, layout and typesetting are considered attempts to render as closely as possible the form of the original documents'. The typographic version he had designed was published in 1960.

14
Hommage à Chrysler Corp.

1957
Oil, metal foil and collage on panel
122 × 81 (48 × 32)
Private Collection

Together with 'Hers is a lush situation' (no.15) this is the first Pop work to synthesise imagery and thematic motifs in a manner inspired by Duchamp's *Green Box*. Correspondences of shape, colour, function and idea between separate elements with different origins are accentuated, with a view to each painting's imagery reading as a continuous system.

The subject matter springs from a topic originally aired by Reyner Banham in the Independent Group discussions of the early 1950s on the 'rhetoric of persuasion' written into car design, advertising, and marketing. The sources of imagery were the texts and photographs collated for the *Man, Machine & Motion* exhibition and the specific passages which deal with the 'Bride apparatus' in Duchamp's *Green Box* notes and preparatory sketches for the 'Large Glass'. Hamilton was fascinated by the similar metaphor at the heart of both sources – a comparison of the automobile's mechanical functions and components with the physiological processes and erotic drives of the female body. Hamilton recalled recently of 1957: 'There are a few Futurist paintings of cars, but ... you have no idea how ... hard it was to find a car in art at that time ... the thing which has probably changed the world more than any other, and it was virtually absent from painting!' (quoted in Andrew Graham-Dixon, 'That Was Then', *The Independent*, 13 August 1991).

The 'Hommage à' of the title was chosen for its high-art associations with the Parisian Cubist milieu of fifty years before and 'Chrysler Corp.' is a *double-entendre* for both a corporated industrial organisation and the body (corps) of a car or woman. The female body can be identified with a car chassis just as her breasts can be the car headlamps. The association of automobile and lover is a cliché of product promotion technique. As Hamilton said 'My sex symbol is, as so often happens in the ads, engaged in a display of affection for the vehicle.' (bib. D5) The 'dream boat' joins the 'dream car'. 'Hommage' is the first of five Pop paintings (nos.14–17, 19) to explore the allusive play of idea and image between girls and machines.

It is also the first of Hamilton's works in which paint and photographic print are integrated and it uses a composite of themes derived from automobile advertising. Pieces are taken from Chrysler's Plymouth and Imperial ads, and others from General Motors and Pontiac material. The sex symbol, constructed from the Exquisite Form bra diagram and the lips of Voluptua, star of an American late night television show, stands behind the car, which she caresses. She evokes, in Hamilton's words 'a faint echo of the "Winged Victory of Samothrace"' (bib. D5).

The setting is a showroom in the International Style as represented by Mondrian and Saarinen; the hovering lips and floorboards parallel to the picture plane are quotations from 're Nude' (no.11); the horizontal black bar (shorthand for modern architecture) is so placed that it recalls the catalogue and exhibition of *Man, Machine & Motion*; the dotted line, lower right, signifies movement; and the spiral configuration of the Exquisite Form bra brings to mind organisms from *Growth and Form*.

an Exhibit

fig.12 Installation view of *an Exhibit* 1957, Hatton Gallery, Newcastle-upon-Tyne

Victor Pasmore, Lawrence Alloway and Hamilton conceived *an Exhibit* as 'a game/an artwork/ an environment' The exhibition was first shown at the Hatton Gallery, Newcastle-upon-Tyne in 1957 and later that year at the ICA, London (fig.12). It was an abstract, non-thematic exhibition, consisting of a kit of standard-sized sheets and suspension devices which enabled the artists to place panels anywhere within a notional 16 inch rectangular grid. Nylon threads held thin acrylic panels (each 4 foot × 2 foot 8 inches) in varying degrees of transparency, at varying heights. A standard size of module and panel permitted freedom of choice in determining the position of the panels.

The installation was empirical; no plans were preconceived and the position of each panel was determined solely as a result of consideration of the space and the location of earlier placement of panels. Each installation would result in a completely different improvisation to create a constructivist work of art on an environmental scale.

Hamilton's role was to design and organise the components. Victor Pasmore, who had for eight years been producing increasingly geometrical abstractions in two and three dimensions, disposed the panels by joint decision with Hamilton. Pasmore then placed cut paper shapes on them wherever he chose. Alloway contributed to discussions on the theoretical concept and wrote the catalogue text.

Two years later a revised version, *Exhibit 2*, was shown only at the Hatton Gallery (fig.13). Because of the difficult, labour-intensive installation demands of *an Exhibit* a marriage was made between the modular framework of *Man, Machine & Motion* and the acrylic panels of *an Exhibit* to create a self-supporting structure which allowed something of the flexibility and improvisatory nature of the earlier show.

an Exhibit, reminiscent of the architectonic conceptions of De Stijl, blurred the boundaries between the formulative framework and the exhibited object and, at the same time, invited the viewer to an exhibition experience of a quite novel kind.

fig.13 Installation view of *Exhibit 2* 1959, Hatton Gallery, Newcastle-upon-Tyne

A Gallery for a Collector

Hamilton was among a group of designers invited to contribute proposals (it could be anything from kitchen to bedroom to music room) for an interior to be shown in the Daily Mail Ideal Home Exhibition, 1958. His proposal for a living room cum exhibiting space was among the schemes adopted (fig.14).

fig.14 Terry Hamilton in *A Gallery for a Collector* Ideal Home Exhibition, 1958

An extremely simple, elegant room with all its storage and appliance requirements placed in a single, slender, centrally placed unit was maximally functional as a gallery for the type of large-scale art just emerging in Europe. Works decorating the space included a battered humanoid sculpture by Paolozzi, an Yves Klein, a Sam Francis and Hamilton's own 'Hommage à Chrysler Corp.' (no.14). A floor-to-ceiling picture-window enabled an avant-garde car, the Citroen DS parked outside, to be appreciated on equal terms with the works of art. Integration with popular culture was further represented by modernist chairs designed by Harley Earl, chief stylist of General Motors, which would not have been known to Hamilton had they not been published in the popular magazine *Look*.

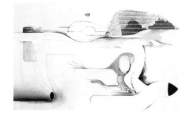

15
Hers is a lush situation
1958
Oil, cellulose, metal foil and collage on panel
81 × 122 (32 × 48)
Private Collection

In the American magazine *Industrial Design*, containing an annual review of automobile styling, the analysis of a 1957 Buick ended with: 'The driver sits at the dead calm center of all this motion; hers is a lush situation'. The painting aims to merge three interconnecting spaces – the girl in the car; the car among others in a flow of traffic; and a cityscape (New York in the vicinity of the United Nations building which, collaged, doubles as a windscreen).

The painting has many common references and similarities with 'Hommage' (no.14) yet the treatment here is more complex. There is a pronounced linear emphasis in which forms continually overlap or share a common outline, and shallow relief (sprayed and sanded to a high finish) is used to convey the pressed steel quality of automobile bodies. Sophia Loren's collaged lips, reasonably placed anatomically but isolated in space above the car, are among the few references to the 'her' of the title.

Hamilton's text 'Urbane Image' (bib. A19), an evocation of all his paintings from 'Hommage à Chrysler Corp.' to 'AAH!', included the following commentary on 'Hers is a lush situation': 'In slots between towering glass slabs writhes a sea of jostling metal, fabulously wrought like rocket and space probe, like lipstick sliding out of a lacquered brass sleeve, like waffle, like Jello. Passing UNO, NYC, NY, USA (point a), Sophia floats urbanely on waves of triple-dipped, infra-red-baked pressed steel. To her rear is left the stain of a prolonged breathy fart, the compounded exhaust of 300 brake horses.'

Although this is the first of many paintings by Hamilton which employ relief, projection from the pictorial surface goes back to the etchings of his Slade period – a hole cut in the plate produces a raised area in the print. This is an example of the kind of direct interaction that can take place between one fine art medium and another but Hamilton's adoption of relief was also an acceptance of the changed sense of surface brought about by new developments in the cinema. Where painting had traditionally represented a 'window' on a scene and had then, from the late nineteenth century, increasingly stressed the surface itself, he instinctively felt that it should now reflect the new world of space opened up by CinemaScope and 3-D projection, in which the image was thrust from the screen to meet its audience.

16
$he

1958–61
Oil, cellulose and collage on panel
122 × 81 (48 × 32)
Tate Gallery. Purchased 1970

'$he' was the outcome of an investigation into domestic appliances for Hamilton's Independent Group lecture 'Persuading Image' (bib. A7). A recollection of the phrase 'Women in the Home', announced with a leer by Groucho Marx, as though it were a title for the long monologue he was about to deliver straight to camera, directed his thoughts while working on '$he'.

The source of imagery is American advertising. '$he', the overt sex symbol, a creature of the media, is derived from an *Esquire* photograph of Vikki ('the back') Dougan. The ambiguous combination of front and back views shows the backless dress as an apron topped by an airbrush-smooth shoulder/breast. The Cadillac-pink fridge is inspired by high-shot photographs favoured in American car advertisements and the toaster/vacuum incorporates an overlapping of presentation styles and techniques. Dotted lines are once more diagrammatic of movement. The plastic eye, a late addition, winks as the spectator moves. Ten of Hamilton's sources of imagery for '$he' are reproduced in bib. A16.

In his 'An exposition of $he' (bib. A16), Hamilton commented that 'The worst thing that can happen to a girl, according to the ads, is that she should fail to be exquisitely at ease in her appliance setting . . . Sex is everywhere, symbolized in the glamour of mass-produced luxury – the interplay of fleshy plastic and smooth, fleshier metal . . . This relationship of woman

and appliance is a fundamental theme of our culture; as obsessive and archetypal as the western movie gun duel.'

Lawrence Alloway observed in 1961 (see bib.): '"$he" is characterized by the cool, clean, hygienic surface of kitchen equipment. It embodies the possibility of identification that the advertising of household appliances offers to women which, until now, her clothes alone had done.' He added that Hamilton had candidly exposed the sources of his imagery in American ads 'in the proud spirit in which Constable could point to Suffolk and say "these scenes made me a painter"'.

17
Pin-up

1961
Oil, cellulose and collage on panel
122 × 81 (48 × 32)
Lux Corporation, Osaka

'Pin-up' embodies the essence of Pop Art expression – fine art motifs with Pop ingredients in a diversity of stylistic language: stylised hair; stockings and shoes in advertising shorthand; three-dimensional moulded breasts in a pseudo-Constructivist style; the gestural brushwork of the Tachistes and naturalistic illusionism (cf. a photograph of an actual bra collaged onto the painting).

In the 1940s Hamilton was invited to join a group of students in an occasional practice studio established by *Vogue* magazine for potential fashion artists. Fashion drawings provided him with a readymade iconography of stance and gesture, posture and positioning. It was a source upon which he was to draw for 'Pin-up' as he freely used the 'sophisticated and often exquisite photographs in *Playboy* magazine, but also the most vulgar and unattractive to be found in such pulp equivalents as *Beauty Parade*' (bib. D5).

The fine-art odalisque has become a 'Pin-up'. This temptress recalls

Matisse and his flat paint surfaces, the restricted colour range of flesh tints Picasso, and there is a conscious analogy with works by Renoir and Pascin. Hamilton's flesh tones are those produced by photographers of girlie magazines with their particular colour printing requirements and limitations. The treatment of the motif recalls 're Nude' (no.11) and Duchamp's theme of the Bride stripped bare. The striptease image alludes simultaneously to the denuding of the consumerist myth and the 'stripping bare' of styles of pictorial representation.

All elements additional to the figure reflect *Playboy* magazine's obsession with significant accessories. A telephone (the Princess by Bell) and a record player named the Wundergram have a psychological role in implying the subject's availability. 'Pin-up' is an essay in accessibility: by technology, by divestment and by projection into the spectator's space.

Details of the imagery in 'Pin-up' include the merging of telephone and record player (comparable to that of toaster and vacuum cleaner in '$he', no.16), references in the breasts to sunbathing and to lactation (both indicated through the crisp line dividing two hues, the lower one white) and the adumbration of movement, both in the different breast positions and in the dotted line suggesting a kicking leg.

18
Glorious Techniculture

1961–4
Oil and collage on asbestos panel
122 × 122 (48 × 48)
Private Collection

Hamilton's first thought for a title was 'Anthology', since the work was conceived as a compilation of the principal myths of popular culture and the styles and techniques in which these were rendered. It became 'Glorious Techniculture', a punning reminder of a lecture titled, 'Glorious

Technicolor, Breathtaking Cinema-Scope and Stereophonic Sound' (a line from a song in a Hollywood musical of the period), which Hamilton delivered in 1959 with a battery of slide projectors, pop music, and an early demonstration of the Polaroid camera (bib. A5).

This is a reworking of a painting produced at the request of Theo Crosby for the Congress of the International Union of Architects, London, July 1961 (fig.15). The conference was held in a pavilion on the South Bank giving on to twin open-air patio areas isolated from the public by eight-foot high hoardings decorated externally with lettering by Edward Wright. In addition to sculptures, the patios included works of art by some of Crosby's artist friends which were attached to the internal side of the hoardings. Hamilton's picture was of a dream New York cityscape with a simulated giant wide-screen outdoor projection of Charlton Heston as Moses at the top of a skyscraper. The original 8 foot × 4 foot panel was found by Hamilton to be too large and heavy to house, so the cut-down bottom half was heavily modified to become the present work. It is the first of Hamilton's paintings not to be unified into a credible whole.

Hamilton draws on a wide range of visual material: the crisp black line, top centre, is derived from a diagrammatic cross-section of a General Motors Corvair engine. Inserted into the profile of a rifle, in a space suggesting the interior of a car, is a bride. Two figures (like tiny knights in armour) result from partial obliteration of a complete cross-section of a car engine with certain parts painted out; the little one bounces on something freely adapted from the Corning Glass prismatic lens for airfield illumination.

The guitar lying flat on the picture plane recalls Cubism and is derived from a *Life* magazine photograph of the pop musician Tony Conn, whose name was written in string on his guitar. Hamilton's paintings of this period often use three-dimensional objects and material glued in shallow relief to articulate the surface.

19
AAH!
1962
Oil on panel
81 × 122 (32 × 48)
Hessisches Landesmuseum, Darmstadt

Tony Conn's name (used in 'Glorious Techniculture', no.18) and the stylised lettering of the onomatopœic 'AAH!' (ballooned in comic strip style) introduce lettering into Hamilton's paintings for the first time since the word 'Slow' loomed large in perspective through a car windscreen as it approached a crossroad in a painting of 1954. (See also 'POP' in no.13.) It is a device which is to play a significant role subsequently.

'AAH!' is concerned with the phenomenon of depth of field. Things are either sharp or out of focus in varying degree; photographic idiom is translated into painterly codes. It is one of the earliest manifestations of Hamilton's continuing interest in photographic qualities and their representation in paint, for 'Much of the hedonism comes from the lush visual pleasure that only photographic lenses can provide' (bib. D5).

A car interior, showing the dashboard and gear switch, was a logical follow-up to the exteriors of cars dealt with in nos.14, 15 and 18. Yet in 'AAH!' the original theme of the car interior has become subordinate to the overall sensuality. The fleshy photographic quality and metaphoric overtones of engagement (advertising's concept of 'finger touch control' here becomes a visual pun on the creation of man as represented by Michelangelo in the Sistine Chapel) make the painting the erotic culmination of a dominant theme in Hamilton's works since 'Just what is it . . . ?'. The association of sexual gratification and wonder at the sight of consumer goods is one that advertisers relish. Ronson had been advised by their motivation research consultant to play up the sexual symbolism of the flame in their advertising. An exaggerated flame from the Varaflame cigarette lighter ads is seen to the right of the painting.

The secondary source is purely graphic in its language. It was appropriated from the paperback cover of van Vogt's novel *The Weapon Shops of Isher*. The 'Isher Weapon' is pictured in the mechanomorphic style favoured by science fiction illustrators and of which they are the masters.

fig.15 **Glorious Techniculture** (first state) in the IUA exhibition, 1961, with Shell Building under construction behind

A definitive statement on the coming trends in men's wear and accessories

The idea for this group of paintings came directly from a text – an annual feature on male fashion in *Playboy*. Hamilton added the word 'Towards' to the article's headline for his title because he found the 'definitive' a trifle presumptuous. He wrote: 'fashion depends on an occasion, season, time of day and, most importantly, the area of activity in which the wearer is involved. A definitive statement seemed hardly possible without some preliminary investigation into specific concepts of masculinity' (bib. D5).

The concepts he explored were (a) man in a technological environment; (b) sport; (c) timeless, classical aspects of male beauty; and all three areas were combined in (d). Each work contains an appliance thought of in a *Playboy* context as a typical adjunct of the male persona – (a) transistor radio, (b) telephone, (c) chest expander, (d) jukebox. They recapitulate the main stylistic vocabulary of the period. The first three paintings continue Hamilton's thesis of the interchangeability of ideas by contributing something to a larger, final working of the theme in (d), which Hamilton found to be no more definitive than the rest.

Frames for the three small paintings were specially made by Hamilton to extend the particular ambience of each.

20

Towards a definitive statement on the coming trends in men's wear and accessories (a) 'Together let us explore the stars'

1962
Oil and collage on panel
61 × 81 (24 × 32)
Tate Gallery. Purchased 1964

The first of the 'definitive statements' is derived from photographs, transmitted back to earth, of astronauts in the early orbits; top right are painted scan lines acknowledging the television source. The treatment harks back to the ancient myths of Icarus and Mercury. The accessories refer to several related contexts: a helmet from a Lucky Strike ad; a racing driver's stitched headguard; a five-pointed knob, as much a sheriff's star as the control device from which it was taken. Technology is represented by a transistor-radio printed circuit and a fruit machine dial. Top left is derived from the reflex systems of the Canon cine camera. The painting was completed on the day that one of the great Soviet space orbits was announced (15 August 1962). 'CCCP' was introduced into the camera sight-line in recognition of the event.

The astronaut's face is that of US President John F. Kennedy and the sub-title 'Together let us explore the stars' is a phrase from a famous Kennedy speech inviting all peoples to join together in the great tasks awaiting mankind.

21

Towards a definitive statement on the coming trends in men's wear and accessories (b)

1962
Oil and collage on panel
61 × 81 (24 × 32)
Anthony d'Offay Gallery

Hamilton mixes references to racing motoring (windscreen, aluminium rivets, upright numeral), American football (helmet, slanting numerals) and gambling (the face of a man in the New York Stock Exchange looking through binoculars at the latest share prices) for the sporting look. The surface is modulated by relief (helmet, rivets) and illusion (contrasting orientation of numerals). The spattering of the windscreen was achieved by throwing a pad of paint-soaked cotton wool at the panel.

When reprinted in *Collected Words*, 'Urbane Image' was accompanied by small reproductions of sixteen source images for Pop works and of the cover Hamilton made for *Living Arts* 2, 1963 (fig.16). This wrap-around cover (photographed by Robert Freeman) was a 'self-portrait' in which he appears as a baseball player surrounded by some favourite objects which had either influenced or appeared in his Pop paintings.

22

Towards a definitive statement on the coming trends in men's wear and accessories (c) Adonis in Y-fronts

1962
Oil and collage on panel
61 × 81 (24 × 32)
Private Collection, courtesy of Raymond Danowski

The theme is 'timeless aspects of male beauty', yet of the series it is perhaps the most concerned with contemporary interpretations of the theme; indeed, the painting's sub-title, 'Adonis in Y-fronts', is an adaptation of the title of a current pop song, 'Venus in Blue Jeans'.

Man is shown as a figure in a bare Hellenic landscape. Three separate contours, each taken from a different profile of the 'Hermes' of Praxiteles as found in a group of photographs in *Life* magazine, uncertainly define the left of his torso, as if pentimenti. These serial profiles simulate movement, in this case, expansion and contraction, a suggestion sustained by a chest-expanding appliance enlarged from an advertisement in a muscleman magazine (fig.8 on p.43).

Pictorial and diagrammatic functions are doubled – in the implications of movement and in the brand of underpants, which, as stressed in their advertising, are functional for comfort (indicated by the recurrent Hamilton motif of dotted and crossed lines). Twin rivets double as nipples and as parts of the appliance.

fig.16 Photograph used for the cover of *Living Arts* 2, 1963 (photograph by Robert Freeman)

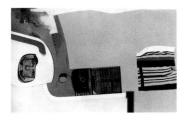

23
Towards a definitive statement on the coming trends in men's wear and accessories (d)

1963
Oil, collage and Perspex relief on panel
122 × 81 (48 × 32) or 81 × 122 (32 × 48)
Museum Ludwig, Cologne
[Not exhibited]

An amalgam of themes from the three smaller paintings. The American football headgear of no.21 evolves into a NASA spaceman's helmet. John Glenn, who made the first American orbital space flight on 20 February 1962, substitutes for John Kennedy (Glenn made a bid to become Democratic presidential candidate in the 1984 presidential election). The number '1' is repeated from (b) and the rivets, in another application, from (c). The striped trunks, like the striped T-shirt in (c), are copied directly from a men's fashion photograph in *Playboy*. The detail of a jukebox, extracted from a page in *Esquire*, shows a music machine in the Times Square subway, New York, the only jukebox known to Hamilton which plays a selection of classical music.

The painting may be hung in any orientation, attesting the lack of gravity in outer space. One view, however, horizontal with the head on the right, is less favoured.

24
'AAH!' in perspective

1963 (second version, 1973)
Oil on board
26 × 17 (10¼ × 6¾)
The artist

Joe Tilson asked his friends to provide a small painting, of prescribed dimensions, for his contributive picture 'A–Z Box of Friends and Family' 1963 (repr. in col. *Pop Art*, exh. cat., Royal Academy, 1991, p. 187). This consisted of rows of vertical panels in which contributors were designated by either fore- or surname initial. Hamilton was allocated 'R' for Richard but he preferred the pun 'R' for 'AAH!'. The upright panel was the wrong way round for Hamilton's original version of 'AAH!' (no.19) so he took a sidelong, perspective view of his 1962 painting to force it to a new proportion. Because Hamilton was unable to borrow the original, he made a second version for his retrospective at the Guggenheim Museum, New York.

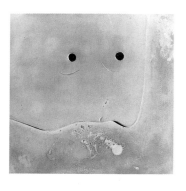

25
Study for 'Portrait of Hugh Gaitskell as a Famous Monster of Filmland'

1963–70
Copper on aluminium relief and collage on motorised disc
45.5 × 45.5 (18 × 18)
The artist

Though begun as a trial to test the effects of relief and of an overall copper priming which could gleam through later applications of oil paint, the base of metallic paint proved so unsatisfactory that the study was developed in a quite different direction from the painting.

Holes one-inch in diameter were drilled through the board to stand for eyes and there was found to be a change of mood when the relief was placed by chance on different backgrounds. This gave Hamilton the idea of attaching a motorised aluminium disc behind the relief so that fragments of coloured paper and printed matter (including a photograph of Harold Wilson, Gaitskell's successor as Leader of the Labour Party) produced a slowly changing sequence through the holes.

The original plywood relief was used to make a mould from which an aluminium casting could be taken. This was then electroplated with copper and treated to encourage a mottled green oxidisation.

26
Portrait of Hugh Gaitskell as a Famous Monster of Filmland

1964
Oil and collage on photograph on panel
61 × 61 (24 × 24)
Arts Council Collection. The South Bank Centre, London

Hamilton's paintings since 1956 had often been interpreted as 'satirical' in intention, though an equal body of opinion was disconcerted by what it considered to be a 'glorification' of the American way of life. Neither of these readings was seen to be appropriate by the artist. He has consistently argued that his purpose at that time was to demonstrate an amoral position in line with the non-Aristotelian philosophic tendencies of the 1950s. That is to say value judgements, the concepts of good and bad, might be seen as an irrelevance in the context of certain kinds of scientific and mathematical or indeed art thinking.

An awareness of the difficulty experienced by his audience in grasping the ironic contradictions which were the means adopted to express his null-A aspirations (the Independent Group's hip synonym for non-Aristotelian was adopted from van Vogt's novel *The World of Null-A*) brought Hamilton to a consideration of what form a truly satirical painting might take. Hugh Gaitskell (Leader of the Labour Party for seven years in opposition) seemed to him an ideal target for acerbic treatment. The left wing of the Labour Party was feeling bruised by Gaitskell's successful overthrow of a majority opinion within the party that the British government's determination to hold on to 'an independent nuclear deterrent' was absurd and dangerous jingoism. Hamilton, as an advocate of nuclear disarmament and a Labour supporter, was glad to find a vehicle for the bitterness felt by many in the Labour Party at what was seen as a betrayal. Hamilton's wife, Terry, a more ardent CND activist than he, and to whom the painting was a tribute, died in a car accident in 1962, a few months before Gaitskell's death. Hamilton overcame his doubts about continuing the project; 'there were good reasons for suppressing any squeamishness that Gaitskell's death might have occasioned.' (bib. A51, p.58)

In the 1950s, Hollywood and Hammer films had given renewed life to the monster myth, along with the publication of *Famous Monsters of Filmland*, a magazine devoted to film stills, publicity pictures and make-up shots. 'In the search for archetypes the monster emerges inevitably along with those other primal figures: the hero of the western, the pin-up girl, the spaceman.' (ibid)

Hamilton used a photographic enlargement of a newspaper picture of Gaitskell as the painting's ground. He then overlaid it with a mask inspired by a cover of *Famous Monsters of Filmland* showing Claude Rains in make-up for *The Phantom of the Opera* and placed it against a lurid red background. The head terminates abruptly across the forehead in reference to another film-still of a man-monster (*The Creature with the Atom Brain*), showing the effects of hamfisted brain surgery. Material was drawn from a number of other sources, among them a bloodshot eyeball from a film of *Jack the Ripper* and the determined look of the *The Creature from the Black Lagoon*. Seven of Hamilton's sources for the work are reproduced in *Collected Words*, p.59.

27
Epiphany
1964
Cellulose on panel
122 (48) diameter
The artist

The painting is based on a lapel button found by chance in a joke shop in Pacific Ocean Park (POP) in Venice, Los Angeles, when Hamilton first visited America in 1963. 'Slip It To Me' epitomised what Hamilton most admired in American art at that time: 'its audacity and wit'. It is an ironical fusion of the twin concerns – Pop and Op – of Hamilton's contribution to *This is Tomorrow*. Both its message (enigmatic and open to interpretation, but also understood in the culture of the 1960s as a sexual invitation) and its form clearly relate the button to the fringes of the popular arts, while the colour treatment (a carefully judged pair of complementaries, orange and blue, which cause an optical flicker) puts the object into the sphere of Op art.

The purpose of Hamilton's visit to the United States was to attend the first-ever Duchamp retrospective, at the Pasadena Art Museum. Viewed as a readymade, 'Epiphany' shows its indebtedness. It also owes something to Duchamp's optical work 'Fluttering Hearts' (1936, repr. on the cover of *Cahiers d'Art*), in which the juxtaposition of complementary colours causes the fluttering of the title.

Another of Hamilton's heroes is recalled in this reincarnation of a commonplace object, for the button represents an epiphany, in the sense James Joyce used the word, a manifestation, a revelation, a sudden moment of insight. At a vulgar level the Feast of the Epiphany, with its Magi bearing gifts, could invite the glad reaction 'Slip it to me'.

'Epiphany' was made as a multiple in an edition of twelve in 1989. An aluminium disc fabricated to the form of a button had been an attractive proposition from the beginning but the cost made it impractical. The wooden 'original', shaped by the artist, was a cheaper alternative.

Twenty-five years later a giant metal button was more marketable and production costs were less of a burden.

28
Desk
1964
Oil and collage on photograph on panel
61 × 89 (24 × 35)
Scottish National Gallery of Modern Art, Edinburgh

A number of studies were made for the 'Interior' subject before two large paintings were embarked upon. Three interior collages were developed from a diverse range of collaged elements and several drawings were directed at specific components of 'Interior I'. A desk was drawn on a printed perspective grid used by graphic artists and engineers; it followed the form of the desk in the foreground of the film still (see no.29) which inspired the series. The range of readymade commercial perspective sheets provided empty three-dimensional spaces into which, as into a box or room, or one of Hamilton's earlier paintings of a conceptual space, anything may be inserted.

A photographic enlargement of the drawing provided a base for the painted study, which carries a surprising number of different treatments. There is a Tachiste passage of loose paint lower left. Areas of flat colour in Mondrianesque primaries contradict the strange perspective. The drawer (its woodgraining part painted and part veneered with a printed self-adhesive plastic film simulating wood) and the telephone (here transparent, from a Bell advertisement) are elements which Hamilton, who did not see the film *Shockproof* until 1968, twenty years after it was made, correctly sensed to be crucial in the film's narrative. They both imply connection with the world outside the picture; the telephone in the same way as it did in 'Pin-up' (no.17), and the drawer working like a relief projection into the spectator's space.

Characteristic of Hamilton's work

is the way offshoots from one art object to the next arise as explorations into the constituent parts of a particular piece. Typical in this respect is the desk which, although a still-life in subject, grew from a study of 'Interior I'.

29
Interior I

1964
Oil and collage on panel with inlaid mirror
122 × 162 (48 × 63¾)
Erna and Curt Burgauer Collection

'Just what is it . . . ?' (no.13) began an involvement with the domestic interior theme which was to develop in the 1960s through a chance encounter. Hamilton became intrigued by a photograph of a modern interior that surrounded a mysteriously transfixed actress (Patricia Knight) in a publicity still for the film *Shockproof*, 1948 (fig.17), in which she co-starred with her husband Cornel Wilde.

He noticed that the studio photograph conveyed in a single exposure more of the film's plot and mood than one would expect from a split-second image taken from the action. The magic of the still resulted from the peculiarities of cinematographic technology as much as from the masterly control of *mise en scène* exercised by the great director Douglas Sirk working on a B movie. 'A very wide angle lens must have been used because the perspective seemed distorted . . . Since the scale of the room had not become unreasonably enlarged, as one might expect from the use of a wide angle lens, it could be assumed that false perspective had been introduced to counteract its effect – yet the foreground remained emphatically close and the recession extreme. All this contributed more to the foreboding atmosphere than the casually observed body on the floor, partially concealed by a desk.' (bib. D5).

The curtain on the left-hand side of the film still assumes a stronger role in the drama when replayed by

Hamilton. It is brought more to the foreground in an attempt to place the witness outside the action. The importance of the curtain is confirmed in three small collaged studies, all of which, though quite different in other respects, rely heavily on a curtain to turn the observer into a *voyeur*.

Again allusion and ambiguity play their part: the mirror behind the woman is real and it reflects back the spectator's space, a further endeavour to bring the area in front of the picture plane into the action. A real pencil glued on the desk points towards the focus of attention. Hamilton used part of a colour supplement feature showing Berthe Morisot's daughter, the elderly Mme Rouart, in her drawing room, hanging in which was a Morisot painting, 'The Cherry Tree'. Hamilton painted this passage in the drab greens, greys and ochres of the printed image, which are quite unlike the colours of the original Morisot painting: thus 'Interior I' acknowledges the possibility of transformation of an artwork into a new image by the processing it receives through photography and printing and back again into painting. Included upper right is a photograph of 'Interior I' at an earlier stage – like 're Nude' (no.11) in other ways, the painting tells the story of its own making.

30
Interior II

1964
Oil, cellulose, collage and metal relief on panel
122 × 162.5 (48 × 64)
Tate Gallery. Purchased 1967

The pair of 'Interior' paintings were born together. Two large panels were primed ready, a photo silkscreen of Patricia Knight was prepared by Christopher Prater who came to Hamilton's studio with black screen ink and the figure was squeegeed on the white surface in a more or less arbitrary position – no composition had been established for either

picture nor preliminary thought given to the placement. The figure of Patricia Knight therefore compelled all subsequent elements to relate to it.

When 'Interior I' was completed, Hamilton approached his second 'Interior' with the benefit of experience. The first painting had been pushed by its sources into a period atmosphere. He was conscious of the fact that 'Any interior is a set of anachronisms, a museum, with the lingering residues of decorative styles that an inhabited space collects' (bib. D35). The more contemporary treatment of 'Interior II' tries to press home this point.

The polished back of the Eames 'La Fonda' chair, constructed in relief rather than painted, reflects the spectator's space. Both paintings show a view into another room; here the secondary space is derived from a colour photograph of Larry Rivers's studio published in *Esquire*. The artwork leaning against the wall in the far room is an Yves Klein monochrome, a radical example of 'modern' painting emphasising the historical range of the art adorning the two 'Interior' paintings. A fragment of wall and ceiling in a low-angle shot at top right is an extreme view of an interior and absurdly unrelated to the many perspective viewpoints in the painting.

Appearing on a television screen, presented more as a picture than an actual TV, is a colour film of the assassination of John F. Kennedy on 22 November 1963 (unnoticed by the occupant of the room) which introduces 'an element of blatant drama as an aside, offstage, unnoticed' (bib. D35). In the film still the desk obscures the body of a man Patricia Knight has just killed in a struggle for a gun. In the painting 'The dramatic role of the dead man is transferred to the lurid colour treatment of the carpet.'

Both 'Interior' paintings have an overt dramatic intention. They appear to tell a story but the narrative is masked with ambiguities, red herrings, diversions and abstraction. Attempts to read the pictures are forced back to an acceptance of their totality. The drama is felt at first sight or not at all – we await the punchline in vain.

fig.17 Publicity still from the film *Shockproof* 1948

Photography

After his exhibition at the Hanover Gallery in 1964, which followed the long gap since his first in 1955, Hamilton's longstanding engagement with photography became a central rather than a contributory factor in his work. It had already played a generative role; collages almost entirely constructed from photographs ('Just what is it . . . ?', no.13) and those painted on a photographic base ('Portrait of Hugh Gaitskell', no.26) confirm the importance the artist placed upon photography as a source of subject matter and as part of his medium.

Preoccupation with how we see what we see leads Hamilton to investigate means of construction and illusion. Photographs can be simply reproduced and are therefore ideal vehicles for Hamilton's continued reflection on sustaining and elaborating ambiguity.

With his interest in figuration Hamilton is a forerunner of other contemporary trends towards adopting photography as a foundation for painting, for example, in the work of Robert Rauschenberg, Andy Warhol, and Gerhard Richter. In the 1960s many artists were using the camera to transfer imagery onto their canvases. 'Direct photographic techniques, through half-tone silkscreen, for example, have made a new contribution to the painter's medium. In my own case there was a time when I felt that I would like to see how close to photography I could stay yet still be a painter in intent.' (bib. A29)

'I would like to think that I am questioning reality. Photography is just one way, albeit the most direct, by which physical existence can modulate a two-dimensional surface. Painting has long been concerned with the paradox of informing about a multi-dimensional world on the limited dimensionality of a canvas. Assimilating photography into the domain of paradox, incorporating it into the philosophical contradictions of art is as much my concern as embracing its alluring potential as a medium.' (bib. A29)

In selecting photographic subjects for his paintings Hamilton's approach was systematic and analytical. As he was continuing to do with pop imagery, he asked how photography as generally experienced broke down into categories and then dealt with the subdivisions of high style photography (nos.31, 32, 57–68); with the commonplace photography of holiday postcards (nos.33, 55–6), amateur snaps (no.84) and flashbulb photo-journalism (nos.48–54); and with his own photographs (nos.92–103). He went on to examine photographs modified electronically by computer (nos.91, 104) and images which owe more to the computer than to the camera (no.89). He asks whether clear boundaries exist beyond which a photograph ceases to fulfil its function of communicating information, and submitted photographs to extreme enlargement (no.34), near obliteration (no.45) and colour reversal (no.46). Equally vitally, in a field where the intended image is customarily read as a photograph's only texture, he scrutinised the facture of the emulsion itself.

31
My Marilyn
1965
Oil and collage on photograph on panel
102.5 × 122 (40¼ × 48)
Stadt Aachen, Ludwig Forum für Internationale Kunst

Marilyn Monroe's contract with photographers gave her a right to approve their work for publication and to veto those exposures she regarded as unsuitable. In the months following her death George Barris and Bert Stern felt able to publish some of the sheets she had marked-up to indicate her wishes. 'My Marilyn' starts with the signs she made on proofs and transparencies and elaborates on the possibilities they suggest.

These markings include crossings-out, scratches, ticks and words of approval, notes for retouching, even the venting of physical aggression by attacking the emulsion with a nailfile or scissors. The marked photographs have become rich illustrations, in themselves, of media-mixture and of the juxtaposition of types of visual communication. This interference of brutal marks made in direct conflict with high photographic quality coincided with Hamilton's interest in seeing conventions mix, and in relationships which multiply the levels of meaning and ways of reading.

The individual shots are spread across the panel like a comic strip – four photographs are each repeated three times on a different scale and show various stages in the combination of photography and painting, from the straight reproduction of the source to a free reworking of it. Unlike in previous pictures the perspective is respected only within each frame. Hamilton crops the photographic sources and makes us aware of the calculated effort behind the media image of a carefree Marilyn.

'My Marilyn' is essentially an assisted readymade and almost reads like a contributive picture (cf. no.24) with compartments filled with works by de Kooning, Wesselmann and Peter Blake. Hamilton possibly had de Kooning's 'Woman' series in mind. Aspects of the latter's Marilyn Monroe are imitated here. The colouring, too, is reminiscent of de Kooning. There are half-quoted phrases from Francis Bacon's style. The spots obscuring the figure in the bottom left cross-refer to Bert Stern's photographs of Marilyn with a spotted veil.

32
Still-life
1965
Photograph with sprayed photo tints
89.5 × 91 (35¼ × 35¾)
Museum Ludwig, Cologne

Eleven years after Hamilton's first 'Still-life?' (no.12) his return to the genre is based closely on a photograph, rather than on direct observation as previously. Here he comes closest in his quest to retain the essentially photographic nature of his material.

'My Marilyn' (no.31) used a photograph as a base but the work is an

exploration of the many possibilities of enriching the picture's surface; from flat areas of colour to collage from a magazine, word to image, crude outline to subtle infill, impasto to staining. 'Still-life' explores the opposite extreme of intervention. Whereas Hamilton's earlier works had often been thought of as anthologies, collections of parts which retain their character and idioms, here the still-life is an entity in itself and the photograph pure and intact (or so it appears).

'Still-life' is a readymade with minimal assistance. It is an enlargement of a high-style commercial photograph from a Braun catalogue of electrical appliances showing one corner of a portable combination grill. The original qualities of the illustration are not particularly enhanced; though some sprayed photographic dyes have been added surreptitiously to tint the background it is evidently not expected that the colour will make the work more 'painterly'. There is no cropping of the original photograph, other than that proposed by the designer of the brochure. Only one change is made, the spelling of the brand name Braun is anglicised to the 'Brown' of German pronunciation. The only significant contributions made by the artist are the choice of his subject and his decision to enlarge it.

Two factors influenced that choice. Duchamp, in his nomination of a readymade, was explicit in his avoidance of any aesthetic bias in his selection. He did not 'choose' an object because he admired, or indeed, had the slightest interest in its form. Hamilton, in a spirit of experimentation, reversed the principle and asked what happens if an object of aesthetic quality, an admired form by an admirable designer, Dieter Rams, is chosen. A second consideration was another polarisation. What would be the consequence of espousing a high-style, well-designed commodity instead of the meretricious subject matter normally associated with Pop, the art movement into which Hamilton found himself neatly slotted?

33
Whitley Bay
1965
Oil and photograph on panel
81 × 122 (32 × 48)
Private Collection

Picture postcards provided Hamilton with the material for several works with figures on a beach as subject (see also no.34). 'Whitley Bay' examines a small area of a postcard view of the beach in this seaside town on the North-east coast of England. All the usual summer activities are taking place, people swimming and paddling, playing with boats and balls and making sandcastles. Enlargement takes the scene to a state where the halftone dots introduced by the printing process are unable to carry information about details of form. Holiday-makers are reduced to blobs which we read as representing human beings simply because their relationship with other blobs tells us that this is so.

A black and white enlargement was mounted on a panel and colour applied with loose washes of dye, in much the way that a photographic retoucher might have applied colour had he been working on the original scale.

34
People
1965–6
Oil and cellulose on photograph on panel
81 × 122 (32 × 48)
The artist

'People' was also derived from a Whitley Bay postcard but one which was unusual in being a real photograph printed on emulsion, rather than a halftone reproduction. It also had the fascination of showing a vast area of beach which, when magnified through many stages of photographic enlargement, provided a rich store of information about many thousands of people. 'As this texture of anony- mous humanity is penetrated, it yields more fragments of knowledge about individuals isolated within it as well as endless patterns of group rela- tionships.' (bib. A29)

The scene was examined piecemeal in a procedure allied to zooming. A 35mm negative was made of a detail in the postcard, using an extension bellows on the camera which allowed extreme close up. An 8 × 10 inch enlargement was printed and the pro- cess repeated with another negative from the enlargement and so on until the prints lost legibility. At this stage an analysis was made to assess just where a figurative reading became impossible. It was found that the breakpoint in the photograph, where contact was lost between an abstract shape and a recognisable person, could be precisely located.

'People' touches the fringes of per- ception, the narrow line between semblance and abstraction. In the chosen frame the figures at the bot- tom still imply specific ages, activities and human relationships, whilst to- wards the top coherence is dissolved. Hamilton's additions, all black and white, are slight yet important. Their main purpose is to give the photo- graphic surface some further textural interest without destroying the essen- tially photographic values. There are touches of matt and gloss black paint, apparent when close-to, which rein- force the figures yet which, once noticed, can tip the reading into abstraction. Other painted and sprayed forms towards the top of the picture hint at a figure or deny it completely.

35
Landscape
1965–6
Mixed media on photograph
81 × 244 (32 × 96)
Museum moderner Kunst, Ludwig Collection, Vienna

'Landscape' takes the divergent pro- positions of 'My Marilyn' (no. 31) and 'Still-life' (no. 32) and restates them in one picture. A postcard is a handy, portable image. Substantial enough to be carried around in a pocket or propped on a shelf, postcards have a unique convenience of form and they effortlessly offer themselves as objects of study. Available everywhere, the postcard will fascinate and instruct.

The source of 'Landscape' was unusual in format, an elongated card showing a panoramic, aerial view of the South Downs. It was a hand- tinted photographic postcard, so each example was marginally different. The girls who tinted the black and white prints worked speedily on batches of hundreds, therefore no great accuracy or precision could be expected – the result is a charming mixture of coloured dyes loosely dis- posed over a perspective of roughly rectangular shapes.

If a copy negative had been made from the postcard and then enlarged the quality would be likely to suffer, so Hamilton decided to search for the postcard's source. Enquiries led him to Hunting Aerosurveys who had a research library in Central London. An exploration of the 'South Downs' files produced a negative number, and an eight-foot wide print of the area shown in the postcard was ordered. 'Painting' consisted of adding many different types of mark to the long panel, ranging from filling in different fields with transparent dyes or opaque colour to adding pas- sages which bear little or no relation to the subject. Some parts, on the other hand, are made more specific in their representation of the scene, with tiny houses modelled in false perspective from balsawood and glued to the surface and areas of woodland made from colour-soaked sponge (cf. fig. 1 on p. 27).

Duchamp's 'Large Glass' (1966)

fig. 18 Marcel Duchamp and Richard Hamilton **The Bride Stripped Bare by her Bachelors, Even (The Large Glass)** 1915–23, replica 1965–6 Mixed media on glass *Tate Gallery*

After his immersion in Duchamp when working on a typographic version of his *Green Box* notes, Hamilton was a natural choice as organiser of the second of only two retrospectives held before Duchamp's death in 1968. The exhibition at the Tate Gallery took place three years after the first, organised by Walter Hopps, in Pasadena in 1963.

'The Bride Stripped Bare by her Bachelors, Even' (*La Mariée mise à nu par ses célibataires, même*) (fig. 18) – better known as the 'Large Glass' – cannot be moved from its home in the Philadelphia Museum of Art. A retrospective of Duchamp without the 'Large Glass' is like *Swan Lake* without the swan, so Hamilton spent a year recapitulating the procedures followed by Duchamp in his construction of 'The Bride Stripped Bare . . .'. As well as the resulting 'Large Glass' now owned by the Tate Gallery, the studies were reconstructed. These devotional exercises, a retracing of the path taken by Duchamp over a period of twelve years, took less time for Hamilton. Some diminu- tion of his output is apparent during the years 1957–60 and 1965–6 when a great deal of time was lost to his own creativity by working on Duchamp, but the dates of this close involvement with Duchamp coincide with positive stages in his own development.

36
Trafalgar Square
1965-7
Oil on photograph on panel
81 × 122 (32 × 48)
Museum Ludwig, Cologne

Hamilton adapted the principle of the Whitley Bay series to an urban post-card scene. The detail chosen for elaboration gives the painting a quite distinct character: an uneven distribution of elements, some massive or speck-like, some geometrical or fluid and others isolated or clumped. There is even greater room for ambiguity and, in line with the photo-tinter's crude exaggerations, a sharper range of even bolder colour.

Hamilton has more fully 'embedded' the printed screen into his semi-invented imagery; here it intensifies the wavering character of all the forms and confounds any sense of constant illusion.

The Guggenheim Museum

Between 1964 and 1967 Hamilton produced an interior, a still-life, a landscape, a self-portrait, a mother and child and a scene of bathers. His approach to subject matter was to think in terms of categories. During this time he also examined buildings as a possible class of subject matter. Piranesi's romantic ruins, Lichtenstein's paintings of classical temples and Artschwager's sky-scrapers are examples of the genre. Hamilton's choice of building represents a structural anti-thesis to the post and lintel or steel-frame grid but he was interested to know if a successful work could be based on a new building – one conceived as a work of high art in itself, an aim related to his use of Braun appliances.

Hamilton's ventures into perspective are wide ranging; from the extreme of side-stepping the issue in 'Still-life' (no. 32) to the mockery of the convention apparent in 'Just what is it . . .?' (no. 13). When he does undertake a serious project involving perspective it is liable to be absurdly problematic. His 'Five Tyres remoulded', 1971 (fig. 19), which required putting into accurate perspective the patterns on the double curve of a torus, was solvable only with the help of a computer. The expanding helix in false perspective of the Guggenheim Museum is another such exercise.

The Solomon R. Guggenheim Museum on Fifth Avenue in New York was designed by Frank Lloyd Wright between 1943 and 1946 and was built 1956-9. The spiral form of the museum looks back to the shells and horns of *Growth and Form* and, like the spiral structure of the Exquis-ite Form bra, encourages a false illusionistic reading as concentric circles (here stacked). The spectator is again made very conscious of shifting viewpoints and the use of heavy relief is the culmination of a preoccupation originating in 1951.

In both their appearance and the process of their making the Guggenheim reliefs contrast with Hamilton's work to date. A single centralised image represented a departure from anthol-ogies of shape, technique and source, and the careful preparatory plan, elevation and section drawings he made were quite different from previous 'studies' for his paintings, being analogous to the blueprints for a building. These constitute an account of Frank Lloyd Wright's magnum opus which Hamilton went to great lengths to distil for this essay on style. They show Hamil-ton's interest in process – whether aesthetic or technical – the reliefs echoing the design and con-struction. He writes: 'It was an attempt to mirror the whole activity of architecture in the con-fines of a 4 feet square panel.' (bib. c8)

Although the form of each relief is the same there is a considerable variation of treatment in the cellulose lacquer finish, always applied with an air-gun. All six treatments disembody the building's dramatic three-dimensional form by transposing it into a skin of colour and texture with quite independent associations and effects.

fig. 19 Several screenprints from portfolio **Five Tyres remoulded** 1971

37
The Solomon R Guggenheim (Black and White)

1965–6
Fibreglass and cellulose
122 × 122 × 18 (48 × 48 × 7¼)
Solomon R. Guggenheim Museum, New York

Painted to contradict the facts of relief by giving the appearance of a drawing or a diagram flat on a sheet; an effect exaggerated by hard, false shadows.

39
The Solomon R Guggenheim (Black)

1965–6
Fibreglass and cellulose
122 × 122 × 18 (48 × 48 × 7¼)
Solomon R. Guggenheim Museum, New York

Arises directly out of the possibilities seen in the recessed bands of the 'Black and White' Guggenheim (no.37). A high gloss black surface is highly reflective. The result of spraying the relief entirely black produced a distorting mirror so that the surface throws back a deformed image of its surrounding environment: hence a form of marked clarity becomes the vehicle for a total fluidity.

41
The Solomon R Guggenheim (Metalflake)

1965–6
Fibreglass, acrylic and metalflake
122 × 122 × 18 (48 × 48 × 7¼)
Private Collection

Refers back to Hamilton's car-styling interests. 'Metalflake' is a brand of automobile finish in which particles of anodised aluminium are mixed with a clear lacquer to produce a glossy crystalline surface beloved by the car customising industry of California. Among the 'colours' offered is a mixture of the individual tints called 'bouquet'; each particle retains its own colour in a shimmering blend.

It is the most pictorial of the reliefs and the only one which isolates the building from its background, sprayed with 'Sky Blue' Metalflake.

38
The Solomon R Guggenheim (Neapolitan)

1965–6
Fibreglass and cellulose
122 × 122 × 18 (48 × 48 × 7¼)
Tate Gallery. Purchased 1970

Derives its colour and shading from the modulated fall of light. Hamilton sprayed a relief with an even coat of white then photographed it with careful lighting. It was then sprayed a creamy tint (vanilla), and over this he sprayed a graduated soft colour (strawberry) to simulate tonal articulation of the lighting in the photograph; the recessed bands were then sprayed a pale green tint (pistachio) to complement the general effect of soft blushes. The analogy of both colour and form with icecream is direct.

40
The Solomon R Guggenheim (Gold)

1965–6
Fibreglass, cellulose and gold leaf
122 × 122 × 18 (48 × 48 × 7¼)
Louisiana Museum of Modern Art, Humlebaek, Denmark

Covered with gold leaf, the form becomes an object of special veneration. Gold gives the relief quite special properties, in that it appears to absorb light and then to emit it as a magical radiance.

42
The Solomon R Guggenheim (Spectrum)

1965–6
Fibreglass and cellulose
122 × 122 × 18 (48 × 48 × 7¼)
Solomon R. Guggenheim Museum, New York

The form of the Wright building from a low vantage point is reminiscent of a rainbow. To reinforce the banded structure with arcs of colour, overlaying one rainbow on another, would have been too obvious. By rotating the colour through 90 degrees Hamilton turns the Guggenheim into the crock of gold at the fairy-tale end of the rainbow.

Studies show an intended painterly freedom of treatment to oppose the relief's smooth lines in this version but the controlled gradations of the spray gun were maintained for the sake of the unity of the series.

43
Toaster

1966–7 (reconstructed 1969)
Chromed steel and Perspex on colour photograph
81 × 81 (32 × 32)
The artist

Like 'Still-life' (no.32), 'Toaster' and its related print (fig.20) is derived from promotional material for Braun domestic goods. In the print version Hamilton added text compiled from Braun brochures for several different products and from technical data particular to the print, modified only by an occasional word change. The peculiarities of the writing style (evidently translated to English from a German original) and the minutiae of the typographical layout are wholly faithful to precedents set by Braun literature.

The object was in shallow relief set against a black and white photographic background. On its return from an exhibition in Germany in 1968 the work was found to be in a badly damaged state. After the usual protests from a German insurance company that the collection of broken and scratched parts, wrapped in brown paper and tied with string, were unlikely ever to have been a work of art, it was reconstructed. Hamilton made a new out-of-focus photograph for the background, this time in colour, and substituted chromium-plated sheet steel for an aluminium slab. The colour-photograph background itself was sprayed, almost imperceptibly, to bring it

closer to the desired colour modulations.

The absence of depicted shadow asserts the reality of the work of art as a relief constructed with almost banal simplicity from rudimentary elements – only the shadows are literal, anti-illusionistic, cast against a flat background across the shallow depth of a few millimetres (cf. Hamilton's observations on Duchamp's Chocolate grinder, No.2, 1914, in bib. A20). The juxtaposed textural extremes of blurred background and crisp machine-wrought steel unexpectedly switch roles, the clean rectangle becoming a container of shifting unfixed reflections – the colour emulsion and atomised paint read as an accumulation of discrete spots. The Braun logotype was replaced by the artist's own so that the object should be clearly seen as no longer a toaster nor an advertisement for one but Hamilton's conceptually operating work of art.

In response to a request from the International Design Centre, Berlin, on the occasion of an exhibition of the work of Dieter Rams, chief designer for Braun (and of their toaster), Hamilton wrote: 'My admiration for the work of Dieter Rams is intense and I have for many years been uniquely attracted towards his design sensibility; so much so that his consumer products have come to occupy a place in my heart and consciousness that the Mont Sainte-Victoire did in Cézanne's'.

44
Bathers I

1966–7
Mixed media on photo-sensitised fabric
84 × 117 (33¼ × 46¼)
Museum Ludwig, Cologne
[Not exhibited]

Hamilton continued his examination (nos.33–6), of the limits of recognition of the human image through photographic marks. His practice had been to accept readymade photographs, often in the convenient form of postcards. While on holiday in

Greece in 1965, with the opportunity of frequent sightings of people bathing, he used his camera to record gatherings of people on beaches and elsewhere. The source for both 'Bathers I' and 'Bathers II' (no.45) was a 35mm colour transparency taken on a Greek island mainly used by German families on vacation. Both are enlargements of the original slide but the photograph is integrated into the painting surface more closely by the use of photo-sensitised canvas instead of the earlier practice of mounting a photograph on board. 'Bathers I' had a piece of printed fabric suggestive of a particularly hideous bathing costume sewn to the canvas beside a two-dimensional reconstruction of a bathing cap covered with rose coloured petals.

fig.20 **Toaster** 1967
Offset lithograph in 4 colours, screenprinted from 4 stencils, and collaged with metalised polyester

45
Bathers II

1967
Oil on colour photo-sensitised fabric
76 × 114.5 (30 × 45)
The artist

'Bathers II' is unique in being a primitive experiment in putting colour emulsion on a canvas. Here everything except the figures and anything manmade (boats, rafts, kicked-up spray) has been obliterated with white paint applied in a gradation of impasto – rough in the foreground and becoming smoother in the distance. The individual figures, so unnaturally isolated, appear to have been placed by collage rather than by a reverse process. Yet from these scattered indications of incomplete bodies, varying depths of water, the purpose of assembling in one place, the activities pursued and a general topography can all be discerned.

46
I'm dreaming of a white Christmas

1967–8
Oil on canvas
106.5 × 160 (42 × 63)
Ludwig Collection, Kunstmuseum Basle

The idea of a painting based in reversed, negative colour emerged from material researched for a lecture (bib. A5); like most of Hamilton's subjects it had been with him for several years. The project had been put aside because Jasper Johns's 1965 version of the Stars and Stripes in colours complementary to red, white and blue seemed to pre-empt the exercise. Hamilton's intentions were sufficiently distinct to overcome this reluctance. There was the extreme complexity of translating a figurative subject into an opposite colour sense, and again there is the ambiguous space of the film industry's interior designs.

The motifs are similar to those in the 'Interior' paintings (nos.29, 30): a film still, a figure in an interior with further spaces beyond, the spectator drawn into the picture space. '"I'm dreaming . . ." almost fits the category of an "Interior" but the emphatic human presence makes it more a "portrait"' (bib. D35). Bing Crosby is seen in a hotel lobby in the film *White Christmas*, 1954 (a musical rejig of *Holiday Inn*, 1942), whose theme song became a smash hit, thereby representing the epitome of 'formula' mass culture commodity.

The reversal of the imagery suggests that the spectator is gazing into a mirror-world through the medium of a photograph (which contains, in a literal manner, its obverse). Scientific thought posits that a non-world exists adjacent to our world, and that this world has as real an existence, in an opposite phase, as the one we experience. The photographic negative becomes a readymade token of this.

Bing Crosby in negative also becomes racially reversed (the song makes an apt title); he becomes a sharp American black. His clothes are colour reversed – a black shirt, white hat, yellow cardigan and light blue coat. The exterior seen through the window is lurid too, the normally blue sky is orange, the green trees red. 'In many ways the scene becomes that much more magical and mysterious and beautiful and more rewarding when meditated upon than the scene as we would normally know it.' (bib. A29)

The initial idea was formulated in a watercolour study, additional sketches were made while the painting was in progress and ideas for prints continued after the completion. The subject was brought full cycle with a print titled 'I'm dreaming of a black Christmas' (fig.21) which reversed the painting back into a positive.

47
Picturegram

1968
Oil on photograph on photo-sensitised fabric
101.5 × 65 (40 × 25½)
The artist

Hamilton was one of a large number of artists asked to contribute a work inspired by Guillaume Apollinaire and his ideas to the exhibition *Tout Terriblement – Guillaume Apollinaire* at the ICA, London in 1968. The starting point for his homage was Apollinaire's concept, in his calligrammes, of words (poetry) constituting a visual work of art in which the same topic is expressed at both a literary and a pictorial level simultaneously.

'Picturegram' is an elaboration of Apollinaire's calligramme 'Il pleut'. It is painted on a photographic enlargement on canvas of Apollinaire's original handwritten version of 'Il pleut'. Faintly visible through the paint are the printed ruled lines and the rubber-stamped monogram 'PAB' (Pierre-Albert Birot, publisher of the calligrammes in 1916) on the original manuscript, now owned by the Bibliothèque Nationale in Paris.

Taking Apollinaire's pictorial calligraphy into a painterly extension whereby the verbal allusions could be further reinforced by colour and tonal nuances has a special relevance to Hamilton. There are strong connections between 'Picturegram' and his painting of Marilyn Monroe's notations on photographs (no.31), since in each painting he elaborated marks in the very forming of which, originally, another hand had revealed much about its owner's mind and feelings. Equally, the restrained tonal range, the masking of a photographic base, and the quality of an abrupt, insistent impasto have a close correspondence with 'Bathers II' (no.45).

In the manner of his painting Hamilton seeks to evoke the mood of Apollinaire's poem, in which the observation of falling rain is fused with nostalgic sadness. Painted at the time of Duchamp's death in October 1968, 'Picturegram' became (through its analogy with tears) a personal expression of sorrow showing a curious synchronicity, since both Hamilton and Apollinaire – involved with the same calligramme fifty years apart – had been personal friends of Duchamp.

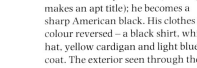

fig.21 **I'm dreaming of a black Christmas** 1971 Screenprint on collotype, plus collage

Swingeing London 67

Police raided a party at the home of Keith Richard of the Rolling Stones on 12 February 1967. Among the guests were Mick Jagger, lead singer of the group, Marianne Faithful and Hamilton's art dealer Robert Fraser. Keith Richard was charged with allowing his house to be used for the smoking of cannabis resin; Jagger and Fraser were charged with being in possession of different drugs, and after court proceedings both were sentenced to imprisonment (Fraser for six months; Jagger's sentence was commuted on appeal to a twelve months conditional discharge).

The arrest and prosecution of the Rolling Stones was front page news for weeks. Fraser's gallery closed but the secretary continued to receive a vast collection of press cuttings from an agency the gallery employed to collect exhibition reviews. Every mention of Robert Fraser's name was duly snipped and delivered. Fraser's secretary agreed to Hamilton's request to give him the large bundle of cuttings. It proved to be a mine of extraordinary information, or misinformation. There were innumerable reports of the same incident, each varying at the whim of reporters; colour of clothes, age of accused, food carried from restaurants to prisoners, police statements, judges' opinions, all were savoured to the utmost. It led to a collage published by a distributor of art posters in Italy (fig.22).

fig.22 **Swingeing London 67– poster** 1968 Photo-offset lithograph

A press photograph (upper left on the collage) by John Twine showed Mick Jagger and Robert Fraser handcuffed together, seen through the window of a police van as they arrived at the court in Chichester to be charged for unlawful possession of drugs. This photograph was the source of a series of paintings titled 'Swingeing London', an ironic comment on the contrast between excesses of individualism and freedom of behaviour attributed to the London pop world of 1967 and the restraints on privacy and personal choice and freedom represented by the Jagger/Fraser prosecution and the sentences imposed. A *Time* magazine cover (15 April 1966) had blazoned an article on 'London: the Swinging City' which focused on the social revolution towards light-hearted permissiveness and gave international currency to the phrase 'Swinging London'. That slogan, and a reported statement of the judge presiding over the hearing, that 'There are times when a swingeing sentence can act as a deterrent', were combined for Hamilton's title.

The character of the image – the action and formal analogy with successive frames of film – is cinematic. It is also yet another variant on the theme of the relationship of the human figure to a motor vehicle. The blurred photographic quality and the slanting angle of the upright of the window almost fit it as an exhibit in *Man, Machine & Motion*. It extends Hamilton's interpretations of inner and outer spaces, transparency, varied focus and photographic marks. It combines the directness of the socio-political concern of the Gaitskell portrait (no.26) with the compassion for the socially inflicted suffering of a public image seen in 'My Marilyn' (no.31).

Hamilton proposed to make a work which captured the sense of the handcuffed 'swingers' in the police van. The frame was to be like the window of a van through which the picture is seen. The first task was to obtain a copy of the original photograph from the *Daily Mail* picture library. This was enlarged and retouched to remove the outside of the van and extend the interior to provide a photographic image that could be silkscreened in black over a coloured, conventional oil painting. The uncertainty inherent in the process required tests to be made so Hamilton prepared six versions of the subject.

With the linear outline of his composition transferred to six canvases Hamilton painted them in contrasting texture, colour, intensity and style, some academically painted and others broadly worked, one with flat areas of poster-like colour. When completed, black pigment was screened over the paintings. Common to all is a basic colour scheme (allowing wide variations) derived from press reports, and the colouring of the two windows behind the figures. The right-hand window always suggests sky or landscape, to represent the freedom left behind, and the left-hand window is the colour of brick, symbolising impending enclosure; the press photograph was taken by flash light as the van drove from the street past the gatepost of the court building.

48
Swingeing London 67 (a)
1968–9
Oil on canvas and screenprint
67 × 85 (26½ × 33½)
Rita Donagh

Here the underpainting was as straightforward as possible, the aim being a clear simplicity of image and maximum smoothness of surface. The painting hidden by the screenprint was the most developed and self-sufficient of the group.

50
Swingeing London 67 (c)
1968–9
Oil on canvas and screenprint
67 × 85 (26½ × 33½)
Private Collection
[Not exhibited]

An airbrush was used to give soft modulations and a slightly softer quality.

52
Swingeing London 67 (e)
1968–9
Enamel on canvas and screenprint
67 × 85 (26½ × 33½)
Private Collection

Heightened colour was applied evenly in well-defined areas. Instead of oil paint the medium was enamel, creating a markedly harsh and gritty texture in the screened black.

49
Swingeing London 67 (b)
1968–9
Oil on canvas and screenprint
67 × 85 (26½ × 33½)
Museum Ludwig, Cologne

Contrasting with (a) (no.48), painted with heavy impasto, vigorous brush-work and academic flamboyance.

51
Swingeing London 67 (d)
1968–9
Oil on canvas and screenprint
67 × 85 (26½ × 33½)
Private Collection, Switzerland, courtesy Massimo Martino S.A.

The paint was again applied with heavy impasto, but with a dramatically exaggerated colour; fierce oranges and purples were applied at the places where the screen would print darkest, to allow the pigment to glow through the black deposits.

53
Swingeing London 67 (f)
1968–9
Screenprint on canvas, acrylic and collage
67 × 85 (26½ × 33½)
Tate Gallery. Purchased 1969

The last variation was an exception; a canvas primed with white was screened with the black image and the oil colour applied on top. It was also different from others in the group in that collage was added; it was used for the views through both windows and for the handcuffs. Realisation of the handcuffs presented the particular problem of how to give them adequate definition while remaining true to their out-of-focus vagueness in the photograph. Hamilton's solution was to formalise the glinting, rather uninformative shapes in the photograph into a progression of arbitrary-seeming discrete elements sculpted in way that the La Fonda chair in 'Interior II' (no.30) is formed from thick aluminium.

54

Swingeing London 67

1968

Relief, screenprint on oil on photograph on hardboard

58.5 × 79 × 7.5 (23 × 31⅛ × 3)

Private Collection

The version of 'Swingeing London' to which the testing was directed is slightly smaller than the trials. There is another major difference: the painting was done on a smooth primed hardboard surface rather than on canvas. The style of its underpainting was closest to version (a) (no.48) but the lack of surface texture allows the halftone screenprint to print more cleanly.

Where the final version achieves its finality is in its box-frame presentation. The figures return to the police van, confined within the bounds of the frame, but they are seen through a plywood simulation of the van with sliding glass windows. A marked departure from its source photograph is that the window frame is sloping, instead of upright. This is clearly designed to increase the picture's direction of impulsion – the movement is clearly from right to left. Dieter Roth, a great friend of Hamilton, once explained to him that when he (Roth) pictured a man on a motorbike going from right to left he is leaving home. If the motorcyclist goes from left to right he is returning there.

55

Chicago project I

1969

Acrylic on photograph on board

81 × 122 (32 × 48)

The British Council

An invitation from the Museum of Contemporary Art, Chicago, to participate in their *Art by Telephone* exhibition, to be held in November–December 1969, demanded a conceptual solution. Hamilton decided there could be interesting possibilities in trying to create a painting through the medium of a message passed over the telephone wire. He prepared a schedule which was designed to produce an acceptable painting by prescribing rigid procedures but introducing wide tolerances within that framework.

It was agreed that a young Chicago painter would paint the picture according to telephoned instructions. The artist who offered his services is now a distinguished member of the Chicago School of painters. The instructions dictated to Ed Paschke on the telephone were these:

'Get a coloured postcard in the Chicago area of a subject in Chicago. Either get it yourself or, if you are worried about the aesthetic responsibility of choosing something, ask a friend to provide it. [The postcard obtained by Ed Paschke was an upright of the tall Prudential building in Chicago with part of Grant Park in the foreground (fig.24).]

'Take a piece of paper and cut a hole in it 1 inch high by 1½ inches wide. The hole should be square with a corner of the paper 1 inch to the left of the edge and ¾ inches from the bottom edge. Place this in the bottom right-hand corner of the postcard. Get a photographer to enlarge the area of postcard revealed in the hole to a size of 2ft 8in × 4ft, preferably on sensitized canvas but if this isn't possible have a paper print dry mounted onto hardboard (Masonite).

'Leave 20 per cent of the surface untouched black and white. Paint 40 per cent in roughly the colours apparent in the postcard. Paint 40 per cent in complementaries of the colours apparent in the postcard. Either transparent stains or opaque colours, some thick, some thin, which areas at your discretion'.

The Chicago Project takes further the ideas expressed in nos.33–6, Hamilton's interest being in the potential of extraction from any given material. Even if the responsibility for selecting source material and final motif are removed as far as possible from the artist or anyone else, the result will have a vitality independent of its source and a distinct visual dialect. This and no.56 are among the most formal of all Hamilton's works. The arrangement of a figure amid shadows and foliage reinforces the inherent ambiguity of the photographic marks: a sinister elusiveness

which is also seen in Antonioni's film *Blow Up* and in the vastly enlarged amateur photographs of scenes adjacent to John F. Kennedy's assassination.

There is an arbitrariness about the way a coloured postcard of Chicago was selected and a detail enormously enlarged. We eavesdrop a scene which seems to have disclosed some seductive possibilities as might a view stolen through a keyhole, or overlooked by a telescope. The hand application of colour to an enlargement is a metaphor of the postcard retoucher's craft, which Hamilton had been examining for several years.

'Such "painting by dictation" compels a radical redefining of what is understood by the creative act. The traditional concept of creativity as a wholly "original" event is put into question. It is deliberately pictured as a much more "secondhand affair" – something which can be done "by proxy" – implying that it is more a matter of "copying and altering", than of inventing from scratch.' (Sarat Maharaj in thesis, 1985; see Bibliography.)

56

Chicago project II

1969

Oil on photograph on canvas

81 × 122 (32 × 48)

The British Council

When Hamilton saw the Chicago postcard which had been used for no.55 he decided it would be interesting to follow his own instructions to see what differences might result. The second painting was made in Highgate, London.

A postcard designed by Hamilton was published in 1974, with the title 'Composer' (dedicated to John Cage). This was a plain white card with a rectangular hole exactly as prescribed for the Chicago project. Printed at the top of the card was the instruction 'place "composer" over any picture postcard so that the bottom and right hand edges align then examine the chance composition defined by the rectangular hole'.

fig.23 Source postcard for **Chicago project I**

Fashion-plate

The 'Cosmetic studies' continue the consideration of genres in our culture that called for assimilation into fine art. It was Hamilton's intention to produce a life-size, perhaps three-quarter length, figure painting, a 'fashion-plate' based on contemporary photography such as that found in *Vogue*, *Harper's Bazaar* and *Queen*, from which much of the collage material here is taken. The studies are a bizarre combination of the irrational and fantastic emotions projected by models' expressions (whether seductive, frigid, rapturous or distraught); the magazines' obsession with colour, stylistic innovation, or accentuated bodily gesture of the moment; and the magazines' instructional emphasis concerning make-up, skin culture and hair.

They are a further example of Hamilton's tendency to elaborate studies until the planned conclusive work is, to some extent, diluted. It is as though the 'studies' become a set of variations which constitute the total work, so the twelve 'Cosmetic studies' should essentially be seen as an integrated group. As is often the case with Hamilton, a subject is first entered in a series of forays armed with different forces using a variety of weapons. Given the objective of a large figure-painting it would be characteristic of him to narrow the problem and begin a research programme through some print medium. His first step, in this instance, was to create an environment in which to place his subject and that, naturally, should be a photographic studio. A photographer friend, Tony Evans, provided the space to photograph a stage empty of performers. Lights and reflectors were set up, to frame a hypothetical model against a white paper background. The black and white photograph they made was printed by lithography on paper in Milan in a sufficient number to provide a common starting point for all the studies and enough to produce an edition of one of the variations.

Full-page heads in fashion magazines are commonly found in the pages devoted to make-up and articles on the application of cosmetics and they often show gross imbalances. Pictorial demonstrations of technique are displayed in such a way that one side of a model's face can be different from the other – a left eye drawn, coloured and decorated quite differently from the right. The fascination lies in the fact that the motif of the artwork, the face of a beautiful woman, can itself be a painted artefact. This theme, the relationship between paint and subject and the varying levels at which intervention can take place, recurs in Hamilton's output (see nos.31, 36, and the serial interference of the self-portraits nos.92–103). These pages of instructions on the use of cosmetics also led to the thought that cosmetics should be the pigment through which his images could be brought about – the message is the medium.

They continue Hamilton's preoccupation with the immediate juxtaposition of contrasting visual languages (cf. nos.17, 31), such as diagrammatic motif next to illusionistic modelling, next to abstract smear of pure pigment. Once again he merges disparate ingredients into new wholes, whilst also stressing the sense of discrepancy and ambiguity between the different parts. In this sense the 'Fashion-plates' are similar to the 'Interior' series (nos.29, 30), in the way they examine how oddly disturbing multiple viewpoints and substitutions may be and yet remain acceptable.

57
Fashion-plate
(cosmetic study I)
1969
Collage, enamel, acrylic and cosmetics on lithographed paper
100 × 70 (39⅜ × 27½)
Whereabouts unknown
[Not exhibited]

A disc of pure colour adjoins the most realistically-painted eye of the series on a doll-like persona owing a lot to Twiggy. The bland, neutral, totally innocent stare is a perfect confection of purity. A sample of real fabric exemplifies the use throughout the series of tokens for substances or concepts (see 'Bathers I', no.44). This work was purchased from Waddington Galleries by a gallery in Johannesburg and was lost by the shippers.

59
Fashion-plate
(cosmetic study III)
1969
Collage, enamel, acrylic and cosmetics on lithographed paper
100 × 70 (39⅜ × 27½)
Private Collection

Here the proportion of collage to paint is reversed. 'Study III' began with a complete face in collage which was then altered. The relationship of word and colours, lower right, is intended to be evocative of mood and sound in much the same way as the word 'Brown' in no.32. Each of the collaged fragments has been placed next to the nearest painted approach in the adjoining paint to the colour it describes.

61
Fashion-plate
(cosmetic study V)
1969
Collage, acrylic and cosmetics on lithographed paper
100 × 70 (39⅜ × 27½)
Private Collection

The leaps of scale which are common to the series are demonstrated by the small area below the neck, formerly a complete set of shoulders.

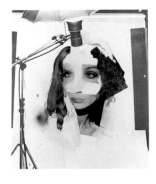

58
Fashion-plate
(cosmetic study II)
1969
Collage, enamel, acrylic and cosmetics on lithographed paper
100 × 70 (39⅜ × 27½)
Private Collection

Contrasts with the other eleven studies in starting with the painted image and moving towards the collage so the proportion of paint to collage is high. The swathed hair, right, is that of Jane Holzer, Andy Warhol's first superstar.

60
Fashion-plate
(cosmetic study IV)
1969
Collage, enamel and cosmetics on lithographed paper
100 × 70 (39⅜ × 27½)
Private Collection, Switzerland

Nine of the 'Cosmetic studies' contain a constant element: Varushka's lips and part of her neck was printed on all but a few sheets in black and white as the first stage in an editioned 'Fashion-plate'.

62
Fashion-plate
(cosmetic study VI)
1969
Collage, enamel and cosmetics on lithographed paper
100 × 70 (39⅜ × 27½)
Massimo and Francesca Valsecchi

A grotesque character appears for the first time in the series. The impression of constructed personality puts the model into the 'Bride of Frankenstein' class. In the first five examples the disparate elements add up to a distinctive, plausible personality. If the elements are attractive in themselves it is possible to maintain an appeal in the whole. Unlike all others there is a wide disparity here between not only the size of the eyes but also the directions in which they look.

  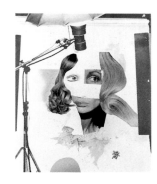

63
Fashion-plate
(cosmetic study VII)
1969
Collage, pastel, acrylic and cosmetics
on lithographed paper
100 × 70 (39⅜ × 27½)
Private Collection

This study developed into a country
girl; wearing gingham, cherries and
violets, she also has a picture hat, its
wide brim defined at one point by the
negative collage of part of a neck.

65
Fashion-plate
(cosmetic study IX)
1969
Collage, acrylic, pastel and cosmetics
on lithographed paper
100 × 70 (39⅜ × 27½)
Rosenthal and Rosenthal

Most of the twenty-four eyes in the
series are collaged but none is a true
pair. Within the photographic range
there are many different treatments:
false lashes, eye shadow of various
colours, mascara, penciled eyebrows
and eye linings. This model accepts
the fact of drawn features and her
right eye is copied faithfully from a
cartoon-like eye by Roy Lichtenstein.

67
Fashion-plate
(cosmetic study XI)
1969
Collage, acrylic and cosmetics on
lithographed paper
100 × 70 (39⅜ × 27½)
Danae Art International

Apart from the surrounding props
and Varushka's lips there are other
motifs recurring on one or two exam-
ples of the series. A token breast, an
eye, a hank of hair returns inverted
(see study 'III', no.59), a piece of jew-
ellery. These shared elements do not
give the studies a common identity. A
curious property of the 'Cosmetic stu-
dies' is their tendency to recall for any
spectator particular people, in terms
of personality as well as appearance.

64
Fashion-plate
(cosmetic study VIII)
1969
Collage, enamel, acrylic and pastel on
lithographed paper
100 × 70 (39⅜ × 27½)
Massimo and Francesca Valsecchi

Here the magazines' preoccupation
with white face-packs is pushed in
the direction of ritual which the asso-
ciations of masks imply; the lips are
painted in an aperture of the mask.
Hamilton had in mind the photo-
graphs like those in Boris de Rache-
wiltz, *Black Eros* (1963, first English
edition 1964), where black girls'
faces are whitened by thick plaster.

66
Fashion-plate
(cosmetic study X)
1969
Collage, enamel, pastel and cosmetics
on lithographed paper
100 × 70 (39⅜ × 27½)
Private Collection

Make-up comparisons are sometimes
made with a sharp dividing line
between 'before and after' – the split
personality is emphatic here. While it
is difficult to identify specific models a
glimmer of Jean Shrimpton carries
through the mask.

68
Fashion-plate
(cosmetic study XII)
1969
Collage, pastel and cosmetics on
lithographed paper
100 × 70 (39⅜ × 27½)
Private Collection

The last of the series projects a quality
typical of the species 'fashion model',
a look of haughty disdain. Perhaps
the series' most striking feature when
seen, evenly spaced around the spec-
tator at eye level, is the hieratic, awe-
some, ambiguous but timeless char-
acter of these twelve images.

69
The critic laughs

1971–2
Electric toothbrush with teeth, case
and instruction book
27 × 11 × 6.5 (10¾ × 4¼ × 2½) (cased)
The artist

When given a giant-sized set of edible
teeth (a block of sugar in the form of
an upper denture) as a present by his
young son who had been on holiday
in Brighton, Hamilton fixed the teeth
to his Braun electric toothbrush. He
was delighted that the assisted-ready-
made brought a recollection of Jasper
Johns's sculpture 'The Critic Smiles'
(1959), showing a normal tooth-
brush with molars substituted for the
bristles, so the grotesquely shudder-
ing teeth were given the title 'The cri-
tic laughs'. Johns followed his tooth-
brush with 'The Critic Sees' (1961),
representing a pair of spectacles,
behind which the eyes have been rep-
laced by open mouths which reveal
teeth. This dealt with the art critic's
'optical apparatus', a metaphor for
the shortsightedness or critical myo-
pia of his or her aesthetic perception.
'The Critic Smiles' and 'The critic
laughs' denote the 'oral apparatus', a
metaphor for the critic who 'bad
mouths' artists.

Hamilton's assemblage remained
in his studio until, in 1968, René
Block asked some artists to donate a
print to the Documenta Foundation
in Kassel. Hamilton conceived of a
laminated offset-litho print, and pho-
tographed 'The critic laughs' in the
style of promotional material for a
product. With time, the sugar
became sticky and began to crystal-
lise so Hamilton asked Hans Sohm (a
dentist and Fluxus archivist) to repro-
duce the sweet teeth in dental plastic.
It was when he was asked by René
Block to produce a multiple for his
Berlin gallery in 1971 that the idea of
making a small edition in the style of
a mass-produced consumer product
developed. It was possible to get a
headstart by purchasing the mecha-
nical part from the manufacturer.
Packaging and presentation
problems were solved by the design of

a case styled and made (indeed they
were produced by the company
which modelled prototypes for
Braun) in the manner of the box for
the Braun Sixtant electric razor. An
instruction leaflet and guarantee card
completed the analogy, although as
Hamilton acknowledges 'art usually
comes without a guarantee' (bib.
A51, p.73). The cycle of product,
packaging and promotional matter
was followed precisely.

Nine years later the BBC asked
Hamilton for a contribution to 'The
Shock of the New', a television series
written and presented by Robert
Hughes, on art since 1880. Since the
interview form held no appeal for
Hamilton he proposed to the pro-
ducer that he should make a 'TV
commercial' advertising 'The critic
laughs' (fig.24) and he wrote a
'script' for his product. The story-
board calls for a beautiful young
woman to enter a luxurious bath-
room bearing a gift for her partner
who, bemused at the sight of the
assembled teeth and electric brush,
realises that the vibrating object is
more for Her than for Him. Mean-
while the voice-over says the
following:

'For connoisseurs who have every-
thing . . . at last, a work of art to
match the style of modern living . . .
"The critic laughs" . . . a perfect mar-
riage of form and function . . . created
for you and yours by Europe's caring
craftsmen in an exclusive edition of
only sixty examples . . . "The critic
laughs" . . . Feel the thrill of owning
. . . "The critic laughs".

'Hamilton is proud to present its
new multiple . . .

'"The critic laughs" . . . by
Hamilton.'

70
Soft pink landscape

1971–2
Oil on canvas
122 × 162.5 (48 × 64)
*Hungarian National Gallery, Ludwig
Collection, Budapest*

A group of advertisements for a new
coloured line of Andrex toilet papers
became visible in the early 1960s. It
was not until 1980 that Bridget Riley
told Hamilton of her role as visualiser
for the promotion of the product
when she worked in the advertising
agency from which the campaign
emanated. The full-page photographs
showed two girls posed equivocally in
a forest glade. Hamilton described
this encounter with lyrical advertis-
ing in equally lyric terms:

'Nature is beautiful. Pink from a
morning sun filters through a tissue
of autumn leaves. Golden shafts
gleam through the perforated vault-
ing of the forest to illuminate a stage
set-up for the Sunday supplement
voyeur. Andrex discreetly presents a
new colour magazine range. A pink
as suggestively soft as last week's
blue – soft as pink flesh under an
Empire négligé. The woodland
equipped with every convenience. A
veil of soft-focus vegetation screens
the peeper from the sentinel. Poussin?
Claude? No, more like Watteau in its
magical ambiguity.' (bib. D19)

In 'Soft pink landscape' there are
paint marks which have little to do
with a likeness of anything, they exist
as paint on a surface and mean little
else. There are also sprayed marks.
While they could also be read as
meaning only themselves, they intro-
duce a confusion because they are
reminiscent of the results of out-of-
focus photography. Something
intruding into the frame, close to the
lens, will produce a blurred haze.
These effects are used in 'Soft pink' to
give an impression of concealment, as
though the viewer is watching through
a screen of vegetation.

fig.24 Still from 'The critic laughs'
television commercial, 1980

Flowers

Given Hamilton's habit of working through the traditional genres of painting it is surprising that the 'flower-piece' escaped his attentions for so long. Over a period of twenty years the main subjects had been covered: nude, interior, portrait, seascape, landscape, architecture, still-life, self-portrait. A flower-piece had become inevitable. Perhaps the reason this important genre took so long to assume its rightful place in the oeuvre was its very ubiquity and, as Hamilton said, 'Naturally there are inhibitions to overcome – flowery allure is an irrelevant anachronism in the context of cultural ideas of our period. It takes perversity and a touch of irony to make it tolerable.' (bib. D28)

As is often the case with Hamilton, a subject, once noticed, will be accorded a number of different treatments, but in such a way that the group has a single identity. The two large 'Interior' paintings (nos.29,30), the twelve 'Cosmetic studies' (nos.57–68), the two 'Soft landscapes' (nos.70,77) add up to something more than the individual works. That is even more true of the three 'Flower-pieces'. They lose some of their meaning if they are not hung together.

71
Flower-piece I

1971–4
Oil on canvas
95 × 72 (37½ × 28⅜)
The artist

All three flower-pieces were painted from three-dimensional postcards of the type laminated with a special plastic film. Hamilton made a three-dimensional print in 1974, a self-portrait titled 'Palindrome' (fig.25), and showed a great interest in the lenticular system of photography that made this possible. It is, of course, the material used for the winking eye in '$he' (no.16).

'Flower-piece I', unlike others of the series, bears evidence of its three-dimensional source. There is some duplication in the outlines, a reminiscence of the treatment in 're Nude' (no.11) and in 'Trainsition' (nos.9, 10), and for very much the same reason. This is the consequence of changing the angle of view on the postcard so that relative positions change within the subject. It is these relative changes, dependent on the distance from the focus of the camera, that create the perception of depth. One part of the composition shows no movement and that is the roll of Andrex toilet paper adopted from the concurrent 'Soft pink landscape' (no.70). This was not part of the original postcard and it demonstrates an interesting phenomenon. Sharpness of definition in the lettering as well as the firmness of its outline puts the toilet roll at the point of focus of the image.

The manner of painting is Cézannesque and so is the subject matter. The basket of fruit and the earthenware pot are not unlike Cézanne's still-life subjects. There is another connection with Cézanne in that it has been said that the peculiarity of Cézanne's perspective lies in a possible willingness to let his head move in front of the subject.

The Andrex toilet roll in 'Flower-piece I' has clear associations with 'Soft pink landscape' (no.70) and the intentions are doubtless similar. The toilet roll shows a reluctance to let the sentimentality of the genre get by without some hint of cynicism. 'Flower-piece II' pushes the references further, beyond the bounds of good taste. The introduction of excrement into the elegant arrangement of flowers and fruit appears to throw doubt on the artist's willingness to accept the genre at all, but there are art historical precedents. 'This compulsion to defile a sentimental cliché was perhaps, though subconscious initially, a conformity with a well established tradition in the flower-piece, the convention of placing, often lower right, a memento-mori: an insect, a crab, a skull – some sinister motif which suggests that life is not all prettiness and fragrance.' (bib. D28)

While he was working on the plates for an etched version of 'Flower-piece II' at the studio of Aldo Crommelynck in Paris, Sonia Orwell, a close mutual friend, saw Hamilton's motif for the first time. She took him by the arm, led him apart from the company and sternly said 'You know Richard, life's not all shit and flowers'. Hamilton found the remark, and the tone of motherly concern, hilarious but reflected that without the 'not' her opinion became profound; life was truly 'all shit and flowers'.

The critical response to Hamilton's excremental works had not been favourable, but Marcel Broodthaers, a much respected friend, was one of few to appreciate them (Gustav Metzger and Mark Boyle were

72
Flower-piece II

1973
Oil on canvas
95 × 72 (37½ × 28⅜)
The artist

fig.25 **Palindrome** 1974 Lenticular acrylic, laminated on collotype in 5 colours

others). Broodthaers was moved to write a text he titled '*Éloge du Désespoir*', which Hamilton used to accompany the publication 'Trichromatic Flower-piece progressives' (1973–4), a complete set of colour progressives for an etched version of 'Flower-piece II'. Marcel Broodthaers saw Hamilton's flower-piece as a frank acceptance of the natural cycle. 'These flowers, ... remote from seeds and seasons, do not speak the language of the heart as once was the fashion ... such beauty ... effaces the reservations we may have had about the excremental form lying low ... Like manure nourishing the colour in the blossoms (the conventions of horticulture are fully respected) it accompanies each stage of the progression and builds a definitive mass. And indeed it is a question of form and mass, obliterating direct reference to reality. It would seem that the subject is not flowers but technique.' Broodthaers, in his choice of an archaic style of language (the original was written in old-world French), is sensitive to the atavistic pictorial treatment and he recommends to us a transcendental reading of the image.

73
Flower-piece III

1973–4
Oil on canvas
95 × 72 (37½ × 28⅜)
The artist

The 'abstract' intention of the third flower-piece is indisputable. The washes of colour, apart from a few hints, have little relationship with specific floral forms. The subject is evoked with colour and its placement. What is important is the difference between two shades of green, or the balance between opaque and transparent, between a mark that looks drawn and another that is merely a stain. The formal emphasis is stressed in all three flower-pieces by the loosely floating character of the

painted marks – each brushstroke retains a calligraphic quality which would be lost if it were required to abut the hard line of the canvas edge. 'The boundaries of the worked area in the flower-piece paintings, like those of the print, are loose because a severe conjunction of image and edge seemed alien to the freedom of the painted mark.' (bib. D28)

74
Sign

1975
Vitreous enamel on steel
34.7 × 80 (13¾ × 31½)
Anthony d'Offay Gallery

Trademarks appear with regularity in individual works by Hamilton. 'Still-life' (no.32), 'Toaster' (no.43), 'Flower-piece I' (no.71) all incorporate some label and the logos are always the name of a manufacturer or company rather than a monogram or an abstract design – Braun, Andrex, Ricard – as though there might be some meaning to be gained from the word if it could only be decoded. At times Hamilton has appropriated a Braun product ('The critic laughs', no.69) and branded it with his own name.

The Ricard trademark (designed by Paul Ricard, who heads the company producing one of the two best selling anis-flavoured drinks in the South of France) is immensely bold and self-assured; it produced in Hamilton an explosion of self-advertisement. In 'Still-life' there is a change of two characters, Braun becomes Brown. There is one small modification to Paul Ricard's image; Ricard has only an h inserted to make Richard. The vitreous enamel signs were manufactured in London for a brief exhibition (a weekend only) in a small gallery in Cadaqués, Spain. The gallery was 'hung' with variant groupings of the single 'Sign', singles, pairs, triplets and so on. Ricard provided free pastis and tapas in the gallery for the whole weekend and a good time was had by all.

The preferred presentation in exhibitions is to show a group of three 'Signs', juxtaposed one above the other, together with a 'Carafe' (no.78) and an 'Ashtray' (no.79).

75
Sunset

1975
Oil on canvas
61 × 81 (24 × 32)
The artist, courtesy of the Anthony d'Offay Gallery

There were four sub-groupings within the fifty-one entries in the catalogue for Hamilton's scatological exhibition *Paintings Pastels Prints* held at the Serpentine Gallery, London, in 1975; soft landscapes based on Andrex advertisements, prints and drawings inspired by postcards from Miers (the French spa famed for the laxative properties of its waters), flowers, and sunsets. Nine pastels, 'Sunset (a–i)' and one 'Sunrise', all derived from postcards of the typical romantic image of the setting sun – skies shot with gorgeous colour from orange to violet, all with a giant turd in the foreground despoiling the sentiment.

While the exhibition had a kitsch aspect, Hamilton has referred to some less frivolous implications. Having used a postcard of Cadaqués for the one sunrise (Cadaqués faces east), with a turd covering the town's glory, its church, he encountered a famous description by Jung, in his *Memories, Dreams, Reflections*. Jung describes a reverie which he felt to be of great personal significance. He says 'I saw before me the cathedral, the blue sky. God sits on his throne, high above the world – and from under the throne an enormous turd falls upon the sparkling new roof, shatters it, and breaks the walls of the cathedral asunder.'

Two oil paintings of sunsets, of which this is one, were under way at the time of the Serpentine exhibition. One was completed, the other, with uninvited additions by Dieter Roth, abandoned.

76
Langan's

1976
Oil on photograph on photo-sensit-
ised fabric
92 × 92 (36¼ × 36¼)
Private collection

Hamilton's painting of the interior of
a restaurant is a key work. It reopens
some of the ideas of his early interest
in pictures of pictures in a room (see
'Just what is it . . . ?', no.13 and 'Inter-
ior I', no.29), to which he would
return in later ventures into the
genre.

Peter Langan asked artist friends to
produce paintings for a new brasserie
he planned to establish on the site of
the *Coq d'Or*, an old-style French res-
taurant in Stratton Street. The room
was surrounded by panels lined with
a fabric printed, like the curtains,
with a hunting scene in a rusty pink
colour. Each panel was to be allo-
cated to a different artist. Hamilton
took his camera to the gutted restaur-
ant and photographed the room,
especially the corner which included
the wall due to receive his work. He
wanted his panel to be left exactly as
it was, retaining the original fabric
and its scalloped frame, the image of
which entered his commissioned
painting when he had his photo-
graph of the interior enlarged onto
photo-sensitised fabric.

After the renovation Hamilton
returned to what had been trans-
formed into Langan's Brasserie, set
up his camera in exactly the same
position as before and photographed,
this time in colour, the room that
now included tables laid with the
new-style place settings. A table, laid
ready for a meal, was painted on the
black and white canvas and the
painting was then hung on the panel
that appears in the picture itself. Sit-
ting at the table the diner was in
same perspective relationship to the
space as that represented in the
painting now forming part of his own
visual environment. As well as the
identifiable scalloped frame were
other relics; the 'Exit' sign and door

frame echoed in the painting.

Shortly after the opening there
were complaints from Peter Langan's
partners that the panel, with its
retained *Coq d'Or* printed cotton, did
not match the other panels, and it
was painted cream like the rest of the
place. Hamilton was unhappy that
his concept had been vandalised so
he removed his painting, with the sad
consequence that the work was disso-
ciated from its context.

Pictures of rooms with pictures of
rooms in them hold a fascination for
Hamilton. They offer 'the possibility
of sub-encounters, two-dimensional
simulations of interiors within the
three-dimensional envelope of an
actual interior' (bib. A56). That the
picture should portray itself in its
own setting would be an added
attraction. The idea of a painting spe-
cifically sited to include its environ-
ment as part of the subject was later
revived (see nos.85 and 91).

77
Soft blue landscape

1976–80
Oil on canvas
122 × 162.5 (48 × 64)
Private Collection

The 'Soft blue' and 'Soft pink' (no.70)
landscape paintings were conceived
together (indeed there is a 'Soft blue'
drawing dated 1971), yet there is a
gap of four years between the com-
pletion of the 'Soft pink' painting and
the beginning of work on the 'Soft
blue'. They are clearly a pair and the
relationship is all the more evident
when the two pictures are seen
together. They share their horizon,
the figures in both paintings occupy
an identical perspective space, the toi-
let roll is in precisely the same
position in both pictures, there is a
similar intention in the handling of
paint and, despite their contrasting
titles, the difference in colour is one of
emphasis rather than of total
disparity.

There is, however, a subtle but
important dissimilarity between the
two paintings; it centres on the para-
dox that lies at the heart of all Hamil-

ton's work, the polarity between rep-
resentation and abstraction. Since his
paintings of the 1950s he had shown
a strong awareness of a fundamental
incongruity at the heart of the pictor-
ial arts. Among the skills developed in
Western art has been the ability to
create, through the use of coloured
powders mixed with a binding agent,
a semblance of what the eye sees. By
the twentieth century the mark itself
was taking precedence over what it
signifies.

While 'Soft pink landscape' has
some marks little concerned with
appearance there are many which
stand for 'seen out-of-focus through a
lens'. 'Soft blue' carries a greater con-
viction. It takes a programme and
carries it through to its conse-
quences, as does 're Nude' (no.11).
There is a centre of focus which is
representational, in an almost photo-
realist sense, but as we move further
from the point of focus so do the
marks become increasingly autono-
mous. There is a slow progression
towards abstraction, but it is intro-
duced in such a way that there is no
boundary. There is an indefinable
region in which it is no longer pos-
sible to say 'this brushstroke means
foliage and this gestural mark means
itself'.

78
Carafe

1978
Vitreous enamel on glass
9 × 20 × 6 (3½ × 8 × 2⅜)
Anthony d'Offay Gallery

The opportunity arose to make an edition of the famous Ricard Art Deco water bottle. Paul Ricard gave permission for the 'Carafes' to be made by the same manufacturer who produced them for Ricard with Richard fired on instead.

'Carafe' is a Duchampian readymade in the same sense as Gilbert and George's multiple 'Reclining Drunk', 1973 (an ashtray made from a collapsed gin bottle) or Marcel Broodthaers's, 'The Manuscript', 1974 (a white Bordeaux wine bottle with the words 'The Manuscript' fired onto the glass). Unlike Duchamp's readymades, always nominated for their anonymity and for their lack of appeal as designed objects, Ricard's water bottle is a rightly celebrated form, almost a cult object; Hamilton's perverse intention in appropriating the ubiquitous icon is to make his artwork anonymous: he sees as the ideal placement for his carafe a bar in the South of France, where the change in the logo goes unnoticed.

79
Ashtray

1979
Vitreous enamel on opaque glass
3.4 × 15.5 × 13.5 (1⅜ × 6⅛ × 5⅜)
Anthony d'Offay Gallery

The Richard ashtray was manufactured to complete the set of artworks based on the promotional products made in enormous numbers for the Ricard company for use in cafés (see nos.74,78).

80
Lux 50 – functioning prototype

1979
Aluminium support, cellulose and anodised aluminium
100 × 100 (39⅜ × 39⅜)
Private Collection

'Lux 50' is a response to a commission from Lux Corporation, Osaka, to design a work of art based on their hi-fi equipment. The project, begun in 1973, was to produce a high quality amplifier, in a limited edition, for release in 1975, the date of the fiftieth anniversary of the founding of their company. It was not as unlikely an invitation as it might seem, for Hamilton worked as a draughtsman in the EMI (Electrical and Musical Industries) factory from 1942 to 1945, where he developed an interest in acoustical equipment; he had formed friendships with audio research engineers and collaborated on the design of homemade pick-ups and speakers.

Hamilton had qualms about accepting the proposal because his interests as a painter lay in illusion and paradox, rather than in three-dimensional objects. The resolution was to suggest an amplifier thin enough to be hung on a wall as a picture of itself – a flat portrait of the functioning object represented in the manner of a table-top still-life. The general specification was provided by Hamilton and he designed a control panel to satisfy his own domestic needs for hi-fi. What might be seen as a disadvantage to wall-mounted equipment was made a virtue by putting an input/output panel at the front. A full-size mock-up was painted in 1976 and a functioning prototype was completed in 1979.

There is a slow but persistent move towards the Lux painting through a number of works over more than a decade. 'Still-life' (no.32) is a flat image of a domestic appliance. 'Toaster' (no.43) has a constructed character; it is even fabricated with the same materials as those used to make the object depicted. It portrays

an appliance in shallow relief on a background of soft, out-of-focus colour so that there is a confusion between the photographic nature of its presentation and the urge the depicted object has to assume a reality. 'The critic laughs' (no.69) moves into full dimensionality; it works, but its activity is futile. 'Lux 50' straddles the boundaries between product design and fine art: it is 'a two-dimensional representation of a piece of equipment which also performs the functions expected of the object portrayed' (bib. D45). Hamilton's computer (no.88) crosses the border into full three-dimensional functionality but it looks surprisingly like minimal sculpture.

81
Study for 'The citizen'

1982
Acrylic underpainting and oil on canvas
87.7 × 67.7 (34½ × 26¼)
Cultural Foundation against Apartheid, Paris

The immediate source for this study and for the larger painting which it preceded was images which Hamilton saw on television in England. These were filmed inside the British government's high-security prison at Long Kesh, near Belfast. The prison was also known as the Maze and as the H Blocks. Hamilton's attention was caught first by a Granada Television 'World in Action' programme on Long Kesh, but the main source of the imagery for his painting came from a BBC film on the same subject shown some weeks later.

The conflict in Northern Ireland began to intensify in terms of violence in 1969. After a number of years, IRA prisoners in the Maze demanded to be classified as political rather than criminal offenders, and thus to be accorded a number of rights and living conditions which were being denied them. The British government refusing to grant political status, IRA

fig.26 The citizen installation, Fruitmarket Gallery, Edinburgh 1988

prisoners escalated their protests. Refusing to 'slop out', to wear prison clothes, to cut their hair or to obey any prison regulations, the prisoners lived in their own squalor, wearing only the blankets they were provided as bedding. After five years the 'no wash' protest was deemed a failure so a further tactic was introduced, the hunger strike. One by one, daily, Republican prisoners were refusing to eat and were finally dying, to achieve the objectives of the long protest. In the television film which so greatly struck Hamilton, cameras filmed Republican inmates 'on the blanket', with the result that the British public were able to witness the extraordinary sight of men who lived in the confined space of a prison cell surrounded by walls daubed with their own excrement.

Hamilton saw the image of the blanket man as a public relations contrivance of enormous efficacy. It had the moral conviction of a religious icon and the persuasiveness of an advertising man's dream soap commercial – yet it was a present reality; he decided to make a life-size figure painting. It was a genre not so far attempted in his output, though it touched upon and deepened the significance of earlier themes. He obtained some pieces of the 16mm film shown on television and printed Cibachrome enlargements from selected frames.

Having prepared a canvas, Hamilton decided to colour his acrylic gesso priming with a blue/green/grey tint and to make a quick underpainting in acrylic. This was a method unfamiliar to him, so he tried out the technique on a full-size detail – the head and shoulders of the figure.

82

The citizen

1982–3
Oil on canvas
2 canvases, each 200 × 100
(78¾ × 39⅜)
Tate Gallery. Purchased 1985

Two collage studies established the overall composition. Because the size of the prison cell prevented the 16mm camera from seeing more than a partial view it was necessary to assemble a complete figure from different frames. Hamilton made his first study by fitting together three homemade Cibachrome prints, two of which produced the top and bottom of the figure. The third print was mounted beside the other pair without any attempt at integration. For the second study, prints were sized to provide a better relationship between the parts of the figure. Oil paint was used on both collages to fill up blank areas and to improve the joins in the photographs.

The decision to make a diptych, with each canvas 2 metres × 1 metre, eased the problems of handling in the studio and gave other advantages. In continuance of Hamilton's interest in figuration/abstraction (see no.77) the subject provided an opportunity to present this interdependence in stark conjunction. If the left-hand canvas were to be separated from its neighbour it would be taken as abstract in the milieu of modern art; the right-hand panel is acceptable as an example of mainstream figurative painting.

Hamilton describes the scene as 'a strange image of human dignity in the midst of self-created squalor ... endowed with a mythic power most often associated with art.' It was 'shocking less for its scatological content than for its potency' (bib. A53). It is the first his works in which a religious quality is apparent and unmistakable, however equivocal on Hamilton's part it may be.

The painting's title bears direct reference to the beginning of the present 'troubles' in Northern Ireland, the Civil Rights marches of the late 1960s and early 1970s. The title 'The citizen' is taken from the 'Cyclops' episode of *Ulysses*, in which Bloom, Joyce's hero, comes into conflict with a pugnacious Fenian bar-fly known to all as 'citizen' (Hamilton follows Joyce's invariable use of a lower case 'c'). The citizen is associated by Joyce with an heroic Irish chieftain, Finn MacCool, as well as with the giant Polyphemus of Homer's *Odyssey*. Hamilton recalls that when Rita Donagh traced the name of the particular Maze detainee from his source photograph she was informed 'the young man's name is Hugh Rooney. He's just a little fellow'.

'The citizen' was first shown at the Guggenheim Museum in New York in 1983 and then, in the same year, at the Orchard Gallery, Derry, Northern Ireland, with Rita Donagh's paintings about the H blocks at Long Kesh prison, in an exhibition titled *A Cellular Maze*. The museum's concern about showing the painting in New York was overcome, though the subject was thought to be a sensitive one soon after a controversial St Patrick's Day parade which had been led by an IRA spokesman. The gallery in Derry had no qualms about the painting, in spite of some worried questions from local government officials; having seen the painting they were less perturbed. On the other hand, the artist was asked by a young woman 'why have you made him look so evil?'. In fact, the painting has often been mistakenly thought, particularly by Americans, to be a portrait of Charles Manson. There were four installations in the 1988 Fruitmarket Gallery exhibition in Edinburgh, among them a 'cell' made to house the citizen painting (fig.26). Hamilton decorated the walls in imitation of those in the the protesters' cells at Long Kesh and put a sponge-rubber mattress and a dirty pillow in a corner to complete the furnishing.

83

Treatment room

1983–4
Installation
275 × 550 × 550 (108 × 216 × 216)
Arts Council Collection. The South Bank Centre, London

In 1984 Hamilton was invited by Michael Regan to take part in a show on the theme of rooms. The Arts Council proposal, *Four Rooms*, was that Anthony Caro, Marc Chaimowicz, Howard Hodgkin and Hamilton should each be free to create any environment they wished for a touring exhibition.

Hamilton sees 'exhibition' as a form in its own right. 'It demands mobile involvement on the part of the spectator to absorb whatever idea or information is being presented. The static experiencing of books, television, or movies from which a stream of sequenced material is directed at a captive reader of word or image is quite different from the kinetic interaction of an audience with a contrived space' (bib. A56). 'Treatment room', like all his exhibition projects, is planned on the expectation that its audience will circulate within the space; where possible there are openings on opposite sides to allow passage through the room. He took the opportunity in *Four Rooms* to deal with a category of interior he had not considered before, that of the public institution: 'a space ... inspired by the bleak, disinterested, seedily clinical style of the establishment institution ... a space as impersonal (yet loaded), or as neutral (yet disquieting) as a dentist's waiting room, a prison cell, a DHSS Labour Exchange or anywhere in an NHS hospital.' (bib. A56)

The main source of inspiration for 'Treatment room' was Hamilton's experience of visiting hospitals for routine diagnosis on several occasions. In particular, the x-ray theatres impressed him with their pronounced display of power; thick cables, protective screens, the circumstance of an examination so intense that there was nothing left to hide, even the bones being laid bare. To simulate the feeling of being scrutinised Hamilton assembled a TV monitor over a table resembling a mortuary slab. It was possible to put a continuously running video image on the screen, so he chose a recording of Mrs Thatcher delivering the final Conservative Party election broadcast in the General Election of 1983.

84
Mother and child
1984–5
Oil on canvas
150 × 150 (59½ × 59½)
Mr and Mrs Keith L. Sachs

While working in Milan on the first stage of 'Fashion-plate' in 1969, Hamilton was pressed, with typically Italian enthusiasm, by a young lithographic printer to go to his flat for a cup of coffee. They sat awkwardly, unable to communicate because neither spoke the other's language.

Then the young Italian had an idea. He grasped his wallet and pulled out the quintessential photograph of his son by an indulgent father; the camera had focused on a smiling infant supported by his mother, whose head is chopped off by the frame. Hamilton, with genuine interest, said that the photograph was beautiful and the father immediately insisted that he should keep it.

The photograph remained in Hamilton's studio for fifteen years, fading a little and getting dusty, until it began to assume its place among the genres as a 'Mother and child'. The painting's proximity in time to 'The citizen' makes it possible to see that the themes of abstraction and figuration are again balanced. Instead of the blatant juxtaposition of two canvases, one abstract the other figurative, or the slow progression to abstraction outwards from a point of focus, the figurative element is framed by an elaboration of the background so that, in so far as the painterly character is concerned, background takes precedence.

85
Lobby
1985–7
Oil on canvas
175 × 250 (69 × 98½) within an installation 305 × 550 × 550 (120 × 216 × 216)
The artist

Postcards had often been the source of Hamilton's subjects. Sometimes they were bought, or picked up from hotel reception desks, but the origin of 'Lobby' came through the mail from an artist friend, Dorothy Iannone, staying briefly at the Europa Hotel, Berlin. The card (fig.27) shows a generous foyer with a glimpse of wide stairs leading to the first floor. There are floor-to-ceiling mirrors on some walls and a free-standing, mirror-faced, rectangular column in the middle of the room which causes the patterned carpet on which it stands to run mysteriously unhindered throughout the structure. To add to the confusion, parts of the ceiling are reflected by the column.

On his next visit to Berlin, Hamilton went to see the Europa Hotel for himself, 'armed with a camera – supposing the space to be a photographer's paradise – a potential mine of source material for paintings. It was a disappointment to find a small hotel with a lobby the size of a domestic living room. There was only one position in which a camera could make an interesting shot and it needed a much wider angle than my 35mm lens. The postcard photographer had found just the spot and s/he possessed the lens to perform the magic.' (bib. D46)

In 1973 a pencil drawing was made, using the complexities of the Europa Hotel lobby as a perspective exercise; watercolour was added and then, a year later, a piece of a Spanish postcard showing a young couple was pasted on. Nearly ten years went by before Hamilton used the watercolour as the basis for a screenprint. A further year passed before an ambitious painting of the subject was begun. It was the largest canvas he had attempted and its scale presented problems. The canvas had to be fixed to a wall of his studio so that the vanishing points of the perspective could be accurately located far beyond the edge of the painting – the studio was just large enough to accommodate the canvas and the threads attached to nails marking the distant vanishing points.

When 'Lobby' was approaching completion after two years of concentrated work Mark Francis approached Hamilton to discuss the possibility of making an exhibition at the Fruitmarket Gallery in Edinburgh. They decided to put together a show of installations, each of them related to a type of institution. 'Treatment room' (hospital) existed, the idea of making a special presentation of the 'Lobby' (hotel) painting was already in Hamilton's mind, and a cell-like setting for 'The citizen' (prison) (no.82) was also possible.

Ideally 'Lobby' should be installed (fig.28) in an area of the same dimensions as 'Treatment room' (no.83). The floor is covered, wall to wall, with a material screenprinted to simulate the polka-dot pattern of yellow spots on a green ground to be seen in the painting. A mirror-faced column stands near the middle of the room, a few treads of a staircase lead directly into the wall, and what purports to be the same staircase returns out of the wall and into the ceiling. 'Lobby' is hung a little to the left of the centre of the wall opposite the entrance. The watercolour study for the painting and the collotype/screenprint are hung to the right of

fig.27 Source postcard for 'Lobby'

fig.28 **Lobby** installation, Fruitmarket Gallery, Edinburgh 1988

the entrance so that the reflected paintings to be seen in the large canvas are echoed by reflections of the small versions of 'Lobby' in the real mirror. Visitors should enter the space to experience physically the uncanny perspective which originally attracted Hamilton to the postcard.

The flowers which form a central feature of the painting proved a problem because there was too little information in the postcard and their organic nature, unlike the rest of the picture, gave no help in systematic extrapolation. Painting flowers from imagination was too taxing. It happened that some special irises, bred by Cedric Morris, had been given to Rita Donagh by Nancy Morris, Cedric's sister, and they were flowering in the Hamilton garden. Some cut blooms and many photographs provided the necessary inspiration. The chrysanthemums (unseasonable companions for irises) are a hangover from earlier attempts at the bouquet, an anachronism which Hamilton enjoys.

The sentimental couple in the watercolour and print disappeared from the painting as Hamilton began to find the supernatural mood of the painting diminished by the human presence. He was 'reminded of *Huis Clos*, Sartre's existentialist play, which is staged in a single set, a public room in a hotel. It is a metaphor for purgatory, the limbo in which we await transit to another condition' (bib. D46, p.47). A person can be seen, but even this marginal hint of habitation is an illusion for he is only a reflection in a mirrored wall of a figure in a dining room located behind the reception desk.

86
Hotel Europa
1986–91
Oil on canvas
100 × 100 (39⅜ × 39⅜)
The artist, courtesy of Anthony d'Offay Gallery

After working on 'Lobby' (no.85) for some months, Hamilton became doubtful about the figures which had been part of his subject from 1974. He decided to make a trial canvas of the part containing a young couple by a red sofa. Before the painted study was complete he returned to 'Lobby' with the decision taken to remove the figures. Not until the larger work was finished did he return to the detail.

87
The subject
1988–90
Oil on canvas
2 canvases, each 200 × 100
(78¾ × 39⅜)
The artist

Northern Ireland is likely to be perceived as a region of dichotomy. Polarities abound – between Catholic and Protestant, republican and loyalist, outsider and insider, have and have not, green and orange. It would not be possible to be gripped by the image of the blanketman seen in 'The citizen' (no.82) without giving some consideration to his antonym. When Hamilton was asked to participate in a group of short television programmes in which artists would use the Quantel Paintbox, the most advanced image-processing computer available, he already had a project in mind, a companion piece to his 'citizen'. His selected material finally included a black and white photograph, a 35mm colour transparency, a still from a video tape he had made from televised events in Northern Ireland and a transparency of his 'citizen' painting. 'The citizen' had been constructed from several parts so the plan was to 'cut and paste' an electronically generated subject. The film, made by Griffin Film Productions for BBC TV, was broadcast in 1987 as part of a series of six programmes called 'Painting with Light'.

The scale and composition of both 'citizen' and 'subject' had to be equi-

balanced if they were to be seen as a pair, or at least two sides of the same coin. Many more components were used for 'The subject' than were used for 'The citizen'. The computer Paintbox allows a much greater fluency in manipulating visual material but the task of creating a match for the less complex 'citizen' was more demanding. One passage from 'The citizen' was transposed into 'The subject'; it is the top right-hand corner of each of the paintings. What is the metal-grilled window of the republican's cell becomes a window on a building seen behind the parading Orangeman. The abstract/figurative dichotomy is common to both paintings. The left-hand, 'abstract' panel of the 'The subject' is from the video tape which shows an 'incident' filmed at night by infra red photography, in which an armoured vehicle is approaching the camera down a street littered with bomb damage. The implication is that the Orangeman, too, is surrounded by ordure.

Quantel's TV Paintbox is far exceeded in power and resolution by another machine, the Graphic Paintbox, designed for the print industry. Hamilton repeated the electronic collaging procedures of the TV Paintbox on the Graphic Paintbox to create a high-resolution image which he went on to use for a dye-transfer print on which his painting 'The subject' is based: this required working with Martin Holbrook, the artist member of the Quantel team which had developed the Paintbox.

Along with the bombings, shootings, and other atrocities defiantly claimed by the IRA, its image of imprisonment is part of a public relations programme with the avowed intention of keeping the subject of Ireland's partition in the news. The fact of separation is also preserved in civic consciousness by the opposing side in its display of symbols of the Orange Order. This secret society, formed in 1795, took its name from William of Orange, who invaded England from Holland with the intention of overthrowing James II. He was then invited to become King William III of England in 1689, in part because he agreed to uphold the established Protestant religion. William crossed to Ireland in pursuit of James, who had landed there as part of his plan to regain the English throne, and whose aim, if restored, would have been to re-establish Catholicism in England. Dutch King Billy was regarded thereafter as a hero by many Irish Protestants, for securing the hegemony of their religion.

Hamilton wrote in 1991 that 'The Orangeman in full ceremonial rig is scarcely less extreme than is the blanket man. The present-day uniform of a member of the Orange Lodge of Freemasons in Belfast consists of a black suit, bowler hat, and well-polished shoes; an orange sash adorned with insignia hangs on his chest and there are large, matching, seventeenth-century-style cuffs on his white kid gloves. Every Orangeman carries a black umbrella on parade except those privileged to possess a 'King Billy' sword which is always held unsheathed and erect. During the marching season the streets of Ulster's towns resound to pipes and drums and the crunch of leather on asphalt that assert allegiance to British rule.

'Apparently eccentric, the Orange garb is well chosen. The hard bowler hat is not unlike a helmet and an umbrella is clearly a substitute for the sword intended to clear Catholicism from Ireland. From beneath the orange frippery emerges a twenties-vintage City of London business man (late of the Brigade of Guards) – the conservative image to which Northern Irish politicians still aspire.' (bib. A69)

Though a pair, it was not Hamilton's intention, or expectation, that the two Northern Irish paintings should be kept together. Since the completion of 'The subject' they have always been shown together. Sometimes side by side. Orangeman on the right, apparently moving towards each other; on one occasion transposed so they appeared to be moving apart; on another they confronted each other across a large gallery. They should always be hung low on the wall, a foot or so above the floor, as though another step would take the citizen out into the viewer's space. In common with 'I'm dreaming of a white Christmas' (no.46), there is a strong sense of the subject moving forward out of the frame by which he is contained.

The title first given to no.87 was 'The Apprentice Boy'. This was changed to 'The Orangeman' when Hamilton became aware that the name 'Apprentice Boy' is specific to members of the Londonderry lodge of the Orange Order – differentiated even to the extent of using a purple rather than an orange sash. In spite of the fact that the painting had been exhibited and catalogued with the title 'The Orangeman' Hamilton's realisation that the opposite of a citizen, in the republican sense, is a subject, one who accepts the dominion of a monarch, begged a further change of title, which he made in 1992.

88
Diab DS-101 computer
1985–9
Mixed media
$70 \times 50 \times 50$ ($27\frac{1}{2} \times 19\frac{3}{4} \times 19\frac{3}{4}$)
Diab Data AB

The Hochschule für Gestaltung, Ulm, the most prestigious industrial design school in post-war Europe, conjectured in its later years that the increasing engagement of industrial designers in consumer product design introduced commercial obligations which would lead to a deviation from the highest standards. A correct moral stance could be maintained only if the designer directed his talent at the design of tools which produced goods rather than at the goods themselves. Hamilton had the opportunity in 1983 to be involved in just such a design project with an invitation from OHIO Scientific (owned by Isotron, a Swedish company) to collaborate on the design of a minicomputer to which he gave an appropriately digital name, '01–110'.

After receiving a list of components, with the overall dimensions of each item, a collection of Polaroid photographs and some of the actual parts, Hamilton came up with a proposal to house the elements in three boxes, divided into the three groups into which they naturally fall:
1. Drive unit: Winchester, floppy disc drive, back up streamer.
2. Central processing unit: card cage, operators I/O panels, system I/O panel.
3. Power supply unit: rectifiers, transformers, etc.

The units would stack, on 1 cm spacers, so that the gaps between the boxes would provide ventilation. The size and proportion of the boxes were carefully planned to be integrated with office furniture. The boxes when stacked make up a block $72 \times 50 \times 50$ cm, the international standards for desk width and height. Isotron went into liquidation before the project was fully realised but a mock-up using a Diab board was available to be shown in London 1986, Stockholm 1987, Edinburgh and Oxford 1988.

In 1986 Diab Data AB, who had

taken over Isotron, decided to make a limited production of Hamilton's concept but employing circuit boards used in other models of their range. This revival of interest was largely due to the enthusiasm for the project shown by Ingvar Larsson, Diab's research director. Work began seriously on the design of the internal engineering of the machine and the utmost precision was necessary to pack the hardware into the small space available, a procedure which would have been impossible without the Computer Aided Design system used by Diab's consultant engineer, Bertil Lohman. The Diab computer was finally brought to completion and exhibited in the Moderna Museet, Stockholm in 1989, by which time the original specifications for power and performance were greatly increased, the design had been refined and elegantly engineered but the proportions of the boxes remained exactly as originally proposed. One reason for Diab's interest in carrying the idea through to completion was that it seemed to fit a gap in their range of products. They had two models, one a large cabinet of rack units and the other a small 'tower' computer designed to go under a desk: all run the UNIX operating system. Hamilton's DS-101 was functionally the equal of the cabinet three times its size; it can serve up to forty users and runs at 25 mips (million instructions per second).

Placed in an art exhibition it is difficult at first to see how the computer fits into the context of Hamilton's work as a painter. When it was exhibited in Stockholm he took the opportunity to photograph the computer in the beautiful installation by Ulf Linde devoted to Marcel Duchamp. The act of photographing a computer designed by an artist beside a urinal chosen by an artist and titled 'Fountain' calls into question the work's status. Duchamp himself suggested that a painting is an assisted readymade 'Since the tubes of paint used by the artist are manufactured and ready made products we must conclude that all the paintings in the world are 'readymades aided' and also works of assemblage.' (Michel Sanouillet and Elmer Peterson (eds.), *The Essential Writings of Marcel Duchamp: Marchand du Sel – Salt Seller*, London 1975, p.142) Hamilton's computer is a work of art in that he does not distinguish between it and his other works and it has been exhibited along with his paintings since it was first produced; its form even has some relationship with Minimal art (Donald Judd's stacked boxes are not dissimilar). Hamilton's computer is different from most other works of art in that it also functions as something other than a work of art. When Duchamp nominated a typewriter cover or a bottle rack as a work of art he did so by depriving it of its separate functionality. Would Duchamp's typewriter cover still be a work of art if it was used to cover a typewriter – even in a museum?

Hamilton has always insisted that his computer should be operative when it is exhibited. In the first showing in 1986 the computer was programmed to enable visitors to relate to it interactively. By choosing from a menu of catalogue listings and texts about the exhibition, they could read on a monitor, or printout, any text or list. Since the 1987 exhibition in Stockholm a graphics board and a colour graphics terminal (not designed by Hamilton) have replaced the simple VDU and keyboard. A sequence of coloured pictures and information relating to Hamilton's art is held in digital form in the computer and repeats continuously during the course of the exhibition.

image on a cathode ray tube and a 'high definition' monitor can provide very good resolution. It can be output to a scanner to make a transparency as large as 10 × 8 inches, but at that size resolution would be unsatisfactory unless the very powerful Graphics computer had been used initially.

An unexpected bonus from the BBC 'Painting with Light' programme of the Orangeman was that, due to the unusual circumstances, the whole of the process of creating the image on the Paintbox had been video recorded so Hamilton was able to review the intermediary stages. Some of these had a crude energy that he thought worth investigating. A transparency was made from a frame of the video editing tape (this accounts for the frame numbers). This was then used to make a Cibachrome print for mounting on canvas. Broad sweeps of enamel paint added to a drama which is evoked by the strangeness of a casually assembled image compounded from fragments of photographs, filtered by coarse TV scanning, to which a further intermediary stage of electronic masking has been applied.

of the auditorium with a packed audience seen from the stage. The cards came in a wide variety of shapes and sizes with many small differences of colour. Hamilton began to build a large collection of variations. The image coincided with a number of his current interests. There was a large massing of humanity, as in 'Bathers' (nos.44–5), 'People' (no.34), 'Trafalgar Square' (no.36); there was the phenomenon of a straightforward colour photograph that was not what it appeared to be; and the image had a humorous relationship with another architectural motif, the Guggenheim Museum – was it the interior, the negative, of the Wright building?

The making of the original black and white photograph was itself a feat of administrative and technical skill. It is clearly not a normal audience; every box is full, every square metre of space except the central aisle is crammed. The cream of Milan is there in full evening dress; it is a unique social document. To evenly illuminate a theatre of this size with sufficient power to produce identifiable portraits of many hundreds of individuals is a remarkable technical feat. Then, the transformation of this into a multiplicity of hand-coloured representation was a perfect example of Hamilton's thesis of the anonymous artist surreptitiously dabbling onto the 'truth' of the lens. Having had the good fortune to find a postcard printed photographically on emulsion rather than halftone reproduction, Hamilton engaged in the same procedures, first in his small etching/screenprint and then, twenty years later, with a painting on a black and white print on sensitised cloth.

89
Countdown
1989
Humbrol enamel on Cibachrome on canvas
100 × 100 (39⅜ × 39⅜)
Hirshhorn Museum and Sculpture Garden, Smithsonian Institution. Holenia Purchase Fund 1991

Working on the Quantel Paintbox (see no.87) was an exciting experience but it posed a large question for Hamilton which he termed 'the hard copy problem'. The computer is incredibly well able to process images and it can store these images in digital form with great efficiency. Sooner or later the image must be given a form that can be perceived with human eyes and it is the output from the computer that presents difficulties for an artist. It is possible to see the

90
La Scala Milano
1989
Oil on photograph on canvas
100 × 144 (39⅜ × 56¼)
Private Collection

Many of Hamilton's prints are studies for paintings; a print more often contributes to a painting than vice versa. There are cases of a print emerging as a review of a subject already executed as a painting. 'La Scala Milano' is a rarity in being a painting based on a print: the print itself was a rarity in being the sole treatment of its subject.

The etching was made in Milan in 1968, while working on an etched stage in the development of 'Swingeing London' (no.54). It was the outcome of seeing an extraordinary proliferation of postcards of the interior of the Scala opera house. Most of them were on the same theme, a view

91
Northend I

1990
Oil on Cibachrome on canvas
100 × 109.5 (39⅜ × 43)
*The artist, courtesy of the Anthony
d'Offay Gallery*

Rita Donagh, Hamilton's wife, while
accepting the necessity, regretted the
wrenching of the Langan picture
(no.76) from its intended site; she
always hoped there would be an
opportunity to repeat the idea of a
painting which depicted the location
in which it was itself intended to
hang. A 35mm transparency existed
from a visit in 1975 to the house
which was to become their home,
Northend Farm. It was a photograph
taken from outside through what had
been a window, looking across a
derelict space to Rita standing in the
second of two doorways which
opened onto a room bathed in light.
As is often the case in Hamilton's
paintings there is a reminiscence of
some classical motif – in this case it is
the figure silhouetted in a doorway in
Velásquez's 'Las Meninas'; though a
background feature in the Velásquez
painting, the image has been dis-
cussed at length by art historians.
There are also overtones of Vermeer,
not only in the colour and the illumi-
nation of the figure, but in the way
the paint is handled to integrate the
painted area into the overall grainy,
photographic quality; the kind of
demands that Vermeer was the
among first to experience when he
used the camera obscura to project
his subject onto the canvas.

The Quantel Paintbox was again
brought into service to square-up the
source photograph; the diagonal
angle of view into the room intro-
duced convergences and warps
which could be forced back into a
clean parallel perspective with elec-
tronic manipulation; in particular,
the door frames were extended and
realigned. While the flaws, dubious
colour quality and camera shake,
were welcomed as an abstract enhan-
cement of the enlarged Cibachrome
print, the door opening, the figure
and the view into the other room
were painted in a pointillist manner
to match the grain of the enlarged
emulsion.

Self-portraits

Since 1968 Hamilton has been engaged in an ongoing project of Polaroid portraits. Three
volumes have been published of the intended four (bib. A36,A45,A55) Each volume contains
thirty-two Polaroid photographs of Hamilton by artist friends and acquaintances.

The first two published volumes had been issued in specially bound limited editions containing
a unique self-portrait Polaroid frontispiece. For the third volume Hamilton decided in 1980 to
unify the individual unique self-portrait photographs by setting up an area in his studio with
flash lights and a sheet of glass with a few marks applied in oil colour, which remained almost
constant. The painted glass was placed between the artist and the camera in such a way that he
could operate the shutter with a foot-operated bulb. Changes of lighting, distance of the glass
from the lens and focus of the camera would create quite dramatic differences of scale, colour
and sharpness of the standard paint marks. Only a few Polaroids were made on any day and only
the best shots were retained; about one in three succeeded. Thick acrylic-colour was applied dir-
ectly to some of the Polaroids afterwards.

The limited edition was not completed and only about twenty Polaroids were made. In 1989
Hamilton used some of the Polaroids to make a group of twelve self-portraits by having the
Polaroids scanned for the Quantel Paintbox. Polaroid photographs often have flaws at the edges
and spots in the middle; they can be very easily retouched on the Paintbox to prepare the
pictures for enlargement. It is also possible to apply additional colour anywhere at this stage.
When the electronic work was completed the portraits were put to a scanner and 10 × 8 inch
transparencies were produced, which were used to make Cibachrome enlargements bonded to
canvas. An additional painting procedure was then undertaken with oil paint on the Ciba-
chromes. The titles give the date on which the photograph was originally made; where there
was more than one useful exposure on any given date an alphabetic character is added.

92
Self-portrait 12.7.80 a
1990
Oil on Cibachrome on canvas
75 × 75 (29½ × 29½)
Anthony d'Offay Gallery

95
Self-portrait 13.7.80 b
1990
Oil on Cibachrome on canvas
75 × 75 (29½ × 29½)
Anthony d'Offay Gallery

98
Self-portrait 04.3.81 c
1990
Oil on Cibachrome on canvas
75 × 75 (29½ × 29½)
Anthony d'Offay Gallery

93
Self-portrait 12.7.80 b
1990
Oil on Cibachrome on canvas
75 × 75 (29½ × 29½)
Anthony d'Offay Gallery

96
Self-portrait 04.3.81 a
1990
Oil on Cibachrome on canvas
75 × 75 (29½ × 29½)
Private Collection

99
Self-portrait 05.3.81 a
1990
Oil on Cibachrome on canvas
75 × 75 (29½ × 29½)
Anthony d'Offay Gallery

94
Self-portrait 13.7.80 a
1990
Oil on Cibachrome on canvas
75 × 75 (29½ × 29½)
*IVAM Centre Julio González. Generali-
tat Valenciana*

97
Self-portrait 04.3.81 b
1990
Oil on Cibachrome on canvas
75 × 75 (29½ × 29½)
Anthony d'Offay Gallery

100
Self-portrait 05.3.81 b
1990
Oil and Humbrol enamel on Cibach-
rome on canvas
75 × 75 (29½ × 29½)
Anthony d'Offay Gallery

101
Self-portrait 05.3.81 c

1990
Oil on Cibachrome on canvas
75 × 75 (29½ × 29½)
Anthony d'Offay Gallery

102
Self-portrait 05.3.81 d

1990
Oil on Cibachrome on canvas
75 × 75 (29½ × 29½)
Anthony d'Offay Gallery

103
Self-portrait 05.3.81 e

1990
Oil on Cibachrome on canvas
75 × 75 (29½ × 29½)
Anthony d'Offay Gallery

104
Northend II

1991
Oil on Cibachrome on canvas
99.3 × 108.7 (39⅛ × 42¾)
Rita Donagh

Rita Donagh was unhappy to see herself in the painting she had initiated (no.91). Hamilton made a second version of 'Northend', replacing her figure with bluebells on a table. On the first encounter with Northend Rita had found a large bunch of fresh bluebells left mysteriously like a welcoming gift in the ruined house. They were in the sunlit room seen in the photograph. The table on which they lie in the painting was given to Hamilton by Rita Donagh in 1982. It is a folding wine table, which appealed to Rita Donagh through the clarity of its geometry. It consists solely of a circle, a triangle and a square.

105
Two gentlemen of Alba

1991
Oil on Cibachrome
100 × 78 (39⅜ × 30¾)
Giorgio and Giò Marconi Collection, Milan

Studio Marconi, Milan, has exhibited Hamilton five times since their first show in 1967. After the latest, in November 1990, Giorgio Marconi arranged a weekend trip to Alba to visit wine-makers and eat white truffles. While waiting for departure to the vineyards in the lounge of their hotel in Alba, Giorgio Marconi and his son Giò were photographed by Hamilton with a 110 format camera. To enlarge a miniature, negative colour frame to a 1 metre wide Cibachrome is optimistic but possible with an intermediary 5 × 4 inch transparency.

This was another of the 'Interior' subjects so beloved by Hamilton. The attraction of the photograph was its 'given' abstract qualities. The picture plane is broken down into more or less rectangular areas. David Sylvester has compared Hamilton with Godard in their shared propensity towards 'planes running parallel to the picture plane' (bib. D47). 'Two gentlemen of Alba' (not far from Verona) is like a stage set in the way it seems to be composed of 'flats'. An abstract arrangement of near-rectangles demanded only literal rectification and this was done with simple blocks of oil paint. To establish an even greater degree of precision some edges were straightened with a pointillist treatment to match the film grain and other parts of the image painted out or extended in simulation of the photograph. The flat treatment is reinforced by colour, the red, green and white, however muted, being appropriately reminiscent of the Italian flag.

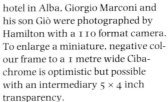

106
War games

1991–2
Oil on Scanachrome on canvas
200 × 200 (78¾ × 78¾)
The artist

The Verein Kornbrennerei, a distillery converted to an art centre in Hanover, Germany, is confronted by a long wall made with concrete posts and beams with brick in-fill. The director of the Kornbrennerei had the idea to commission artists to produce works as a permanent outdoor public exhibition with each artist assigned an area approximately five metres square. Hamilton agreed to make a

fig.29 **War games**, first version (1991) at Kornbrennerei, Hanover

fig.30 **Kent State** 1970 Screenprint

fig.31 Still from BBC 'Newsnight' programme showing Peter Snow in the Sandpit

panel using the computer-controlled Scanachrome system of colour enlargement (fig.29).

In his search for a subject Hamilton resorted to a method similar to that which he had used in 1970 when television offered 'Kent State' (fig.30) to his monitoring camera (see p.51); but here, instead of a camera, he used a video recorder over a period of several days, taping short television sequences of particular interest; these were usually news items. It happened to be the period of the Gulf war of 1991 and the BBC 'Newsnight' programme provided many entries to the tape (fig.31). In these, presenter Peter Snow was seen delivering his famous commentaries on the battle over a model of the war zone dotted with balsawood tanks and pinned with the adversaries' flags – the model itself has achieved some fame as the 'Sandpit' and has been exhibited in the Imperial War Museum, London. Selected still frames from the video were photographed on the TV screen in Hamilton's living room, surrounded by the video equipment associated with it. In the midst of bombs, missiles and general carnage it was the Sandpit which communicated the most telling image of the war. The headline in the newspaper seen in the painting, 'the Mother of Battles' was a threatening phrase coined shortly before the outbreak of hostilities by the Iraqi leader, Saddam Hussein.

Out of many trial 6 × 6 cm exposures one was selected to be enlarged on the Scanachrome machine. The transparency is put in a scanner at one end of the axle of a very large drum. The material to be printed is stretched over the drum. As the drum rotates, four airbrushes controlled by the computer reading the transparency spray blue, red, yellow and black inks to create the picture as the bank of jets move slowly along the axis of the drum. On a large-scale Scanachrome the distance between the scanning lines can be as much as 4 mm; this has the effect of giving the whole image the character of television. Hamilton decided to confuse the issue by himself painting the TV screen, with an assistant, so that the only part of his image without scanning lines is the part where they might be expected. The large, outdoor version of 'War games' must have a limited life expectancy so the need to redo the painting on a gallery scale became an early imperative. The 2 metre square scale gave an opportunity for Hamilton alone to work more meticulously on the painted area.

To a domestic audience, one way in which the war seemed to be being played out was on television. Not only was the action transmitted by satellite to screens in every home but the television screen often showed the participating generals delivering their press conferences with the aid of monitors, so that video replays were replayed on countless television tubes throughout the world: the television set was itself the image on our screens. The irony was emphasised by Peter Snow when the war was transferred to a simulated desert scattered with national symbols and model weaponry. It seemed to Hamilton, as to many others, that the prominence of the war game as a phenomenon in itself obscured the fact that thousands of Iraqi conscripts were dying in their 'sandpit'. Blood can be seen seeping from the bottom of Hamilton's television.

BIOGRAPHICAL CHRONOLOGY

A complete list of Richard Hamilton's one-man exhibitions is given in the Bibliography.

1922

24 February: Richard William Hamilton born at Bendall Street (now a continuation of Bell Street), Marylebone, London. Father, Albert William Hamilton (occupation, motor driver). Mother, Constance Elizabeth, *née* Ellerbeck.

1929

Parents moved to Victoria. Attended primary school, St Peter's, Eaton Square.

1934

Attended evening classes in art at local LCC adult education centres in Pimlico and Southwark, though under age, with the generous encouragement of the teacher, Mr Smith.

1935

Recommended by Sir Guy Dawber for interview with Sir Walter Russell who advised applying for studentship at the Royal Academy Schools when sixteen.

1936

Left elementary school. Worked for a year as office boy in advertising department of electrical engineering firm. Attended evening classes in art at Westminster School of Art, Vincent Square (teachers included Mark Gertler and Bernard Meninsky) and St Martin's School of Art (teachers included William Roberts).

1937

Employed in display department of Reimann School of Art, Regency Street, London sw1 (commercial art school/studios) where he was allowed to draw in the life class in his free time. Teachers included Merlyn Evans and Matvyn Wright. The instructor in stage design, Prof. Haas-Heye, became a mentor; under his guidance saw exhibitions of Picasso's 'Guernica', Man Ray and other modern artists, and met Lady Ottoline Morrell.

Family group, including R.H.'s father (in uniform), grandmother and step-grandfather

Hamilton family outing to Southend-on-Sea (R.H. at left)

R.H. as a schoolboy

1938

Student of painting at Royal Academy Schools (to 1940). Teachers included F. Ernest Jackson, Sir Walter Russell and Walter Bayes. Attended evening classes in etching and lithography at the Central School of Arts and Crafts. Made copies from old masters at National Gallery. Student friends included Michael Greenwood and James Tower. Attended avant-garde theatre and dance.

1939

Travelled to France for summer vacation. Returned in time to hear Chamberlain's declaration of war.

1940

Too young for conscription when the Royal Academy Schools closed. Sent to a Government Training Centre for nine months to learn engineering draughtsmanship.

1941

Employed as jig and tool draughtsman; at Design Unit Group, a bogus engineering design office set up with Jack Jackson (the band leader) as director (to 1942); at EMI (Electrical & Musical Industries), Hayes (1942–45). Rented flat in Newman Street, Soho. Drank at the Wheatsheaf and Fitzroy Tavern with Nina Hamnett, Dylan Thomas, Tambimuttu, etc. First met David Sylvester.

1942

Moved to Paddington and stayed there through the Blitz. Organised music club at EMI for weekly lunchtime concerts of recorded music from HMV archives.

1943

Involved with acoustical engineers, as spare time enthusiasts, in the design of moving-coil pickups and horn speakers. Attended first and many subsequent meetings of the Society for the Promotion of New Music.

Professor Haas-Heye in Berlin, with model

Group of students at R.A. Schools, 1940. R.H. front row, second from left; Michael Greenwood back row far right, standing next to James Tower

1944

Met Terry O'Reilly, a research assistant in the chemistry laboratory at EMI. Around this time had his interest in printmaking stimulated by displays of French artists' books (included publications by Vollard) in foyer of National Gallery.

1945

Awestruck by the exhibitions of Matisse and of Picasso's large wartime canvases at the Victoria and Albert Museum. Attended many concerts at the Wigmore Hall and elsewhere, especially those organised by the French Institute.

1946

Denied permission to leave reserved occupation to return to his art studies, applied to Hardship Tribunal and was permitted to return to re-opened Royal Academy Schools (January). Alfred Munnings had become President of the RA, new teachers included Philip Connard and Thomas Monnington. Expelled (July) for 'not profiting from the instruction given in the Painting School' – as a consequence made liable to call-up. 'Dragged screaming' into 18 months' military service in Royal Engineers. Read English classics (Chaucer to Hardy) from the regimental library and his own two-volume Odyssey Press edition of James Joyce's *Ulysses*.

R.H. (right), 1946, with group around André Lhote at Anglo-French Art Centre, St John's Wood, which R.H. visited occasionally

1947

Began to make studies for illustrations to *Ulysses*. Completed camouflage course (which involved making models of landscapes from an aerial viewpoint) and Army Education Corps. Instructors course. Married Terry O'Reilly (September).

1948

Studied painting at Slade School of Art (to 1951); worked mainly in life class and etching studio (teacher John Buckland Wright). Slade student Nigel Henderson introduced him to his fellow students Eduardo Paolozzi and William Turnbull, to D'Arcy Wentworth Thompson's book *On Growth and Form*, to Marcel Duchamp's *Green Box* and to Roland Penrose, who subsequently commended his idea of an exhibition on the subject of growth and form to the Institute of Contemporary Arts, London.

1949

Siegfried Giedion's *Mechanization Takes Command* became a significant source book. Giedion saw agricultural machinery as being at the interface between technology and nature. Hamilton went to the cinema about three times a week and found a rich source of imagery in the Hollywood films of the period. Invited by art director of *Vogue* magazine to join weekly studio sessions for budding fashion artists; after some months his results were assessed as too artistic. Made models for industrial and government exhibitions. Birth of daughter, Dominy.

1950

Visited Paolozzi in Paris, who took him to Giacometti's studio. Made trip to Chartres and to the Dordogne to look at cave art. Travelled the Pyrenees and first met, by chance, Benn Levy and his wife Constance Cummings, forming a lasting friendship. Designed catalogue/poster (first venture into typography) for ICA exhibition *James Joyce: His Life and Work* and helped to install the show. Exhibition of engravings *Variations on the theme of a reaper* explored different engraving techniques, Gimpel Fils (February). Purchasers included Roland Penrose, Arthur Waley and Lynn Chadwick. Discussed *Growth and Form* exhibition, and collected material from J. D. Bernal, C. H. Waddington, Kathleen Lonsdale, Joseph Needham, Jacob Bronowski, etc. Lived in Abbey Road, St John's Wood; near neighbours, Edward Wright, Lucian Freud and Gerard Dillon. First met Peter Watson and Sonia Orwell, *née* Brownell.

1951

With the help of Peter Gregory (Managing Director of Lund Humphries and one of the small group of founder/patrons of the ICA) met T. S. Eliot at Faber and Faber to discuss the possibility of publishing an illustrated *Ulysses*. Eliot pointed out the difficulty of resetting *Ulysses* for a limited edition. Aided by his wife, made map-models of Harlow, Speke, Stevenage, Basildon, etc. for the Festival of Britain and collaborated with Elidir Davies on the design of the house in Hurst Avenue, Highgate, which he occupied from 1952. Met Jean Hélion. Devised and designed *Growth and Form* exhibition, opened by Le Corbusier, ICA (July–August). First met Reyner Banham.

Catalogue/poster for exhibition *James Joyce: His Life and Work* 1950

1952

Taught ideas developed from *Growth and Form* to students from various craft departments at the Central School of Arts and Crafts, London (to 1953). Fellow teachers included Eduardo Paolozzi, William Turnbull, Victor Pasmore and Anton Ehrenzweig. Founder member of the Independent Group formed at the ICA; others included Lawrence Alloway, Reyner Banham, John McHale (convenors), Toni del Renzio, Eduardo Paolozzi, William Turnbull, Nigel Henderson, Colin St John Wilson, James Stirling, Theo Crosby, Alison and Peter Smithson, Magda and Frank Cordell (see in particular catalogue of Independent Group retrospective exhibition, 1990, in bib., section E).

1953

Appointed lecturer, Fine Art Department, King's College, University of Durham (later University of Newcastle-upon-Tyne), Newcastle-upon-Tyne (to 1966), under Lawrence Gowing, and taught fundamentals of design to first year students. Researched devices which extend man's mobility, with help of student, Arthur Pulford. Restored lapsed etching and lithography facilities in Newcastle, instituted evening classes in the subject and began again to make his own etchings. Commuted weekly from London to Newcastle for the next thirteen years. Installed *Wonder and Horror of the Human Head*, an exhibition of material collected by Roland Penrose and Lee Miller, at the ICA. Studied the representation of motion in Muybridge, Marey, the Futurists, Cubists and Duchamp. Endeavoured to develop a perspective convention to describe a moving spectator.

1954

With the Independent Group discussed the ideas of Korzybski, Norbert Wiener, Claude Shannon, von Neumann and van Vogt. Read science fiction avidly. Victor Pasmore appointed Master of Painting in Newcastle. From now until 1966 one of Hamilton's main roles was to organise and install, with the help of students, exhibitions in the Fine Art Department's Hatton Gallery. Designed catalogues and posters, and produced them using the small resources of the University printing section.

R.H. at the *Masterpieces of Modern Art* exhibition, Tate Gallery 1952 (photograph by R. Saidman)

1955

Exhibited *Paintings 1951–55*, Hanover Gallery, London (January). Devised and designed *Man, Machine & Motion* exhibition and worked with Anthony Froshaug on the design of a catalogue for which Reyner Banham wrote the notes, Hatton Gallery, Newcastle-upon-Tyne (May) and ICA (July). Worked for Sidney Bernstein as a consultant designer for Granada Television before the company began transmissions. Birth of son, Roderic.

1956

With John McHale and John Voelcker, devised an environment on the twin themes of perception and popular imagery as part of *This is Tomorrow* exhibition, Whitechapel Art Gallery (August–September). Theo Crosby masterminded the exhibition, for which 36 artists grouped into teams of three (ideally painter, sculptor and architect). Talked at the ICA on Marcel Duchamp's 'Large Glass' using a diagram he had made of the glass and its relationship to the *Green Box* notes. Wrote to Duchamp enclosing a copy of his diagram with request for correction or confirmation (April). On the recommendation of David Sylvester, worked as designer for *Encounter* magazine. Worked as consultant designer for Churchill Gear Machines, Blaydon-on-Tyne, Co. Durham (to 1962).

1957

Answered a question from Peter and Alison Smithson with a proposal (January) for an exhibition of work based on compliance with the principles of Pop art. He suggested:

Pop Art is:

Popular (designed for a mass audience)
Transient (short-term solution)
Expendable (easily forgotten)
Low cost
Mass produced
Young (aimed at youth)
Witty
Sexy
Gimmicky
Glamorous
Big business

In absence of response from Smithsons began work on 'Hommage à Chrysler Corp.' to examine his own proposition. Received reply from Duchamp (May) to his letter of the previous year, inviting him to collaborate with George Heard Hamilton, Professor in the History of Art, Yale University, on a complete English

Terry Hamilton with 'A bicycle made for 10', *Man, Machine & Motion*, 1955

Terry Hamilton outside the Highgate house, c.1957

R.H. and Terry Hamilton, John McHale and Magda Cordell constructing their stand for *This is Tomorrow*, 1956

Installing *an Exhibit* at the ICA London, 1957. R.H. and Victor Pasmore, with Terry Hamilton behind (photograph by Roger Mayne)

version of *Green Box* notes. With Alloway and Pasmore devised and organised *an Exhibit*, Hatton Gallery, Newcastle-upon-Tyne (June) and a revised installation, ICA (August). Began, at the invitation of Hugh Casson, to teach Interior Design one day a week at Royal College of Art (to 1961). Listened to Buckminster Fuller. First met Richard Smith and Peter Blake.

1958

Corresponded regularly with Duchamp on *Green Box* project. Designed *A Gallery for a Collector*, Ideal Home Exhibition, Olympia (March). Central living unit and chairs (made from design by Harley Earl) transferred to Hamilton's home. Visited the Hochschule für Gestaltung, Ulm, at the invitation of Tomas Maldonado. Kenneth Rowntree took over the Professorship from Lawrence Gowing at Newcastle and Hamilton's teaching was merged with the basic studies set up by Victor Pasmore. Important roots of the course lay in their experience at the Central School (see 1952). Saw the Levys often and met at their home refugees from the Hollywood of the McCarthy era: Carl Foreman, Donald Ogden Stewart, Joseph Losey as well as Labour MPs Aneurin Bevan, Jennie Lee and Michael Foot.

1959

Erected, with Victor Pasmore, a free-standing version of *an Exhibit* called *Exhibit 2*, combining the *Man, Machine & Motion* frame system with the panels of acrylic used for *an Exhibit*, Hatton Gallery, Newcastle-upon-Tyne. Lectured on technical developments in the entertainment industry 'Glorious Technicolor, Breathtaking CinemaScope and Stereophonic Sound' in Newcastle, the ICA, Cambridge and at the Royal College; demonstrated Polaroid camera to each audience by taking a photograph of it. Lectured on 'The Design Image of the Fifties'. *The Developing Process* exhibition held in the Hatton Gallery, Newcastle-upon-Tyne (and national tour), on the basic courses in Newcastle and Leeds. Met Marcel and Teeny Duchamp for the first time at dinner arranged by William and Noma Copley at their house at Longpont, near Paris. Other guests included Jean and Eva Tinguely and Man and Julie Ray. Published illustrated essay on the problems of translating Duchamp into type in *Uppercase 2*. Interviewed Marcel Duchamp for BBC Third Programme.

R.H. at the Hochschule für Gestaltung, Ulm, 1958

1960

Received William and Noma Copley Award. Typographic version of Marcel Duchamp's *Green Box* published by Lund Humphries. *Green Box* book reviewed by Jasper Johns. Wrote to Diter Rot (Dieter Roth) after installing the Edition MAT exhibition in Newcastle, to which he contributed; correspondence and friendship continues.

1961

Invited by students of the Royal College of Art Painting School to give criticism of their paintings. Saw the work of RCA 'Pop art' students for the first time. Awarded prize to David Hockney. First met R.B. Kitaj. First met Cedric Price. Corresponded with Dieter Roth. Began to edit monographs for the William and Noma Copley Foundation (to 1965); *Hans Bellmer* was the first. Wrote article on 'The books of Diter Rot' for *Typographica*. In prison (with many other CND protestors) after anti-Polaris demonstration at Holy Loch.

1962

Interviewed Marcel Duchamp for BBC TV, 'Monitor' programme. First showing of Pop paintings, with Hockney, Kitaj, Peter Blake, etc. at Arthur Jeffress Gallery. First met Emmett Williams, Robert Fillou, Ben Vautier and other Fluxus members on the occasion of the *Festival of Misfits* exhibition at Gallery One, London, and the ICA. Death of wife Terry in car accident (November). Reyner Banham wrote of her 'She was, among other things, protest-oriented, but one of the beautiful, electric protestors, not one of the drips' (In 'Representations in protest', *New Society*, 8 May 1969).

1963

Invited by Duchamps to visit them in Cadaqués, Spain. First visit to USA, to attend the Marcel Duchamp retrospective at the Pasadena Museum, California (October), at the invitation of Walter Hopps, the exhibition's organiser. Lectured on the 'Large Glass' at the Guggenheim Museum, New York, Yale University, Pasadena and Boston. Travelled with Duchamps from New York to California. First meetings with Warhol and Oldenburg, who both had important exhibitions in Los Angeles, made acquaintance with Larry Bell, Billy Al Bengston, Joe Goode, Bob Irwin and Alison Knowles. Weekend outing to Las Vegas with Duchamps and party.

R.H. on CND Polaris protest, Holy Loch, 1961

Terry Hamilton in the Highgate house, 1962

R.H. with Richard Smith (left) teaching in Newcastle foundation year, *c*.1962

At the Stardust Hotel, Las Vegas, 1963. Left to right: Teeny Duchamp, R.H., Betty Factor, William N. Copley, Donald Factor, Walter Hopps, Betty Asher, Marcel Duchamp

Visited Pacific Ocean Park and purchased button-badge with legend 'SLIP IT TO ME'. Spent a day with Joseph Cornell in Utopia. First screenprints made with Christopher Prater. Began 'Five Tyres', a complex perspective problem, and abandoned it. Went regularly to poetry readings at the Morden Tower in Newcastle where Tom Pickard conducted readings by Basil Bunting, Allen Ginsberg, Lawrence Ferlinghetti, Robert Creeley, etc.

1964

Exhibited *Paintings etc. '56–64*, Hanover Gallery (October–November). Went, at the request of the Arts Council, to investigate the condition of the Schwitters Merzbarn at Ambleside. Hamilton recommended extensive protective measures, that the work should be restored in situ and taken under the stewardship of the Arts Council but this was deemed impossible. Began to experiment with extreme close up. With Ronald Hunt, organised first Picabia retrospective, Hatton Gallery, Newcastle. Worked with Nancy Thomas on BBC TV 'Monitor' film on Jean Tinguely. First met Dieter Roth and through him Nam June Paik. Asked by Arts Council of Great Britain to organise Duchamp retrospective.

1965

Further deterioration of the Schwitters Merzbarn made it essential to move the work from Ambleside and Hamilton persuaded Newcastle University to allocate funds for the purpose. Began reconstruction of Duchamp's 'Large Glass' and of the studies made between 1912 and 1915. Designed first edition of *The Spoils* for Basil Bunting. Publication of Eduardo Paolozzi's *Kex* and the Dieter Roth *Copley Book*, edited by R.H. for the William and Noma Copley Foundation. First met Jasper Johns, John Cage, Merce Cunningham and Jim Dine.

1966

Finished reconstruction of the 'Large Glass' and presented it with all the studies in the Hatton Gallery. Wrote notes for the catalogue designed by Gordon House and installed *The Almost Complete Works of Marcel Duchamp* at the Tate Gallery (June). First exhibition at Robert Fraser Gallery, London (October). Gave up full-time teaching to become professional artist. Students had included: Adrian Henri, Ian Stephenson, Noel Forster,

R.H. with Marcel Duchamp at the Museum of Modern Art, New York, 1963 (photograph by George Cserna)

R.H. as a baseball player with Apollo capsule, 1963. Photograph by Betsy Scherman in connection with cover for *Living Arts*

R.H. in Schwitters Merzbarn, Ambleside, 1965 (photograph by Mark Lancaster)

Rita Donagh in Diane Logan hat, 1965 (photograph by Richard Hamilton)

Matt Rugg, John A. Walker, John Walters, Rita Donagh, Mark Lancaster, Mary Webb, Stephen Buckley, Tony Carter, Mali Morris, Bryan Ferry, Tim Head, Nick de Ville. Attended 'Destruction in Art Symposium'; first met Gustav Metzger, Wolf Vostell, Hermann Nitsch, Yoko Ono. Schwitters Merzbarn arrived in Newcastle.

1967

First exhibition in Germany (March). First New York exhibition (May). First exhibition in Italy (November). First screenprint with Domberger, Stuttgart. Met John Heartfield.

1968

Began series of *Polaroid Portraits* after being photographed by Roy Lichtenstein in Lichtenstein's New York studio (March): the project consists of R.H. offering a Polaroid camera to an artist friend or acquaintance with the request, 'take a photograph of me'. Designed sleeve and inserts for *The Beatles*, known also as 'the white album', presenting it as a mock small press publication in a limited edition of 5,000,000. Showed in Documenta 4 in Kassel where first met Marcel Broodthaers. Worked in Milan with various printers, including etching with Grafica Uno. First collaboration with Dieter Roth. Visited Joseph Beuys in Düsseldorf after seeing his exhibition in Eindhoven. Saw M.C. Escher retrospective, Gemeentemuseum, The Hague. Completed edition of Marcel Duchamp's 'The oculist witnesses'. Marcel Duchamp died. Visited Canada as juror for the exhibition *Canadian artists '68*, met Greg Curnoe, Iain Baxter and General Idea.

1969

Bought a ruin in Cadaqués and began restoration. First dye-transfer print with Creative Colour, Hamburg. Awarded joint first prize (with Mary Martin) in John Moores exhibition, Liverpool. Cremated one of his own paintings for a Clive Barker sculpture to be placed in an 'Urn'. Attended Gilbert and George's performance 'Underneath the Arches' in Cable Street.

R.H. in Highgate studio with Paul McCartney, 1968, while working on insert for 'the white album' (photograph by Rita Donagh)

R.H. cremating a painting for Clive Barker's 'Urn', 1969 (photograph by Rita Donagh)

Location shot by R.H. for final sequence in James Scott's film on him for Maya Productions, 1969

1970

First museum retrospective (Tate Gallery, March–April). First screenprint with Dieter Dietz, Lengmoos, Bavaria. First collotype with Heinz Häffner, Stuttgart. The shooting of students by National Guardsmen at Kent State University, Ohio shocked R.H. into making a screenprint on the subject in an edition of 5000. Awarded Talens Prize international by jury of Dutch museum directors.

1971

Returned to Five Tyres subject, using computer programming to solve the perspective problem. Completed edition of Marcel Duchamp's 'Sieves'. Invited by Barbara Rose to participate in Marcel Duchamp symposium at University of California, Irvine. Taught at University of Wisconsin, Madison, for one semester. Designed an adjustable jointing device for the mitres of canvas stretchers and applied for a provisional patent.

1972

Made a print for Release, an organisation providing legal support for people accused of infringements of drug laws.

1973

First of many prints with Aldo Crommelynck, 'Picasso's meninas', for publication of sixty prints by different artists intended as a homage to Picasso on his 90th birthday in 1971. Began 'Trichromatic Flower-piece' with Crommelynck as an experiment in three-colour printing with hand-etched plates (until 1974).

1974

First exhibition in Spain (July); made postcard based on 'Chicago Project' in homage to John Cage. First visit to Japan, to discuss commission by Lux Corporation of hi-fi painting (March). Stayed briefly in Berlin under DAAD scheme. First met James Lee Byars and Mario Merz.

1975

Lithograph with Ken Tyler experimented further with the possibilities of manual colour separation and trichromatic registration.

Interior of Hamilton's house, Cadaqués, 1970

R.H. with Joseph Beuys at the Tate Gallery, 1972

R.H. at Café Meliton, Cadaqués, with 'Sign' (photograph by Bob Janz)

R.H. with Marcel Broodthaers, Cadaqués, c.1974 (photograph by Maria Gilissen)

1976

'Collaborations' made with Dieter Roth in Cadaqués (summer). First exhibition in Canada. Bought derelict farm complex in Oxfordshire and began the process of restoration and adaptation with the help of architect Stephen Mullin.

1977

'INTERFACEs' begun with Dieter Roth in Cadaqués (summer), completed in London (autumn).

1978

Moved home to Oxfordshire. At the National Gallery, selected paintings from the collection and created an installation for them. This exhibition, *The artist's eye*, incorporated an ironing board, a working television set and chairs by Breuer and Eames.

1979

First experiments with photogravure.

1980

First use of large format Polaroid camera in Amsterdam to make an edition of 'Instant painting'. Made TV 'commercial' for 'The critic laughs' for the BBC series 'Shock of the New'. Invited to open major exhibition of the work of Dieter Rams at the Internationales Design Zentrum, Berlin.

1981

With Aldo Crommelynck in Paris made etching 'In Horne's house', to honour Joyce centenary; this initiated resumed activity on the *Ulysses* series of illustrations. First Polaroid 'Self-portraits' made by photographing through paint on glass.

1982

Collected Words published. It brings together, in one volume, the full range of Hamilton's writings and lectures. Started to use Epson laptop computer.

1983

'The citizen' first shown at the Guggenheim Museum, New York, in an exhibition titled *Aspects of Postwar Painting in Europe*. From New York it went to the Orchard Gallery, Londonderry, to join Rita Donagh's 'Irish' work in the exhibition *A Cellular Maze*. World Print Council Award.

R.H. with Dieter Roth, 1977

The artist's eye installation, National Gallery, 1978

R.H. with Rita Donagh and Shem at Northend, 1978 (photograph by Greg Curnoe)

R.H. with Jean Tinguely at the Tate Gallery, 1982

1984

First exhibition in Sweden. Acquired Altos computer and began to use the UNIX operating system: the process of programming his own environment continues. Asked to design OHIO scientific computer for a Swedish computer company (Isotron), he proposed a set of stacked boxes with separate functions. Participated in Arts Council touring exhibition, *Four Rooms*, with Anthony Caro, Marc Camille Chaimowicz and Howard Hodgkin.

R.H. with Francis Bacon, 1983 (photograph by Barry Joule)

1986

First print with Kurt Zein. First showing of OHIO prototype computer at Riverside Studios.

1987

Participated in a group of films, 'Painting with Light', made for the BBC by Griffin Film productions in which six artists were invited to experiment with the Quantel TV Paintbox. Hamilton took the opportunity to treat a subject complementary to his painting 'The citizen', using the Paintbox to 'collage' media images of Orange parades. *This is Tomorrow* 'fun house' reconstructed for exhibition at the Clocktower, New York.

R.H. with Aldo Crommelynck, 1985

1988

Reworked the Orangeman painting on Quantel Graphic Paintbox, at higher resolution, as study for 'The subject'.

R.H. Digital Logo for his computer, 1986

1989

Diab computer, based on the OHIO concept, completed and exhibited at the Moderna Museet, Stockholm.

1990

Reconstructed a version of *an Exhibit* for the exhibition *The Independent Group; Postwar Britain and the Aesthetics of Plenty* for the showing in Valencia.

1991

Delivered the William Townsend Memorial Lecture at University College London, on the *The Hard Copy Problem*, which discussed the proliferating technology of the computer paintbox and the questions it poses for artists. Married Rita Donagh (July).

BIBLIOGRAPHY

Richard Hamilton is unusual among artists in maintaining on computer an extensive record of publications by and about him. This bibliography has therefore been prepared by the artist and Nigel McKernaghan, but with important contributions by Meg Duff, Angela Ford and Alan Hopkinson of the Tate Gallery Library, and from Fiona Robertson. The bibliography was formatted on a work of art by Hamilton, the Diab computer, of which an example is no.88 in this catalogue. In differing degrees according to the sections, the bibliography is selective; this applies in particular to newspaper articles, a comprehensive review of which has not been possible. The frequent references to *Collected Words* are to item A51 in this bibliography. Each section is listed chronologically. Numbering is to aid cross-referencing from the text.

Writings by the artist

See also all other sections

A1   'Hommage à Chrysler Corp.,' *Architectural Design*, vol.28, no.3, pp.120–1, March 1958. Description of sources for the painting: reprinted in *Collected Words*.

A2   'U-L-M Spells H.f.G,' *The Architect's Journal*, vol.128, no.3307, pp.73, 75, 17 July 1958. On a visit to the Hochschule für Gestaltung, Ulm: reprinted in *Collected Words*.

A3   'Ulm,' *Design*, no.126, pp.53–7, June 1959. On the Hochschule für Gestaltung, Ulm: reprinted in *Collected Words*.

A4   'Diagrammar,' in *The Developing Process*, pp.19–26, University of Durham, Newcastle-upon-Tyne, 1959. Catalogue of exhibition: work in progress towards a new foundation of art teaching as developed at the Department of Fine Art, King's College, Durham University, Newcastle-upon-Tyne and at Leeds College of Art: reprinted in *Collected Words*.

A5   *Glorious Technicolor, Breathtaking Cinema-Scope and Stereophonic Sound*, 1959. Lecture on technical innovations in the entertainments industries; first published in *Collected Words*.

A6   'Towards a Typographic Rendering of the Green Box,' *Uppercase 2*, 1959. On the problems of typesetting Duchamp: reprinted in *Collected Words*.

A7   'Persuading Image,' *Design*, no.134, pp.28–32, February 1960. Published version of lecture, 'The designed image of the fifties': reprinted in *Collected Words*.

A8   'Art and Design,' in *Popular Culture and Personal Responsibility*, pp.135–56, October 1960. Lecture, chaired by Herbert Read, followed by discussion. Verbatim report of National Union of Teachers Conference, Church House, Westminster, London: reprinted in *Collected Words*.

A9   'First year studies at Newcastle,' *Times Educational Supplement*, 1960. Reprinted in *Collected Words*.

A10 *The Bride stripped bare by her bachelors, even*, Lund Humphries, London, 1960. Typographic version by Richard Hamilton of Marcel Duchamp's 'Green Box,' translated by George Heard Hamilton. Contains 'Inside The Green Box' by George Heard Hamilton, 'The Green Book' and a diagram of the glass by Richard Hamilton: reprinted in *Collected Words*.

A11 'FoB + 10,' *Design*, no.149, pp.40–51, May 1961. A retrospective view of the 1951 Festival of Britain: reprinted in *Collected Words*.

A12 'The Books of Diter Rot,' *Typographica*, no.3, pp.21–40, June 1961. An appreciation of Dieter Roth's early books: reprinted in *Collected Words*.

A13 'Glorious Techniculture,' *Architectural Design*, vol.21, no.11, p.497, November 1961. Part of 27 pages devoted to buildings and art assembled on the South Bank for the Congress of the International Union of Architects, London with contribution by Hamilton.

A14 'About art teaching, basically,' *Motif 8*, pp.17–23, Winter 1961. On basic teaching in Newcastle: reprinted in *Collected Words*.

A15 'For the Finest Art Try – POP,' *Gazette*, no.1, 1961. On the relationship between the popular arts and fine art: reprinted in *Collected Words*.

A16 'An exposition of $he,' *Architectural Design*, vol.32, no.10, pp.485–6, October 1962. Description of sources for the painting: reprinted in *Collected Words*.

A17 'Artifical obsolescence,' *Product Design Engineering*, January 1963. On the economics of obsolescence: reprinted in *Collected Words*.

A18 *Ark*, vol.34, pp.4, 14–16, 24–6, 34–7, Summer 1963. Issue devoted to theme of incidence and selection of images experienced in everyday life: Hamilton's commissioned contribution consisted of images and text, the latter on pp.37–8.

A19 'Urbane Image,' *Living Arts 2*, pp.44–59, June 1963. Text, wrap around cover and inside cover photographs: reprinted in *Collected Words*.

A20 'Duchamp,' *Art International*, vol.7, no.10, pp.22–8, January 1964. Review of Duchamp's 1963 Pasadena retrospective: reprinted in *Collected Words*.

A21 'Portrait of Hugh Gaitskell as a Famous Monster of Filmland,' 1964. First published in *Collected Words*.

A22 *NOT SEEN and/or LESS SEEN of/by MARCEL DUCHAMP/RROSE SELAVY 1904–1964*, Cordier & Ekstrom Inc., New York, January 1965. Introduction and notes for the Mary Sisler Collection catalogue.

A23 *Copley Book*, William and Noma Copley Foundation, 1965. An assemblage of loose pages by Dieter Roth with an introduction by Hamilton. Printed by Lund Humphries.

A24 *KEX*, William and Noma Copley Foundation, 1965. A collection of Eduardo Paolozzi's scrapbook pages with text and illustrations. Edited into a continuous text by Hamilton. Printed by Lund Humphries.

A25 *The almost complete works of Marcel Duchamp*, The Arts Council of Great Britain, London, June 1966. Introduction and catalogue notes for the Duchamp retrospective at the Tate Gallery.

A26 *The Bride stripped bare by her Bachelors even again*, University of Newcastle-upon-Tyne, 1966. An account of the reconstruction of Duchamp's 'Large Glass': reprinted in *Collected Words*.

A27 'Urbanismer,' *Konstrevy*, no.3, Stockholm, 1967. Swedish translation of 'Urbane Image' by Leif Nylén.

A28 'Roy Lichtenstein,' *Studio International*, vol.175, no.896, pp.20–4, January 1968. Reprinted in *Collected Words*.

A29 'Photography and painting,' *Studio International*, vol.177, no.909, pp.120–5, March 1969. On the integration of paint and photographic emulsion, front and back cover: partly reprinted in *Collected Words*.

A30 'Magical Myth For Our Time,' *The Sunday Times*, 22 February 1970. Review of *The Complete Works of Marcel Duchamp* by Arturo Schwarz: reprinted in *Collected Words*.

A31 'Colour television: seven singular choices,' *Radio Times*, 12 November 1970. With others.

A32 'Letter,' *Catalyst*, p.78, January 1971. On the subject of museum admission charges.

A33 'Propositions,' *Catalyst*, p.20, May 1971. Conceptual art axioms: reprinted in *Collected Words*.

A34 'Work in Progress,' *Chroniques de l'Art Vivant*, no.29, pp.10–11, April 1972. With French translation of 'Propositions'.

A35 '5 Tyres remoulded,' *Studio International*, vol.183, no.945, pp.276–7, June 1972. On the development of computerised perspective project: reprinted in *Collected Words*.

A36 *Polaroid Portraits*, vol.1, Edition Hansjörg Mayer, Stuttgart, London and Reykjavik, 1972. Polaroid photographs of Hamilton by 32 artists.

A37 'Thesen,' in *Kunst Praxis Heute: Eine Dokumentation de Aktuelle Aestetik*, p.25, Cologne, 1972. With German translation of 'Propositions'.

A38 'The Large Glass,' in *Marcel Duchamp*, ed. Anne d'Harnoncourt and Kynaston McShine, pp.57–67, Museum of Modern Art, New York, 1973. Published on the occasion of Marcel Duchamp retrospective. First publication of Hamilton's 'Large Glass' lecture: reprinted in *Collected Words*.

A39 'Marcel Broodthaers,' *Art Monthly*, no.1, October 1976. An obituary acrostic.

A40 *Collaborations of Ch. Rotham*, Edition Hansjörg Mayer with Galerie Cadaqués, Stuttgart, January 1977. Texts and play *Die Grosse Bockwurst* by Dieter Roth and/or Richard Hamilton.

A41 'Letter,' *Art Monthly*, March 1977. On the removal of a painting from the *Collaborations* exhibition.

A42 'The books of Diter Rot,' *Sondern*, no.2, 1977. Text of *Typographica* (1961) article updated to include later work. German translation: reprinted in *Collected Words*.

A43 *The artist's eye*, National Gallery, London, July 1978. Catalogue introduction: reprinted in *Collected Words*.

A44 'The little world of Dieter Roth,' *Sondern*, no.3, pp.34–57, Zürich, 1978. Transcript of Dieter Roth BBC Radio Three interview.

A45 *Polaroid Portraits*, vol.2, Edition Hansjörg Mayer, Stuttgart, London and Reykjavik, 1978. Polaroid photographs of Hamilton by 32 artists.

A46 *Contemporary British Artists with Photographs by Walia*, 1979. On the human figure (statement originally made to Yoshiaki Tono in 1971).

A47 *Sondern*, no.4, pp.154–68, Zürich, 1979. Conversation between Dieter Roth and Richard Hamilton on the subject of 'INTER-FACEs'.

A48 'Letters,' *Aspects*, no.11, Summer 1980. Letters of 1970 and 1980 on inaccurate reporting by Peter Fuller.

A49 'Hamilton's Plaint,' *Art Monthly*, no.49, September 1981. Letter in response to Peter Fuller article (*Art Monthly*, June 1981).

A50 'When the fan hits the XXXX,' *Art Monthly*, no.51, pp.25–6, November 1981. Open letter to Peter Fuller.

A51 *Collected Words*, Thames and Hudson, London, 1982. Compilation of writings by Richard Hamilton.

A52 *In Horne's house*, Waddington Graphics, London, 1982. Monograph on etching illustrating the 'Oxen in the Sun' episode of James Joyce's *Ulysses*: reprinted in *Collected Words*.

A53 *A Cellular Maze*, Orchard Gallery, Londonderry, August 1983. Pamphlet with texts by Rita Donagh and Richard Hamilton, published on the occasion of a joint exhibition.

A54 'Der Widerstand von Long Kesh,' *du*, no.513, pp.32–5, November 1983. German translation of text *A Cellular Maze*.

A55 *Polaroid Portraits*, vol.3, Edition Hansjörg Mayer, Stuttgart, London and Reykjavik, 1983. Polaroid photographs of Hamilton by 32 artists.

A56 *Four Rooms*, Liberty's, London, March 1984. Arts Council of Great Britain exhibition curated by Michael Regan: with a text by Hamilton.

A57 *The Expendable Icon: Works by John McHale*, pp.45, 47, Albright-Knox Art Gallery, Buffalo NY, May–July 1984. Contribution to catalogue of John McHale memorial exhibition.

A58 'Statement by the artist,' in *Twentieth century artists on art*, ed. Dore Ashton, pp.143–4, Pantheon, New York, 1985.

A59 'Recollections of Joseph Beuys,' *Art Monthly*, no.94, pp.10–11, March 1986. On the death of Beuys.

A60 *The transmogrifications of Bloom*, Waddington Graphics, London, 1986. Monograph on etching illustrating the 'Circe' episode of James Joyce's *Ulysses*.

A61 'A wholemeal loaf for Joseph,' in *Ohne die Rose tun wir's nicht: für Joseph Beuys*, pp.148–9, Heidleberg, 1986. A recipe for making wholemeal bread: in homage to Beuys.

A62 'John Latham,' in *John Latham: early works 1954–1972*, pp.7–16, Lisson Gallery, London, January 1987. Essay on Latham's *Report of a Surveyor*.

A63 *INTERFACEs*, Roth's Verlag, Basle, 1988. Double volume with 120 images by Dieter Roth and Richard Hamilton echoing the format of 30 INTERFACE triptyches.

A64 'Endangered Species,' *The Tamarind Papers*, vol.13, Albuquerque, 1990. On old print technologies and the preservation of craftsmen.

A65 'Anteckner om fotographie,' *Konst Magasinet*, no.12–13, pp.20–3, Malmo Konsthalls Vanner, Malmo, September 1991. Swedish translation of article on photography and painting.

A66 'The visual arts under attack,' *The Guardian*, 21 November 1991.

A67 'Making their mark,' *The Independent*, 17 December 1991. On Colin Self.

A68 'The ship on the wall,' *Lovely Jobly*, vol.II, no.III, p.22, Hercules Fisherman, London, 1991. Comment on Patricia Scanlan's interview (see *Lovely Jobly*, vol.II, no.II).

A69 *Carnegie International 1991*, The Carnegie Museum of Art, Pittsburgh, 1991. Two part catalogue: includes statement by Hamilton.

B5 'Das Sofortbild Polaroid,' *der Löwe*, pp.12–16, October 1977. Interview by Gerhard Johan Lischka on the occasion of an exhibition at Aktionsgalerie, Bern.

B6 'The Distant Involvement of Richard Hamilton,' *Vanguard*, vol.7, no.6, pp.12–14, October 1978. Interview on the occasion of an exhibition in the Vancouver Art Gallery.

B7 'Hamilton's Progress,' *Alba*, no.9, pp.40–3, Talbot Rice Art Centre, University of Edinburgh, 1988. Interview by Bill Hare and Andrew Patrizio recorded at Fruitmarket Gallery, Edinburgh.

B8 'The Apollo Portrait: Richard Hamilton,' *Apollo*, vol.131, no.336, pp.101–4, February 1990. Inteview by James Hall.

B9 'My love of art came from museums,' *Art International*, no.10, pp.51–2, Paris, Spring 1990. Interview by Jonathan Watkins.

B10 'The reconstruction of Ducamp's Large Glass,' *Art Monthly*, no.136, pp.3–5, London, May 1990. Interview by Jonathan Watkins.

B11 'Pop-Dialoge,' *Kunstforum*, no.111, pp.110–17, January–February 1991. Interview by Jürgen Zänker on the occasion of an exhibition at the Kestner-Gesellschaft, Hanover.

B12 'A Colloquio con Richard Hamilton,' *Arte in*, no.6, pp.45–6, Edizione IA, Venezia-Mestre, February 1991. Interview by Valerio Vivian on the *Image and Process* exhibition at Marconi, Milan.

B13 'That was then,' *The Independent*, 13 August 1991. Interview by Andrew Graham-Dixon on the Pop movement.

B14 'HAIKU-OHIO,' *Lovely Jobly*, vol.II, no.II, p.45, Hercules Fisherman, London, 1991. Strangely transcribed interview by Patricia Scanlan.

B15 'Richard Hamilton interviewed by Richard Cork,' in *Pop Art*, ed. Andreas C. Papadakis, pp.26–33, Art & Design, London, 1992.

Printed interviews with the artist

B1 'Son of the Bride stripped bare,' *Art and Artists*, vol.1, no.4, pp.22–8, July 1966. Interview by Mario Amaya on Hamilton's reconstruction of Duchamp's 'Large Glass'.

B2 'What Kind of Art Education,' *Studio International*, no.172, pp.132–3, September 1966. Interview by Victor Willing.

B3 'Slick it to me: Polaroid portraits, Vol.1,' *Studio International*, vol.184, no.949, pp.198–200, November 1972. Article consists mostly of comments from the artist on the origin and production of the book: interview by Elizabeth Glazebrook.

B4 'Richard Hamilton,' *der Löwe*, no.5, p.9, July 1975. Interviewed in New York in 1973.

Films, audio tapes, radio and television programmes

Broadcast items are included whether or not a transcript or recording exists

C1 *This is Tomorrow*, BBC Third Programme, 17 August 1956.

C2 *Art-Anti-Art*, BBC Third Programme, 13 November 1959. Interview with Marcel Duchamp.

C3 *Artists as Consumers: the Splendid Bargain*, BBC Third Programme, 11 March 1960. Discussion between Lawrence Alloway, Basil Taylor, Richard Hamilton and Eduardo Paolozzi in series 'Art-Anti-Art'.

C4 *Comment*, BBC Third Programme, 19 January 1961.

C5 BBC Third Programme, 11 March 1961. Discussion.

C6 *New Comment*, BBC Third Programme, 18 November 1964. Interview by Andrew Forge produced by Leonie Cohn. Broadcast in part, 18 November 1964 on 'New Comment'; in full on April 5, 1965.

C7 *The Obsessive Image*, BBC Third Programme, 15 May 1968. Discussion with Christopher Finch, Anne Seymour and Allan Jones, produced by Leonie Cohn. Recorded 3 May 1968.

C8 *Conversation with Christopher Finch and James Scott*, Maya Film Productions, 1968. Unpublished pre-edited transcript of tape made for James Scott film.

C9 *Richard Hamilton*, Maya Film Productions, London, 1969. Film (25 minutes) directed by James Scott, made for the Arts Council of Great Britain.

C10 *The Arts This Week*, BBC Third Programme, 18 March 1970.

C11 *Perspective – In Camera*, BBC Radio Three, 30 April 1971. Interview with John Donat.

C12 *Moving From Chaos To Form*, BBC Radio Three, 21 June 1972. Joseph Beuys interviewed by Hamilton.

C13 *Kaleidoscope*, BBC Radio Four, 9 April 1973. Interview on Picasso.

C14 *A Tear is Better than a Bad Word*, BBC Radio Three, 14 July 1974. Dieter Roth interviewed by Hamilton.

C15 *The Independent Group: The Impact of American Pop Culture in the Fifties*, The Open University, 1975. Talk by Hamilton. First broadcast by BBC Radio for the A351 course, 'Modern Art from 1848 to the Present Day'.

C16 *Canciones de Cadaques*, Edition Hansjörg Mayer and Galerie Cadaqués, July 1976. Double album of EP records by Dieter Roth and Richard Hamilton, with sleeve photographs by Rita Donagh.

C17 *Audio Arts*, vol.2, no.4, 1976. Marcel Duchamp's 1959 BBC interviews with George Heard Hamilton and Richard Hamilton.

C18 *Interview by Nigel Finch*, February 1977. Dieter Roth and Richard Hamilton interviewed on the occasion of the *Collaborations* exhibition at the ICA, London.

C19 *Collaborations Readings*, Audio Arts, London, 1978. Tape recordings of readings from *Collaborations* by Dieter Roth, Richard Hamilton and Duncan Smith.

C20 *Fathers of Pop (The Independent Group)*, The Arts Council of Great Britain, London, 1979. Film (40 minutes) by Reyner Banham and Julian Cooper.

C21 *Kaleidoscope*, BBC Radio Four, 6 March 1980. Talked about his exhibitions at Anthony d'Offay Gallery and Waddington Gallery.

C22 *Shock of the New*, BBC 2 Television, 1980. 'Commercial' by Hamilton for 'The critic laughs,' included in Robert Hughes' art series for television.

C23 *Kaleidoscope*, BBC Radio Four, London, 6 February 1981. Review of Jasper Johns exhibition.

C24 *Kaleidoscope*, BBC Radio Four, 11 November 1982. Interview by Paul Vaughan to mark the publication of *Collected Words*.

C25 *Audio Arts*, vol.6, no.1 side 1, 1983. Interview by Michael Compton recorded at the ICA, London, on 4 November 1982 to mark the publication of *Collected Words*.

C26 *Kaleidoscope*, BBC Radio Four, 30 March 1984. Interview on exhibition at the Museum of Modern Art, Oxford.

C27 *Conversations with Artists: Epiphanies*, BBC Radio Three, 4 April 1985. Conversation with Richard Cork.

C28 *Looking into Paintings: Episode 1: Meanings – or how Art Doesn't Imitate Life*, Malachite Productions for Channel 4, London, 13 November 1985. Interview by Alistair Smith about 'The citizen'.

C29 *Painting with Light*, Griffin Film Productions, London, 1987. One of a series of six television programmes of artists working on the Quantel Paintbox.

C30 *Third Ear*, BBC Radio Three, 28 March 1988. Interview by Julian Spalding.

C31 *Audio Arts*, vol.9, no.2, Autumn 1988. Tape recording of Roy Lichtenstein and Richard Hamilton in conversation with Marco Livingstone, discussion at Museum of Modern Art, Oxford.

C32 *Artists talking. Richard Hamilton/1: Paths of Parody and Pastiche*, Lecon Arts, 1989. Tape/slide conversation with Sarat Maharaj.

C33 *Artists talking. Richard Hamilton/2: Coolness or Satire?*, Lecon Arts, 1989. Tape/slide conversation with Sarat Maharaj.

C34 *Talking Art: Richard Hamilton*, 14 February 1990. In conversation with Michael Craig-Martin on the occasion of the *Independent Group* exhibition at the ICA, London.

C35 *Late Show*, BBC 2, 20 February 1990. On the occasion of the *Independent Group* exhibition.

C36 *Late Show Special*, BBC 2, 6 September 1991. Discussion with Andrew Graham-Dixon on the occasion of the *Pop Art* exhibition at the Royal Academy, London.

C37 *Den som gapar . . .*, SRT Kanal 1 TV, Stockholm, 8 March 1992. Interview on the crash in the art market.

One-man exhibitions

D1 *Variations on the theme of a reaper*, Gimpel Fils, London, February 1950. Single page list of exhibits.

D2 *Growth and Form*, Institute of Contemporary Arts, London, July–August 1951. Exhibition devised and designed by Hamilton: catalogue designed by Herbert Spencer.

D3 *Richard Hamilton: Paintings 1951–55*, Hanover Gallery, London, January–February 1955. Single page handlist (12 works).

D4 *Man, Machine & Motion*, University of Durham, Newcastle-upon-Tyne, May 1955. Exhibition devised and designed by Hamilton: Catalogue: text by Reyner Banham, introduction by Hamilton and Lawrence Gowing, designed by Anthony Froshaug for exhibition in the Hatton Gallery. Also shown at the ICA, London, July, 1955.

D5 *Paintings 1956–1964*, Hanover Gallery, London, October–November 1964. Catalogue designed by Gordon House, notes by Hamilton.

D6 *The Solomon R Guggenheim: six fibreglass reliefs*, Robert Fraser Gallery, London, October–November 1966. Poster and two foolscap sheets (16 works).

D7 *Richard Hamilton: Collagen, Zeichnungen und Seriegraphien*, Galerie Ricke, Kassel, March 1967. Folded card.

D8 *Paintings 1964–1967*, Galerie Alexandre Iolas, New York, May 1967. Catalogue designed by Sergio Tosi: notes by Hamilton.

D9 *Richard Hamilton: dipinti e disegni 1957–1968*, Studio Marconi, Milan, November 1968. Folded 12 page sheet (23 works), Italian translation, by Daniela Palazzoli, of 'Urbane Image'.

D10 *Richard Hamilton: Swingeing London '67, People, Graphics 1963–68*, Robert Fraser Gallery, London, April–May 1969. Four page handlist (35 works).

D11 *Richard Hamilton: graphic work since 1963*, Württembergischer Kunstverein, Stuttgart, May–June 1969. Folded card, German text (16 works).

D12 *Bilder + Zeichnungen sowie das graphische Gesamtwerk*, Galerie Hans Neuendorf, Hamburg, November–December 1969. Format and printing on one side of sheet as Studio Marconi, November 1968. With phonetic German translation by Dieter Roth of 'Urbane Image'.

D13 *Cosmetic Studies*, Studio Marconi, Milan, December 1969. Travelled to Galerie René Block, Berlin, January 1970. Folded card.

D14 *Richard Hamilton*, Tate Gallery, London, March–April 1970. Retrospective catalogue, text by Richard Morphet (100 pages). Travelled to Stedelijk van Abbemuseum, Eindhoven, and Kunsthalle, Berne.

D15 *Richard Hamilton: Prints*, National Gallery of Canada, Ottawa, September–October 1970. Unillustrated catalogue, commentary by Hamilton. Separate French language version. Travelled to Regina, Calgary, Vancouver and other towns in Canada until December 1971.

D16 *Recent Editions*, Studio Marconi, Milan, January 1971. With Italian translations of Hamilton text.

D17 *Richard Hamilton: Prints and Multiples*, Stedelijk Museum, Amsterdam, February–March 1971. With parallel Dutch translation of Hamilton text (44 pages).

D18 *Richard Hamilton*, Galerie René Block, Berlin, July 1971. With German translations of Hamilton text.

D19 *Prints, multiples and drawings*, Whitworth Art Gallery, Manchester, January–February 1972. Introduction by John Russell: commentary by Hamilton.

D20 *Hamilton*, Studio Marconi, Milan, December 1972. With Italian translations of Hamilton text.

D21 *Kent State*, Galerie René Block, Berlin, February 1973.

D22 *The Prints of Richard Hamilton*, Davison Art Center, Wesleyan University, Middletown, Connecticut, September–November 1973. Exhibition curated by Richard S. Field, text by Field. Travelled throughout the USA until March 1975.

D23 *Richard Hamilton*, Solomon R. Guggenheim Museum, New York, September–November 1973. Introduction by John Russell: commentary by Hamilton.

D24 *Richard Hamilton Graphics*, Scottish Arts Council, Edinburgh, April–May 1974.

D25 *Richard Hamilton*, Nationalgalerie, Berlin, July–August 1974. Extended German edition of Guggenheim catalogue.

D26 *Richard Hamilton: Das Graphische Werk*, Galerie Herbert Meyer-Ellinger, Frankfurt a.m., August–October 1974.

D27 *Obra Grafica Y Multiples 1964–74*, Galeria Eude, Barcelona, May 1975. Introduction by A. Cirici.

D28 *Paintings, Pastels, Prints*, Serpentine Gallery, London, October–November 1975. Commentary by Hamilton: travelled to Amsterdam, Maastricht and Arnhem.

D29 *schilderijen, pastels en grafiek*, Stedelijk Museum, Amsterdam, February 1976. Exhibition curated by Marja Bloem: travelled to Maastricht and Arnhem until October 1976. With Dutch translation of Hamilton text (16 pages).

D30 *Richard Hamilton*, Fontana d'Or, Gerona, July 1976. Folded card, 6 pages A4 (54 works).

D31 *Drawings and Graphics: Richard Hamilton*, Musée – Place de Verdun, Grenoble, February–April 1977. Introduction: French translation of John Russell's Guggenheim catalogue text. Travelled to Musée des Beaux-Arts, Chambéry, May 1977.

D32 *Release: Stage proofs and related works 1968–9 and 1972*, Tate Gallery, London, August–October 1977. Unillustrated catalogue: text by Elizabeth Underhill.

D33 *Richard Hamilton: Studies*, Kunsthalle Bielefeld, Bielefeld, April–May 1978. Exhibition curated by Michael Pauseback. Texts by: Thomas W. Gaethgens, Toni del Renzio, Karl-Egon Vester, Michael Pauseback, and 'Motion/Perspective' by Hamilton. Also travelled to Tübingen and Göttingen.

D34 *Richard Hamilton Graphics*, Vancouver Art Gallery, Vancouver, July–September 1978. Introduction by George Knox.

D35 *Interiors 1964–79*, Waddington Galleries, London, February–April 1980. Text by Hamilton.

D36 *Richard Hamilton: Drawings, prints and paintings 1941–55*, Anthony d'Offay Gallery, London, February–March 1980. Introduction by Anne Seymour.

D37 *Richard Hamilton (1922): Kent State 1970*, pp.63–6, Stedelijk Museum, Amsterdam, 1981. Part of loose-leaf publication by the Education Department, Stedelijk Museum on the occasion of exhibition of 'Kent State' screenprint and related material.

D38 *Image and Process*, Provinciaal Museum, Hasselt, September–November 1982. Broadsheet, Dutch text.

D39 *Image and Process*, Tate Gallery, London, December 1983–February 1984 and tour. Exhibition of studies, stage and final proofs from the graphic works 1952–82 curated by Richard S. Field. Catalogue Edition Hansjörg Mayer. Foreword by Hamilton. Introduction and commentary by Richard S. Field.

D40 *Richard Hamilton: Grafik 1953–81*, Nationalmuseum, Stockholm, May–June 1984. Exhibition curated by Ragnar von Holten.

D41 *Prints 1939–83*, Waddington Graphics, London, November–December 1984. A complete catalogue of graphic works published by Waddington Graphics + Edition Hansjörg Mayer.

D42 *Interactions*, Thordén Wetterling Galleries, Stockholm, January 1987. Text by Hamilton.

D43 *Richard Hamilton*, Fruitmarket Gallery, Edinburgh, March–May 1988. Exhibition curated by Mark Francis and Fiona McLeod: text by Mark Francis. Travelled to Museum of Modern Art, Oxford.

D44 *Work in Progress*, Orchard Gallery, Londonderry, September 1988. Catalogue of *Ulysses* material to date. Introduction by Terry Eagleton. Texts by Hamilton include 'Horne's House' and 'Transmogrifications' monographs.

D45 *Richard Hamilton: teknologi < ide > konstverk*, Moderna Museet, Stockholm, April–May 1989. Texts by Olle Granath, Bo Nilsson and Hamilton.

D46 *Exteriors, Interiors, Objects, People*, Kunstmuseum, Winterthur, September–November 1990. Contains essays: Dieter Schwartz, 'Exteriors, Interiors, Objects, People'; Stephen Bann, 'Exteriors/Landscapes'; Richard Hamilton, 'An inside view'; Lynne Cooke, 'Art usually comes without a guarantee'; Sarat Maharaj, 'The orgasmic smile, satire, the scatalogical.' Travelled to Kestner-Gesellschaft, Hanover and IVAM, Valencia.

D47 *Richard Hamilton*, Anthony d'Offay Gallery, London, June–August 1991. Foreword by Anne Seymour, essay by David Sylvester.

Group exhibitions

1956
This is Tomorrow, Whitechapel Art Gallery, London, August 1956. Catalogue designed by Edward Wright. Group 2 environment devised by Hamilton, John McHale and John Voelcker. With statement by Hamilton.

1957
an Exhibit, Hatton Gallery, Newcastle-upon-Tyne, June 1957. Exhibition designed by Hamilton and Victor Pasmore, leaflet designed by Hamilton with text by Lawrence Alloway. Also shown at the ICA, London, August 1957.

1959
Exhibit 2, Hatton Gallery, Newcastle-upon-Tyne, 1959. Freestanding version of *an Exhibit* using the frame structure of *Man, Machine & Motion*. No catalogue.

1964
Carnegie International 1964, Carnegie Museum of Art, Pittsburgh, 1964. Foreword by Gustave von Groschwitz.

Nieuwe realisten, Haags Gemeentemuseum, The Hague, 1964. Newspaper format (4 works).

1966
European Drawings, Solomon R. Guggenheim Museum, New York, 1966. Introduction by Lawrence Alloway (4 works).

Exhibition by artists connected with the Robert Fraser Gallery, London, Studio Marconi, Milan, 1966. Essay by Christopher Finch. Italian text with English translation on accompanying 4 page leaflet (5 works).

1967
Drawing Towards Painting 2, Arts Council Gallery, London, 1967. Text by Anne Seymour. Arts Council touring exhibition, in Great Britain until March 1967 (21 works).

1968
ars multiplicata, Wallraf-Richartz-Museum, Cologne, January 1968. Curated by Gert von der Osten.

Documenta 4, Documenta, Kassel, 1968. Introduction by Arnold Bode, essays by Max Imdahl and J. Leering (9 works).

1969
Pop Art Redefined, Hayward Gallery, London, July–August 1969. Arts Council of Great Britain exhibition curated by John Russell and Suzi Gablik.

1970
British Painting and Sculpture 1960–1970, National Gallery of Art, Washington DC, 1970. Text by Edward Lucie-Smith. An exhibition organised by the Tate Gallery and the British Council (4 works).

Kelpra prints, Hayward Gallery, London, 1970. Introductions by Ronald Alley, Joe Tilson, Gordon House. Arts Council exhibition (7 works).

Métamorphose de l'objet: art et anti art 1910–1970, Palais des Beaux-Arts, Brussels, 1970. Touring in Europe (2 works).

1971
Graphic der Welt: International Druckgraphik der letzen 25 Jahren, Kunsthalle, Nürnberg, August 1971. Text by W. Stubbe.

1973
Graphische Techniken, Neuer Berliner Kunstverein, Berlin, February 1973. Exhibition of prints by Dieter Roth, K.P. Brehmer, Richard Hamilton: curated by René Block (41 works).

Combattimento per Un'Immagine: Fotografi e Pittori, Il Museo Civico di Torino, Turin, 1973. Exhibition curated by Daniela Palazzoli and Luigi Carluccio.

1976
Arte inglese oggi 1960–76, Palazzo Reale, Milan, February–May 1976. Foreword by Gerald Forty, essays by Norbert Lynton and David Thompson. Italian/English parallel text. British Council exhibition (11 works).

Pop Art in England: Beginnings of a New Figuration, Kunstverein, Hamburg, February 1976. Exhibition curated by Uwe M. Schneede. Travelled to Galerie im Lenbachhaus, Munich and to York City Art Gallery.

The Human Clay, Hayward Gallery, London, August 1976. Arts Council of Great Britain exhibition selected by R.B. Kitaj.

1977
Malerei und Photographie im Dialog, Kunsthaus Zürich, May 1977. Exhibition curated by Erika Billeter.

Englische Kunst der Gegenwart, Kunstlerhaus Palais Thurn und Taxis, Bregenz, July 1977.

Documenta 6, Documenta, Kassel, 1977. Introduction by Manfred Schneckenburger, essays by Lothar Romain, Karl Oskar Blase and Bazon Brock (1 work).

1978
INTERFACEs: Artists Statements September 1977– February 1978, Whitworth Art Gallery, University of Manchester, Manchester, March 1978. Text by Richard Hamilton and Dieter Roth. Catalogue/poster folded sheet.

INTERFACEs: Dieter Roth and Richard Hamilton, Waddington and Tooth Galleries II, London, 1978. Folded card, 9 pages (30 works).

The mechanized image: an historical perspective on 20th century prints, Portsmouth Museum and Art Gallery, Portsmouth, 1978. Text by Pat Gilmour. Catalogue published to accompany an Arts Council touring exhibition (5 works).

A treasury of modern drawings: the Joan and Lester Avnet collection, Museum of Modern Art, New York, 1978. Text by William S. Lieberman (4 works).

1979
INTERFACEs, Kunsthalle Bielefeld, June 1979. Introduction by Thomas W. Gaethgens: with conversation between Dieter Roth and Hamilton.

Nachbilder: vom Nutzen und Nachteil des Zitierens Für die Kunst, Kunstverein, Hanover, 1979 (10 works).

1980
Für Augen und Ohren, Akademie der Künste, Berlin, January 1980. Exhibition curated by René Block.

Instantanés, Centre Georges Pompidou, Paris, May 1980. Exhibition of Polaroid photographs curated by Alain Sayag.

Kelpra Studio: The Rose and Chris Prater Gift, Tate Gallery, London, July 1980. Text by Pat Gilmour.

Printed art: a view of two decades, Museum of Modern Art, New York, 1980. Text by Riva Castleman (2 works).

1981
Druckgraphik Wandlungen eines Mediums seit 1945, Nationalgalerie, Berlin, June 1981. Exhibition curated by A. Dückers.

Instant fotografie, Stedelijk Museum, Amsterdam, December 1981. Exhibition curated by Els Barents: contains statement by Hamilton.

British Artists in Berlin, Goethe Institute, London, 1981. Two decades of the DAAD's Artists-in-Berlin-Programme. Preface by Wieland Schmied (3 works).

Westkunst: Zeitgenossische Kunst seit 1939, Dumont, Cologne, 1981. Exhibition curated by Kasper Koenig and Laszlo Gloszer.

1982
Momentbild – Kunstlerphotographie, Kestner-Gesellschaft, Hanover, March 1982. Introduction by Carl Haenlein.

The Print Collection: A selection, Tate Gallery, London, March 1982.

'60'80 attitudes / concepts / images, Stedelijk Museum, Amsterdam, April 1982. Exhibition curated by Ad Petersen.

1983
A Cellular Maze, Orchard Gallery, Londonderry, August 1983. Pamphlet with texts by Rita Donagh and Richard Hamilton, published on the occasion of a joint exhibition.

Contemporary Masters, World Print Council, San Francisco, September 1983. Introduction by K. Tsujimoto: Pat Gilmour on Richard Hamilton.

Photography in Contemporary Art, National Museum of Modern Art, Tokyo, October 1983. Curated by Hisae Fujii. Travelled to National Museum of Modern Art, Kyoto, December 1983.

Art contre/against Apartheid, Les Artists du monde contre l'apartheid, Paris, 1983.

Aspects of British Art from the Solomon R Guggenheim collection, Solomon R. Guggenheim Museum, New York, 1983. Text by Lisa Dennison (3 works).

1984
Four Rooms, Liberty's, London, March 1984. Arts Council of Great Britain exhibition curated by Michael Regan: with a text by Hamilton.

Artistic Collaboration in the Twentieth Century, Hirshhorn Museum, Washington DC, June 1984. Exhibition curated by Cynthia Jaffee McCabe.

The Hard-Won Image, Tate Gallery, London, July–September 1984. Exhibition curated by Richard Morphet.

1985
Pop Art 1955–70, International Cultural Corporation of Australia, 1985. Exhibition touring in Australia, organised by the International Council of the Museum of Modern Art, New York, curated by Henry Geldzahler.

1986
Falls the Shadow: recent British and European art: Hayward Annual, Hayward Gallery, London, April–June 1986. Text by Jon Thompson and Barry Barker. Also a 16 page checklist of works in the exhibition. Arts Council exhibition.

Beuys zu Ehren, Stadtische Galerie im Lenbachhaus, Munich, July 1986.

Antidotes to Madness?: Richard Hamilton, Nam June Paik, Ree Morton, Hannah Collins and Piotr Sobieralski, Riverside Studios, London, 1986. Text by Maureen O. Paley. Folded card with text by Maureen O. Paley.

Studies of the Nude. Marlborough Fine Art, London, 1986. Introduction by William Packer (2 works).

1987
Aldo Crommelynck, Waddington Graphics, London, March 1987. Exhibition of Aldo Crommelynck prints with Braque, Picasso, Hamilton, Dine. Text by Pat Gilmour.

Pop Art USA-UK, Odakyu Grand Gallery, Tokyo, July 1987. Essays by Lawrence Alloway, Marco Livingstone and Masataka Ogawa. Travelled to Osaka, Funabashi and Yokohama.

The International Art Show for the End of World Hunger, Artists to End Hunger, Inc., New York, 1987. Contains statement by Hamilton.

1988
Richard Hamilton and Tom Phillips: A Question of Style, Australian National Gallery, Canberra, March 1988. Introduction by Pat Gilmour, Text by Mark Henshaw.

Zuruck zur Natur, aber wie?, Stadtische Galerie im Prinz-Max-Palais, Karlsruhe, April–July 1988. Curated by Erika Rodiger-Diruf.

this is tomorrow today, Institute for Art and Urban Resources, New York, October–December 1988. Exhibition curated by Brian Wallis: contains reprint of 'Persuading Image'.

1989
Blasphemies, Ecstasies, Cries, Serpentine Gallery, London, January 1989. Exhibition curated by Andrew Brighton.

20a Bienal Internacional de São Paulo, São Paulo, October–December 1989. 'Lobby' installation in British section and print retrospective in international section. Two pages in vol. 1 of catalogue (228 pages) of Bienal. See also 4 page catalogue on Hamilton with essay by Richard S. Field, in folder of catalogues on artists in British section. Print retrospective toured to Brazil, Uruguay and Mexico.

1990
Glasgow's Great British Art Exhibition, Glasgow Museums and Art Galleries, March 1990. Exhibition curated by Julian Spalding.

The Readymade Boomerang: Certain relations in 20th century art, Biennale of Sydney, Sydney, April 1990. Introduction by the exhibition curator, René Block, cover title: 'Art is easy'.

Marcel Duchamp et/en Richard Hamilton, Galerie des Beaux-Arts Galerij, Brussels, September–October 1990. No catalogue.

High & Low: Modern Art and Popular Culture, Museum of Modern Art, New York, October 1990.

The Independent Group: Postwar Britain and the Aesthetics of Plenty, MIT Press, Cambridge, Mass., and London, 1990. Published on the occasion of an exhibition: ICA, London. Travelled to Valencia, Spain, and various locations in the USA. Includes retrospective statement by Hamilton, p.188.

1991
Pop Art, Royal Academy of Arts, London, September 1991. Exhibition curated by Marco Livingstone. Travelled to Museum Ludwig, Cologne and Centro de Arte Reina Sofia, Madrid.

Carnegie International 1991, The Carnegie Museum of Art, Pittsburgh, 1991. Two part catalogue: includes statement by Hamilton.

Sections of books: articles in periodicals and newspapers: unpublished theses

1955
Lawrence Alloway, 'Re vision,' *Art News and Review*, vol.6, no.26, p.5, 22 January 1955.

Reyner Banham, 'Vision in Motion,' *Art*, p.3, January 1955.

Lawrence Alloway, 'Art News from London: All Over the Place,' *ARTnews*, vol.54, no.3, p.11, 65, July 1955. Review of *Man, Machine & Motion*.

Reyner Banham, 'Man, Machine & Motion,' *Architectural Review*, vol.118, no.703, pp.51–3, July 1955. Review of exhibition, ICA, London.

1956
Lawrence Alloway, 'This is tomorrow,' *ARTnews*, vol.55, no.5, p.64, September 1956. Review of exhibition *This is Tomorrow*, Whitechapel Art Gallery, London.

Reyner Banham, 'Miscellany – Exhibitions,' *Architectural Review*, vol.120, no.716, pp.186–8, September 1956. Review of exhibition *This is Tomorrow*, Whitechapel Art Gallery, London.

Theo Crosby, 'This is Tomorrow,' *Architectural Design*, vol.26, no.9, pp.302–4, September 1956.

Theo Crosby, 'This is Tomorrow,' *Architectural Design*, vol.26, no.10, pp.334–6, October 1956.

1958
Reyner Banham, 'Ideal Interiors,' *Architectural Review*, no.734, pp.207–8, March 1958. Review of Ideal Home exhibition room. *A Gallery for a collector*.

1959
Roger Coleman, 'Will success spoil industrial design?,' *Architecture and Building*, pp.296–7, August 1959. Review of ICA lecture *The Design Image of the Fifties*.

1960
Reyner Banham, 'Persuading image: a symposium,' *Design*, no.138, pp.54–7, London, June 1960. Designers, critics and manufacturers from Europe and America comment on issues raised in Hamilton's article, 'Persuading Image,' in *Design*, no.134. Text includes Hamilton's response to the comments.

Jasper Johns, 'Duchamp,' *Scrap*, no.2, December 1960. Review of typographic version of Marcel Duchamp's *Green Box*.

1961
Lawrence Alloway, 'Artists as Consumers,' *Image*, no.3, pp.14–19, February 1961.

1962
Lawrence Alloway, 'Pop Art since 1949,' *The Listener*, pp.1085–7, 27 December 1962.

1963
Jasia Reichardt, 'Pop Art and After,' *Art International*, vol.7, no.2, pp.42–7, 1963.

1964
David Sylvester, 'Art in a Coke Climate,' *The Sunday Times Magazine*, pp.17–23, 26 January 1964.

Charles Spencer, 'Richard Hamilton: Painter of Being Today,' *Studio International*, vol.168, no.858, pp.176–81, October 1964.

Patrick Procktor, 'Techniculture,' *New Statesman*, vol.68, no.1756, p.710, 6 November 1964. Review of exhibition, Hanover Gallery, London.

Norbert Lynton, 'London Letter: Hamilton,' *Art International*, p.43, 10 December 1964.

1965
'Notizen zu Meiner Arbeit,' *das kunstwerk*, pp.3–4 and 13, 18 January 1965.

John Russell, 'Art News from London: Richard Hamilton,' *ARTnews*, vol.63, no.9, p.49, January 1965.

Robert Melville, 'One-Man Show at the Hanover,' *Architectural Review*, vol.137, no.816, pp.141–2, February 1965.

John Russell, 'London/NYC: the two way traffic,' *Art in America*, vol.53, no.2, pp.130–1, April 1965.

Mario Amaya, *Pop Art and After*, New York, 1965.

Mario Amaya, *Pop as Art: a survey of the new super realism*, pp.31–42, Studio Vista, New York, London, 1965.

'Eduardo Paolozzi,' in *Arts Yearbook 8*, pp.160–3, 1965. Interview by Hamilton.

Bryan Robertson, John Russell, and Lord Snowdon, *Private view*, pp.258–9, Nelson, London, 1965.

1966
Andrew Forge, 'In Duchamp's footsteps,' *Studio International*, vol.171, no.878, pp.248–51, June 1966. Hamilton's reconstruction of the 'Large Glass'.

M.G. McNay, 'Big Daddy of Pop,' *The Guardian*, p.7, 25 July 1966.

Reyner Banham, 'Work in progress,' *Architectural Review*, vol.140, no.833, pp.61–2, July 1966. Review of exhibition, Robert Fraser Gallery, London.

Christopher Finch, 'Richard Hamilton,' *Art International*, no.8, pp.16–23, October 1966.

Bryan Robertson, 'Firing Line,' *The Spectator*, 28 October 1966.

Gene Baro, 'Hamilton's Guggenheim,' *Art & Artists*, no.8, pp.28–31, November 1966.

[Richard Morphet], *Studio International*, vol.172, no.884, p.i, December 1966. Advertisement for Peter Stuyvesant Foundation Collection.

Lawrence Alloway, 'The development of British Pop,' in *Pop Art*, ed. Lucy Lippard, pp.26–68, Thames & Hudson, London, 1966.

Enrico Crispolti, *La Pop Art*, Milan, 1966.

The Tate Gallery report 1964–65, pp.38–9, Tate Gallery, London: HMSO, 1966.

1967
Alain Jouffroy, 'Art de demi brume á Londres,' *L'Oeil*, no.149, p.84, May 1967.

Arts Magazine, vol.41, no.8, p.58, Summer 1967. Review of exhibition, Alexandre Iolas Gallery, New York.

Alain Jouffroy, 'l'Actualism,' *Connaissance des arts*, no.186, pp.42–9, 18 August 1967.

Christopher Finch, 'A Fine Pop Art Continuum,' *New Worlds*, vol.51, no.176, pp.15–19, New Worlds, London, October 1967.

1968
Lawrence Alloway, 'Pop Art: The Words,' in *Auction*, vol.1, pp.7–9, New York, February 1968.

Richard Morphet, 'Richard Hamilton's Interior II,' *The Burlington Magazine*, vol.110, no.781, pp.219–20, April 1968.

Christopher Finch, *Pop Art: Object and Image*, Studio Vista, London, 1968.

Aaron Scharf, 'Art and Photography today,' in *Art and Photography*, pp.249–51, Allan Lane the Penguin Press, London, 1968.

The Tate Gallery 1967–8, pp.60–1, Tate Gallery, London, 1968.

1969
Barry Lord, *Artscanada*, vol.26, no.1, pp.27–8, Art Gallery of Ontario, February 1969. Includes discussion of Hamilton's role as juror for the exhibition *Canadian artists '68*.

Norbert Lynton, 'Art out of News,' *The Guardian*, p.10, 25 April 1969.

Simon Field, 'Objects more or less,' *Art and Artists*, vol.4, no.1, pp.57–8, April 1969.

Reyner Banham, 'Representations in protest,' *New Society*, pp.717–18, London, 8 May 1969.

Lawrence Alloway, 'Popular Culture and Pop Art,' *Studio International*, vol.178, no.913, p.3, July–August 1969.

Jasia Reichardt, 'People: Retrospective Exhibition at the Tate Gallery,' *Architectural Design*, no.345, July 1969.

John Russell, 'Pop Reappraised,' *Art in America*, no.57, pp.78–88, July 1969. Review of exhibition, Hayward Gallery, London.

Philip Oakes, 'Profits from the Present,' *The Sunday Times*, 16 November 1969.

'Big Daddy: Pop Pioneer Hamilton,' *Der Spiegel*, no.23, pp.177–9, December 1969. Review of exhibition, Galerie Neuendorf, Hamburg.

H. Flemming, *das kunstwerk*, vol.23, no.3–4, pp.56, 81, December 1969. Review of exhibition, Galerie Neuendorf, Hamburg.

Christopher Finch, *Image as Language: Aspects of British Art 1950–68*, pp.19–35, Penguin, Harmondsworth, 1969.

Atushi Miyakawa, *About Quotation Continued*, pp.65–79, 1969. The title is No.5 in a series called 'Alice in Mirrortown'.

John Russell and Suzi Gablik, *Pop Art Redefined*, pp.73–6, 88–91, Thames & Hudson, London, 1969. Statements by the artist reproduced from *Architectural Design*, October 1962 and *Studio International*, January 1968.

1970
Peter Fuller, 'Close Up,' *Harpers Bazaar*, p.17, February 1970. Preview of Tate Gallery retrospective.

H. Ohff, 'Cosmetic Studies,' *das kunstwerk*, no.23, p.76, Stuttgart, February 1970. Review of exhibition, René Block Gallery, Berlin.

Norbert Lynton, 'The pop of Pop,' *The Guardian*, p.10, 12 March 1970.

Edwin Mullins, 'Father of Pop Art,' *Daily Telegraph Magazine*, pp.45–8, 13 March 1970.

Guy Brett, 'Putting on the style,' *The Times*, 14 March 1970.

Pat Gilmour, 'Richard Hamilton: Painter of Prints and Printer of Paintings,' *Arts Review*, vol.22, no.5, p.137, 14 March 1970.

Bryan Robertson, 'The Legacy of Duchamp,' *The Spectator*, 14 March 1970.

'Pop Daddy,' *Vogue*, vol.127, no.4, pp.90–1, London, 15 March 1970.

John Russell, 'All images are equal,' *The Sunday Times*, 15 March 1970.

Robert Melville, 'The Power of the Word,' *New Statesman*, pp.420–1, 20 March 1970.

Terence Mullaly, 'Father of British Pop Art,' *Daily Telegraph*, 21 March 1970.

Paul Overy, 'Hamilton's world,' *Financial Times*, 25 March 1970.

James Burr, 'The First "Pop" Painter,' *Apollo*, vol.91, no.97, p.238, March 1970.

Peter Fuller, 'Richard Hamilton: The Tate Gallery,' *Connoisseur*, vol.173, no.697, p.196, March 1970.

Pat Gilmour, 'Art Films of James Scott,' *Art and Artists*, no.4, pp.16–19, March 1970.

R.C. Kenedy, 'Richard Hamilton,' *Art International*, vol.XIV, no.3, pp.45–53, 57, March 1970.

R.C. Kenedy, 'Richard Hamilton Visited,' *Art and Artists*, vol.4, no.12, pp.20–3, March 1970.

'Richard Hamilton,' *Album*, no.2, pp.40–2, March 1970.

'Richard Hamilton: Fashion Plates,' *London Magazine*, no.9, pp.82–3, March 1970.

John Russell, 'Richard Hamilton,' *Art in America*, no.58, pp.115–19, March 1970.

Andrew Causey, 'A question of identity,' *Illustrated London News*, p.27, 4 April 1970.

Christopher Finch, 'Richard Hamilton at the Tate,' *Arts Magazine*, no.44, pp.49–50, April 1970.

'Richard Hamilton: est-il le precurseur du pop art?,' *Jardin des Arts*, no.185, pp.60–3, April 1970.

Bernard Denvir, 'Exhibition at the Tate,' *Arts International*, no.14, May 1970.

R. Kudielka, 'Tate Gallery London,' *das kunstwerk*, vol.23, no.9–10, pp.44–5, Stuttgart, June 1970.

Michael Kustow, 'Richard Hamilton à la Tate Gallery,' *Opus International*, no.18, pp.49–53, June 1970.

Cor Blok, 'Richard Hamilton: towards a definitive statement?,' *Museumjournaal*, vol.15, no.4, pp.170–5, September 1970. Dutch text with English summary p.223.

Guy Burn, 'Crónica De Londres,' *Goya*, no.98, pp.104–6, September 1970.

H. Ohff, 'Hamilton Ausstellung,' *das kunstwerk*, vol.23, no.11–12, pp.71–2, Stuttgart, October 1970.

Laszlo Glozer, 'Tod am Bildschirm – oder: Die Kunst und die Medien,' *Frankfurter Allgemeine Zeitung*, 30 December 1970 (reprinted Kunstkritiken, Frankfurt a.m., 1974).

Michael Compton, *Pop Art*, pp.56–61, Hamlyn, London, 1970.

Kenneth Coutts-Smith, *The Dream of Icarus: art and society in the twentieth century*, pp.178–80, Hutchinson, London, 1970.

George Melly, *Revolt into Style: the Pop Arts in Britain*, Allan Lane the Penguin Press, London, 1970.

'Richard Hamilton,' *Mizue*, no.781, pp.65–79, 1970. Japanese text.

The Tate Gallery 1968–70, pp.84–7, Tate Gallery, London, 1970.

1971
art now: Man-Made Nature, Kodansha Ltd, Tokyo, 1971.

1972
F.W. Hawcroft, 'Prints, multiples and drawings by Richard Hamilton,' *Connoisseur*, vol.179, no.720, p.151, February 1972. Review of exhibition, Whitworth Art Gallery, Manchester.

Daniela Palazzoli, 'Viaggio fuori stagione,' *Domus*, no.516, p.52, November 1972.

Van Deren Coke, *The Painter and the Photographer: from Delacroix to Warhol*, pp.247–9, 314–5, University of New Mexico Press, Albuquerque, 1972.

'From Painters, a Different Tack for Photographers,' in *Frontiers of Photography*, pp.105, 108–9, Time-Life Books, New York, 1972.

The Tate Gallery 1970–72, pp.114–19, Tate Gallery, London, 1972.

Gerald Woods, Philip Thompson, and John Williams, *Art Without Boundaries 1950–70*, pp.128–9, Thames and Hudson, London, 1972. Includes statement by the artist on 'Kent State'.

1973
Harold Rosenberg, 'Dogma and Talent,' *The New Yorker*, pp.115–19, 15 October 1973. Review of exhibition, Solomon R. Guggenheim Museum, New York.

Barbara Rose, 'The Decline of the West, The Revolt of the Masses,' *New York Magazine*, pp.112–13, 22 October 1973. Review of exhibition, Solomon R. Guggenheim Museum, New York.

Piri Halasz, 'A Devastating Elegance: Richard Hamilton Master of English Pop Art,' *ARTnews*, vol.72, no.9, pp.86–7, November 1973.

John Loring, 'Not Just So Many Marvellously Right Images,' *The Print Collector's Newsletter*, vol.IV, no.5, pp.98–100, November–December 1973.

James Collins, 'Richard Hamilton the Two Culture Theory,' *Artforum*, vol.12, no.4, pp.58–60, December 1973.

Riva Castleman, *Modern prints since 1942*, pp.138–141, 165, Barrie and Jenkins, London, 1973.

1974
Peter Frank, 'Richard Hamilton at the Guggenheim,' *Art in America*, vol.62, no.1, pp.97–9, January 1974.

Laszlo Glozer, 'Staedische Galerie im Lenbachhaus,' *Pantheon*, no.32, pp.312–13, July 1974.

Andrew DeShong, 'Will the real Richard Hamilton please stand up?,' *Artweek*, vol.5, no.35, pp.1, 16, 19 October 1974.

1975
Michael Greenwood, 'British painting '74,' *Artscanada*, vol.32, no.1, issue no.196/7, pp.29–34, March 1975. Review of exhibition, Hayward Gallery, London.

Michael McNay, 'Painters Talking – 1: Richard Hamilton,' *The New Review*, vol.2, no.16, pp.21–8, July 1975.

Caroline Tisdall, *The Guardian*, p.8, 10 October 1975. Review of exhibition, Serpentine Gallery, London.

Karl Heinz Bohrer, 'Vergiftete Visonen vom Schönen,' *Frankfurter Allgemeine Zeitung*, 3 November 1975. Review of exhibition, Serpentine Gallery, London.

Charles McCorquodale, *Art International*, vol.19, no.10, p.25, December 1975. Review of exhibition, Serpentine Gallery, London.

Mirrors of the Mind, Multiples Inc. and Castelli Graphics, New York, 1975. Pamphlet with portfolio contains text by Nicolas Calas for portfolio of multiples.

Frank Whitford, 'Origines britanniques du pop art,' *Revue de l'Art*, no.30, pp.77–81, 1975. French text with English summary pp.110–11.

1976
Toni del Renzio, 'Style, technique and iconography,' *Art and Artists*, vol.11, no.4, pp.34–9, July 1976. Extended version, in English, of catalogue introduction to group exhibition at the Boymans Van Beuningen Museum, Rotterdam, May–July 1976.

Anne Nicholson, 'Invisibilities in the "Large Glass",' *The Month*, vol.237 (second new series, vol.9, no.11), no.1310, pp.383–7, November 1976.

Stephen Dixon and Michael McNay, 'Bone of Contention,' *The Guardian*, 16 December 1976.

Guido Almansi, 'Watteau escrementizio,' *Nuovi Argomenti*, no.2, pp.191–4, 1976. Review of exhibition, Serpentine Gallery, London.

1977

Josep Iglesias del Marquet, 'Una historia del pop-art,' *Goya*, no.140–1, pp.153–4, September 1977. Review of INTERFACEs exhibition, Galeria Eude, Barcelona.

'Statements by the artist,' in *Towards another picture: an anthology of writings by artists working in Britain 1945–1977*, ed. Andrew Brighton and Lynda Morris, pp.24, 78–9, 122, 148–9, Midland Group Nottingham, Nottingham, 1977.

1978

Carter Ratcliff, *Art International*, vol.22, no.1, pp.87–8, January 1978. Review of INTERFACEs exhibition, Carl Solway Gallery, New York.

Tiffany Bell, *Arts Magazine*, vol.52, no.6, p.33, February 1978. Review of INTERFACEs exhibition, Carl Solway Gallery, New York.

Richard Ehrlich, 'Artist's Eye,' *Art and Artists*, vol.13, no.4, pp.40–1, August 1978.

Keith Roberts, 'Current and Forthcoming Exhibitions,' *The Burlington Magazine*, vol.120, no.905, pp.547–8, August 1978. Review of *The artist's eye*.

Peter Winter, 'Richard Hamilton: Studien 1937–77.' *Pantheon*, vol.36, no.4, pp.374–5, October 1978.

1979

Arthur Perry, 'Richard Hamilton's Graphics,' *Art-magazine*, vol.10, no.42, pp.37–40, February–March 1979.

Handbuch Museum Ludwig: Kunst des 20 Jahrhunderts, Museum Ludwig, Cologne, 1979. Catalogue of Ludwig Collection by Evelyn Weiss.

1980

Guy Burn, 'Richard Hamilton Interiors '64–'69,' *Arts Review*, vol.32, no.6, p.155, 28 March 1980. Review of exhibition, Waddington Graphics, London.

Peter Fuller, 'Richard Hamilton,' *Aspects*, no.10, Spring 1980.

Jeremy Wood, *Pantheon*, vol.38, no.3, p.226, July–September 1980. Review of exhibitions, Anthony d'Offay Gallery and Waddington Gallery, London.

Richard Martin, 'Richard Hamilton,' *Arts Magazine*, vol.55, no.2, p.8, October 1980. Review of exhibition, Charles Cowles Gallery, New York.

Donald B. Kuspit, 'Richard Hamilton at Cowles,' *Art in America*, vol.68, no.10, pp.153–4, December 1980.

1981

Peter Fuller, 'The Necessity of Art Education,' *Art Monthly*, no.47, pp.27–9, June 1981. This article resulted in a lengthy correspondance between Fuller and Hamilton, published in subsequent issues of *Art Monthly*: nos.49, 50, 51 and 53.

Gloria Moure, 'Entavista a Richard Hamilton,' *Cimali*, no.11/12, October 1981.

David Thistlewood, *A continuing process: the new creativity in British art education 1955–65*, Institute of Contemporary Arts, London, 1981. Published on the occasion of an exhibition, focusing on the work of three innovators in art education: Richard Hamilton, Victor Pasmore and Tom Hudson.

1982

Adrian Lewis, 'British avant-garde painting 1945–1956: Part III,' *Artscribe International*, no.36, pp.14–27, August 1982.

Yoshiaki Tono, 'Richard Hamilton,' in *Chatting with Artists*, pp.249–65, Iwanami Publishing Co., Tokyo, September 1982. Chapter in book of conversations.

Tom Phillips, 'Cogent consumerism,' *Times Literary Supplement*, no.4156, p.1294, 26 November 1982. Review of *Collected Words*.

Marina Vaizey, *The artist as photographer*, pp.123–5, Sidgwick & Jackson, London, 1982.

1983

Adrian Lewis, 'Collected Words by Richard Hamilton,' *Artscribe International*, no.39, pp.63–6, February 1983. Review of *Collected Words*.

Richard E. Caves, 'Collected Words, 1953–1982,' *Print Collector's Newsletter*, March–April 1983.

Tanya Harrod, *Art International*, vol.xxvi, no.2, pp.77–8, April–June 1983. Review of *Collected Words*.

Valentine Tatransky, 'Richard Hamilton,' *Art International*, vol.xxvi, no.3, pp.34–8, James Fitzsimmons, Lugano, July–August 1983.

Julian Spalding, 'Collected Words, 1953–82,' *The Burlington Magazine*, vol.125, no.967, pp.631–2, October 1983. Review of *Collected Words*.

1984

Raymond Spurrier, 'A sign of the times,' *The Artist*, vol.99, no.2, pp.16–19, February 1984.

Nena Dimitrijevic, 'Richard Hamilton: Image and Process,' *Flash Art*, no.116, p.42, March 1984. Review of *Image and Process* exhibition at the Tate Gallery, London.

Christiane Bergob, *Kunstforum International*, no.71–2, pp.312–14, April–May 1984. Review of *Four Rooms* exhibition at Liberty's, London.

Charlotte Ellis, 'Four Rooms,' *Architectural Review*, vol.175, no.1046, pp.62–3, April 1984. Review of *Four Rooms* exhibition at Liberty's, London.

Roger Bevan, 'Richard Hamilton: Image and Process,' *Print Quarterly*, vol.1, no.2, pp.138–42, June 1984.

Pat Gilmour, 'Richard Hamilton: graphic retrospective,' *Art Monthly*, no.82, pp.16–17, December 1984. Review of exhibition, Waddington Graphics, London.

Vivian Endicott Barnett, *100 Works by Modern Masters from the Guggenheim Museum*, p.139 and covers, Harry N. Abrams Inc., New York, 1984.

The Tate Gallery 1980–82: illustrated catalogue of acquisitions, pp.252–3, Tate Gallery, London, 1984.

1985

Richard E. Caves, 'Richard Hamilton: Prints 1939–83; Image and Process,' *Print Collector's Newsletter*, vol.15, no.6, pp.221–3, January–February 1985. Book reviews.

Heinz Ohff, 'Prints, 1939–83,' *das kunstwerk*, vol.38, no.4–5, pp.166–7, September 1985. Review of exhibition, DAAD Galerie, Berlin.

Richard Martin, 'A Past as palpable as the present: image and history in the art of Richard Hamilton,' *Arts Magazine*, vol.60, no.2, pp.80–3, October 1985.

Peter Fuller, 'The Hard-Won Image,' in *Images of God, The Consolations of Lost Illusions*, pp.98–108, 1985.

Sarat Maharaj, *The Dialectic of Modernism and Mass Culture: A Study of Pop Art in Britain with special reference to Richard Hamilton's and Eduardo Paolozzi's work (1935–85)*, University of Reading, 1985. Unpublished thesis for doctorate.

1986

Pat Gilmour, 'Symbiotic exploitation or collaboration: Dine and Hamilton with Crommelynck,' *Print Collector's Newsletter*, vol.xv, no.6, pp.194–8, January–February 1986.

Kouichirou Ishizaki, Ben Yama, and Ichiou Haryu, 'Richard Hamilton,' *Hangwa Geijutsu*, no.52, pp.59–83, 1986.

Wenzel J. Jacob, *Die Entwicklung der Pop Art in England*, Peter Lang, Frankfurt a.m., 1986. Thesis for doctorate.

Dawn Leach-Ruhl, *Studien zu Richard Hamilton: Das Fruhwerk*, Ann Arbor: UMI, 8718894, 1986. Dissertation. Ruhr-University, 1986.

Carl Ruhrberg, 'Zwischen Faszination und Kritik,' in *Kunst im 20 Jahrhundert – Auswahlkatalog*, pp.230–2, Das Museum Ludwig, Cologne, 1986.

The Tate Gallery 1982–84: illustrated catalogue of acquisitions, pp.401–5, Tate Gallery, London, 1986.

1987

Christopher Holden and Roy Perry, 'The reconstruction of the lower panel of Duchamp/Hamilton's "Large Glass",' *Conservator*, no.11, pp.3–13, 1987.

1988

Dawn Leach-Ruhl, 'The Chronology of Richard Hamilton's Reaper Series,' *Print Quarterly*, vol.v, no.1, pp.66–71, March 1988.

Frederick Palmer, 'Painting and photography: a love-hate affair,' *The Artist*, vol.103, no.4, pp.21–3, April 1988.

Susan Tallman, 'Richard Hamilton's Ulysses,' *Arts Magazine*, vol.63, no.1, pp.23–4, September 1988.

Michael Tarantino, *Artforum*, vol.27, no.1, p.158, September 1988. Review of exhibition, Fruitmarket Gallery, Edinburgh.

Paul Wood, 'Richard Hamilton,' *Artscribe International*, no.72, pp.77–8, November–December 1988.

Lynne Cooke, 'Dread and Desire,' *Art International*, no.5, pp.73–4, Winter 1988. Review of exhibition, Museum of Modern Art, Oxford.

'Richard Hamilton: Methoden zur Rückeroberung der Bilbweld für die Kunst,' *Künstler Kritisches Lexikon der Gegenwartskunst*, pp.1–16, WB Verlag, Munich, 1988. Issue devoted to Hamilton.

The Tate Gallery 1984–86: illustrated catalogue of acquisitions, pp.371–5, Tate Gallery, London, 1988.

Richard Yeomans, 'Basic design and the pedagogy of Richard Hamilton,' *Journal of Art and Design Education*, vol.7, no.2, pp.155–73, 1988. Examines the foundation course in basic design taught by Hamilton after 1954 at the University of Newcastle, Department of Fine Art.

1989
James Odling-Smee, 'Richard Hamilton: Work in Progress,' *Arts Review*, vol.41, no.2, pp.63–4, January 1989. Review of exhibition of *Ulysses* illustrations at Arts Council of Northern Ireland Gallery, Belfast.

Stephen Coppel, 'Richard Hamilton's *Ulysses* Etchings: an Examination of Work in Progress,' *Print Quarterly*, no.1, pp.10–42, March 1989.

Dawn Leach-Ruhl, 'Das imaginaire Museum der Gegenwart XIV – Richard Hamilton "Lux 50",' *das kunstwerk*, no.1 XLII, pp.63–4, Stuttgart, March 1989.

Brian McAvera, 'Richard Hamilton, *Ulysses* and the Flaxman Factor,' *Art Monthly*, no.124, pp.19–21, March 1989.

Angélica Moraes, 'Festa para os olhos,' *Veja*, pp.150–4, São Paulo, 18 October 1989.

Tilman Osterwold, *Pop Art*, Benedikt Taschen Verlag GmbH & Co KG, Cologne, 1989.

1990
Terry Myers, *Flash Art*, no.150, p.132, January–February 1990. Review of exhibition, Paul Kasmin Gallery, New York.

Robert Mahony, *Arts Magazine*, vol.64, no.7, pp.102–3, February 1990. Review of exhibition, Paul Kasmin Gallery, New York.

Andrew Brighton, 'Hamilton, IG, Mythmaking & Photography,' *Creative Camera*, no.303, pp.28–30, London, May 1990.

Lynne Cooke, 'Richard Hamilton,' *Parkett*, no.25, pp.114–20, September 1990.

Daniela Palazzoli, 'Un lecca-lecca per l'arte,' *Il Giornale*, 25 November 1990.

Flaminio Gualdoni, *Richard Hamilton: Una Collezione '60/'70*, Studio Marconi, Milan, November 1990. Booklet of Giorgio Marconi's collection of works by Hamilton: published on the occasion of an exhibition.

Jutta Martens, 'Keine Angst vor dem Glanz der Reklame,' *Art*, no.11, pp.138–9, Gruner + Jahr AG & Co., Hamburg, November 1990. Review of *Art et Publicité* exhibition, Centre Pompidou, Paris.

Alfred Nemeczek, 'Der Pop-Furst mischt sich ein,' *das kunstmagazin*, no.12, pp.120–1, Gruner + Jahr AG & Co., Hamburg, December 1990. Review of exhibition, Kestner-Gesellschaft, Hanover.

Lynne Cooke, 'The Independent Group: British and American Pop, A "Palimpcestuous" Legacy,' in *Modern Art and Popular Culture*, Museum of Modern Art, New York, 1990. Published in conjunction with the exhibition *High & Low*.

Marco Livingstone, *Pop Art: A Continuing History*, Thames and Hudson, London, 1990.

1991
Peter Winter, 'Die Falltü ist die Boschaft,' *Frankfurter Allgemeine Zeitung*, 15 January 1991. Review of exhibition, Kestner-Gesellschaft, Hanover.

Guido Almansi, 'Humour o tragedia nella provocazione pop?,' *Arte*, no.215, pp.66–9, Giorgio Mondadori, Milan, February 1991.

Andrew Graham-Dixon, 'Richard Hamilton: Father of Pop,' *ARTnews*, vol.90, no.2, pp.102–7, New York, February 1991. Cover portrait by Timothy Greenfield-Sanders.

Lynne Cooke, 'Richard Hamilton, Pop Pioneer and Technophile,' *The Journal of Art*, vol.4, no.3, p.10, New York, March 1991. Adapted from Winterthur catalogue essay.

Peter Winter, 'Richard Hamilton: exteriors, interiors, objects, people,' *das kunstwerk*, vol.44, no.3, pp.64–5, March 1991. Review of exhibition, Kestner-Gesellschaft, Hanover.

Richard Cork, 'POP: Yesterday's Rebels Today's Old Masters,' *Telegraph Magazine*, pp.30–45, *The Daily Telegraph*, 11 May 1991.

Andrew Graham-Dixon, 'Popping On,' *The Independent Magazine*, no.145, pp.56–60, 15 June 1991. Review of exhibition at the Anthony d'Offay Gallery, London.

Tiffany Danneff, 'Hunting down the Pop archetypes,' *The Sunday Telegraph*, 23 June 1991.

Bryan Ferry, 'Still the top of the pops,' *The Independent on Sunday*, p.24, 23 June 1991.

William Feaver, 'Living it up at Hotel Limbo,' *The Observer*, p.52, 7 July 1991.

Sarah Kent, 'Turd man,' *Time Out*, no.1090, p.47, 10 July 1991. Review of exhibition, Anthony d'Offay Gallery, London.

Marco Livingstone, 'l'heritage du pop art anglais leurres: voir double,' *art press*, no.160, pp.18–25, July–August 1991.

Marco Livingstone, 'Anthony d'Offay Gallery: Richard Hamilton,' *The Burlington Magazine*, vol.113, no.1062, pp.635–6, September 1991.

Frank Whitford, 'Veneer All Through,' *Art Monthly*, no.149, pp.3–5, September 1991. Review of exhibition, Anthony d'Offay Gallery, London.

Caroline Kaye, *Art Monthly*, no.151, p.29, November 1991. A response to Frank Whitford's review of d'Offay exhibition.

Elizabeth Mortimer, 'Richard Hamilton,' in *The Swindon Collection of Twentieth Century British Art*, pp.60–2, Thamesdown Borough Council, 1991. Catalogue entry on 'Interior study (a),' 1964.

Simon Wilson, *The Tate Gallery, an illustrated companion*, p.240, Tate Gallery, London, 1991. 2nd ed., revised and expanded.

1992
Michael Compton, 'Pop Art in Britain,' in *Pop Art*, ed. Andreas C. Papadakis, pp.63–73, Art & Design, London, 1992.

'The Pop Art Symposium: General Discussion,' in *Pop Art*, ed. Andreas C. Papadakis, pp.48–61, Art & Design, London, 1992.

LENDERS

Numbers refer to catalogue entries

PRIVATE COLLECTIONS

Anthony d'Offay Gallery 21, 74, 78, 79, 92, 93,
    95, 97–103
Cultural Foundation against Apartheid, Paris 81
The artist 1–4, 7, 8, 24, 25, 27, 34, 43, 45, 47,
    69, 71–3, 75, 85–7, 91, 106
Erna and Curt Burgauer Collection 29
Danae Art International 67
Diab Data AB 88
Rita Donagh 48, 104
Lux Corporation, Osaka 17
Giorgio and Giò Marconi Collection, Milan 105
Private Collections 5, 6, 9, 12, 14, 15, 18, 22,
    33, 41, 42, 50–2, 54, 58–61, 63, 66, 68, 76,
    77, 80, 90, 96
Rosenthal and Rosenthal 65
Mr and Mrs Keith L. Sachs 84
Massimo and Francesca Valsecchi 62, 64
Whereabouts unknown 57

PUBLIC COLLECTIONS

Aachen, Ludwig Forum für Internationale
    Kunst 31
Basle, Kunstmuseum 46
Budapest, the Hungarian National Gallery 70
Cologne, Museum Ludwig 23, 32, 36, 44, 49
Darmstadt, Hessisches Landesmuseum 19
Edinburgh, Scottish National Gallery of Modern
    Art 28
Humlebaek, Louisiana Museum of Modern
    Art 40
London, The British Council 55, 56
London, Arts Council Collection 26, 83
London, Tate Gallery 10, 16, 20, 30, 38, 53, 82
New York, Solomon R. Guggenheim Museum 37,
    39, 42
Stockholm, Moderna Museet 11
Tübingen, Kunsthalle 13
Washington, Hirshhorn Museum and Sculpture
    Garden, Smithsonian Institution 89
Valencia, IVAM Centre Julio González 94
Vienna, Museum moderner Kunst 35

PHOTOGRAPHIC CREDITS

Per-Anders Allsten, Moderna Museet Stockholm; Anthony d'Offay Gallery; Arts Council; Belfast Library and Education Board; Birmingham Museums and Art Gallery; H.R. Clayton; George Cserna; Prudence Cuming Associates Ltd; Greg Curnoe; Rita Donagh; Robert Freeman; Maria Gilissen; Patrick Goetelen; The Guardian; Richard Hamilton; Colorphoto Hans Hinz; Irish Times; Bob Janz; Barry Joule; Mark Lancaster; Salvatore Liciera; Belinda Loftus; Louisiana Museum; Ludwig Forum, Aachen; Eric Luke; Lux Corporation; Roger Mayne; Ciaran McGowan; Nigel McKernaghan; Jörg Müller; National Gallery, London; Dept of Photography at University of Newcastle upon Tyne; Dr Parisini (Museum Moderner Kunst, Wien); Penrose Film Productions; Philadelphia Museum of Art; Rheinisches Bildarchiv (Museum Ludwig Köln); Rosenthal Art Equities; R. Saidman; Betsy Scherman; Sean Smith; Sotheby's; South Bank Centre; Tate Gallery Photographic Department; Vartia; Waddington Galleries; John Webb; Zoltan Wegner; Kunsthaus Zürich.

INDEX

FRIENDS OF THE TATE GALLERY

Since their formation in 1958, the Friends of the Tate Gallery have helped to buy major works of art for the Tate Gallery Collection, from Stubbs to Hockney.

Members are entitled to immediate and unlimited free admission to Tate Gallery exhibitions with a guest, invitations to previews of Tate Gallery exhibitions, opportunities to visit the Gallery when closed to the public, a discount of 10 per cent in the Tate Gallery shop, special events, *Friends Events* and *Tate Preview* magazines mailed three times a year, free admission to exhibitions at Tate Gallery Liverpool, and use of the new Friends Room at the Tate Gallery, supported by Lloyd's of London.

Three categories of higher level memberships, Associate Fellow at £100, Deputy Fellow at £250, and Fellow at £500, entitle members to a range of extra benefits including guest cards and invitations to exclusive special events.

The Friends of the Tate Gallery are supported by Tate & Lyle PLC.

Further details on the Friends may be obtained from:

Friends of the Tate Gallery
Tate Gallery
Millbank
London SW1P 4RG

Tel: 071–821 1313 or 071–834 2742

Tate Gallery Liverpool Supporters

Tate Gallery Liverpool Supporters were established in 1989 to promote the Gallery and help raise funds for its exhibitions and projects.

Members are entitled to unlimited free admission to Tate Gallery Liverpool and London exhibitions, invitations to private previews of Tate Gallery Liverpool exhibitions, a discount of 10 per cent on Tate Gallery Liverpool catalogues and goods in the Tate Gallery London Shop, special events, invitations to the Supporters' annual party, regular information on all Tate Gallery Liverpool activities and *Tate Preview* magazine mailed three times a year.

Further details on the Supporters may be obtained from:

Tate Gallery Liverpool Supporters
Albert Dock
Liverpool L3 4BB

Tel: 051–709 3223

PATRONS OF THE TATE GALLERY

The Patrons of British Art support British painting and sculpture from the Elizabethan period through to the early twentieth century in the Tate Gallery's Collection. They encourage knowledge and awareness of British Art by providing an opportunity to study Britain's cultural heritage.

The Patrons of New Art support contemporary art in the Tate Gallery's Collection. They promote a lively and informed interest in contemporary art and are associated with the Turner Prize, one of the most prestigious awards for the visual arts.

Annual membership of the Patrons ranges from £350 to £750, and funds the purchase of works of art for the Tate Gallery Collection.

Benefits for both groups include invitations to Tate Gallery receptions, an opportunity to sit on the Patrons' acquisitions committees, special events including visits to private and corporate collections and complimentary catalogues of Tate Gallery exhibitions.

Further details on the Patrons may be obtained from:

The Development Office
Tate Gallery
Millbank
London SW1P 4RG

Tel: 071–821 1313

TATE GALLERY FOUNDATION

The Tate Gallery is one of the great art museums of the world. It houses the national collections of British art since 1550, including the Turner Bequest, and of international twentieth-century art. The Gallery attracts an ever-increasing number of visitors who enjoy its lively exhibition and education programmes.

Income is raised through a variety of methods, including commercial sponsorship, appeals corporate membership, a bequest programme and donations from trusts, foundations, corporations and individuals. The Tate Gallery Foundation (charity registration number 295549) was established in 1986 to support the fund-raising activities of the Tate Gallery.

Tate Gallery Foundation

SPONSORSHIP

Tate Gallery, London – Sponsorships since 1989

Agfa Graphic Systems Group
  1991, *Turner: The Fifth Decade* exhibition and catalogue
Barclays Bank plc
  1991, *Constable* exhibition
Beck's
  1992, *Otto Dix* exhibition
British Gas plc
  1989, Education study sheets
British Gas North Thames
  1989, *Colour into Line: Turner and the Art of Engraving* exhibition
The British Land Company plc
  1990, *Joseph Wright of Derby* exhibition
British Petroleum Co plc
  1989, *Paul Klee* exhibition
  1990–93, *New Displays*
British Steel plc
  1989, *William Coldstream* exhibition
Carroll, Dempsey & Thirkell
  1990, *Anish Kapoor* exhibition
Channel 4 Television
  1991–93, The Turner Prize
Clifton Nurseries
  1989–91, Sponsorhip in kind
Daimler Benz
  1991, *Max Ernst* Exhibition
Debenham Tewson & Chinnocks
  1990, Turner *Painting and Poetry* exhibition
Digital Equipment Co Ltd
  1991, *From Turner's Studio* touring exhibition
Drivers Jonas
  1989, *Turner and Architecture* exhibition
Erco Lighting
  1989, Sponsorhip in kind
The German Government
  1992 *Otto Dix* exhibition
The Independent
  1992, *Otto Dix* exhibition
KPMG Management Consulting
  1991, *Anthony Caro: Sculpture towards Architecture* exhibition
Linklaters & Paines
  1989, Japanese Guide to Turner Bequest
Lin Pac Plastics
  1989, Sponsorship in kind
Lloyd's of London
  1991, Friends Room
Olympia & York
  1990, Frameworkers Conference
PA Consulting Group
  1989, Video projector
Pearsons plc
  1992–5, Elizabethan Curator Post
Reed International plc
  1990, *On Classic Ground* exhibition
SRU Ltd
  1989, Market research consultancy
  1992, *Richard Hamilton* exhibition
Tate & Lyle PLC
  1991–93, Friends relaunch marketing programme

TSB Group
  1992, *Turner and Byron* exhibition
  1992–5, *William Blake* series of displays
Ulster Television plc
  1989, *F.E. McWilliam* exhibition
Volkswagen
  1989–92, The Turner Scholarships
Westminster City Council
  1989, Trees project
  1989, *The Tate Gallery Companion* (New Display Guidebook)

Tate Gallery Liverpool – Sponsorships since 1989

Barclays Bank plc
  1989, Sculpture for the visually impaired
BASF
  1990, *Lifelines* exhibition
Beck's Bier
  1990, *Art from Köln* exhibition
British Alcan Aluminium plc
  1991, *Dynamism* and *Giacometti* exhibitions
British Telecom
  1989, Salary for media van
  1990, Outreach Programme
Cultural Relations Committee, Department of Foreign Affairs, Ireland
  1991, *Strongholds* exhibition
Granada Television
  1990, *New North* exhibition
Korean Air
  1992, Sponsorhip in kind
The Littlewoods Organisation plc
  1992–5, *New Realities* display
Merseyside Development Corporation
  1989, Outreach Programme for two years
Miller & Santhouse plc
  1989, Sculpture show for visually impaired
Mobil Oil Company Ltd
  1990, *New North* exhibition
Momart plc
  1989–92, Artist-in-residence at Tate Gallery Liverpool
NSK Bearings Europe Ltd
  1991, *A Cabinet of Signs: Contemporary Art from Post Modern Japan* exhibition
Samsung Electronics
  1992, *Working with Nature* exhibition

DONATIONS

Towards Acquisitions for the Archive

The Sir Nicholas and Lady Goodison Charitable Settlement
The Henry Moore Foundation

Towards Acquisitions for the British Collection

Miss Marjorie Ball
Mr Edwin C. Cohen
Echoing Green Foundation
Ernst & Young
Friends of the Tate Gallery
Mrs Sue Hammerson
National Art-Collections Fund
National Art-Collections Fund (Woodroffe Bequest)
National Heritage Memorial Fund
The Mail on Sunday
The Patrons of British Art
Mr John Ritblat

Towards Acquisitions for the Modern Collection

American Fund for the Tate Gallery
Miss Nancy Balfour
Mr Tom Bendhem
Mr Gilbert de Botton
Mr Edwin C. Cohen
Mr Paul Dupee
Evelyn, Lady Downshire's Trust Fund
Friends of the Tate Gallery
General Atlantic Corporation
Sir Anthony and Lady Jacobs
The Mail on Sunday
National Art-Collections Fund
The Patrons of New Art
Mrs Jill Ritblat
The Hon. Simon Sainsbury
Mr Barry and The Hon. Mrs Townsley

Towards Projects and Activities at Tate Gallery, London

Anonymous donor
The Baring Foundation
BAA plc
Clifton Nurseries
Mrs Dagny Corcoran
The Elephant Trust
The Gabo Trust
The Getty Foundation
The Getty Grant Program
Mr and Mrs John Hughes
The Leverhulme Trust
Linklaters and Paines
Mr and Mrs Robert Mnuchin
The Henry Moore Foundation

The Henry Moore Sculpture Trust
The Andy Warhol Foundation for the Visual Arts, Inc.
Save & Prosper Educational Trust
SRU Ltd

Towards Projects and Activities at Tate Gallery, Liverpool

Anonymous donor
Blankstone, Sington & Co.
Ivor Braka Ltd
British Rail Board
Mr and Mrs Henry Cotton
Fraser Williams Group
Goethe Institute, Manchester
Merseyside Development Corporation
The Henry Moore Foundation
The Henry Moore Sculpture Trust
The Pilgrim Trust
Save & Prosper Educational Trust
Stanley Thomas Johnson Stiftung Foundation
Yale University Press

Towards Buildings at Tate Gallery, London

The Esmée Fairbairn Charitable Trust
Calouste Gulbenkian Foundation
Clothworkers Foundation
The Nomura Securities Co. Ltd
Anthony d'Offay Gallery
The Office of Arts and Libraries
The Rayne Foundation
Dr Mortimer and Theresa Sackler Foundation
Waddington Galleries
Westminster City Council
The Wolfson Foundation

Towards Buildings at Tate Gallery, Liverpool

Arrowcroft Group Ltd
The Baring Foundation
Barclays Bank plc
British Gas plc
Clothworkers Foundation
The John S. Cohen Foundation
Deloitte, Haskins & Sells
The Esmée Fairbairn Charitable Trust
Granada Television and the Granada Foundation
Higsons Brewery plc
The Idlewild Trust
Kodak Ltd
The John Lewis Partnership
The Liverpool Daily Post and Echo
The Manor Charitable Trust
The Henry Moore Foundation

The Moores Family Charitable Foundation
The New Moorgate Trust Fund
Ocean Group plc
Pilkington plc
The Pilgrim Trust
Plessy Major Systems (Liverpool)
Eleanor Rathbone Charitable Trust
Royal Insurance (UK) Ltd
The Sainsbury Family Charitable Trusts
The Bernard Sunley Charitable Trust
The TSB Foundation
United Biscuits UK Ltd
Whitbread & Co plc
The Wolfson Foundation

Towards the Tate Gallery St Ives Appeal

Viscount Amory Charitable Trust
Barbinder Trust
Barclays Bank plc
The Baring Foundation
Patricia, Lady Boyd and Viscount Boyd
British Telecom plc
Cable & Wireless plc
Christie, Manson & Woods Ltd
The John S. Cohen Foundation
Cornish Brewery Co. Ltd (in kind)
English China Clays Group Charitable Trust
The Esmée Fairbairn Charitable Trust
Foundation for Sport and Arts
J. Paul Getty Jr Charitable Trust
Grand Metropolitan Charitable Trust
The Landmark Trust
David Messum Fine Paintings
The Henry Moore Foundation
D'Oyly Carte Charitable Trust
Pall European Limited
The Pilgrim Trust
The Sainsbury Family Charitable Trusts
Southwestern Electricity Board
South West Gas
South West Water
Television South West
The TSB Foundation
Western Morning News, West Briton, Cornish Guardian and The Cornishman
Mr and Mrs Graham Williams
The Worshipful Company of Fishmongers

Partners

Agfa UK Ltd
Barclays Bank plc
The British Petroleum Co plc
Glaxo Holdings plc
Manpower (UK) Ltd
THORN EMI
Unilever plc

Associates

Bell Helicopter Textron
Channel 4 Television
Debenham, Tewson & Chinnocks
Ernst & Young
Global Asset Management Ltd
KPMG Peat Marwick
Lazard Brothers & Co Ltd
Linklaters & Paines
Smith & Williamson
S.G. Warburg Group
Tate & Lyle PLC
Vickers plc